120 GREAT PAINTINGS OF THE *American West*

PLATINUM DVD AND BOOK

Edited by
CAROL BELANGER GRAFTON

DOVER PUBLICATIONS, INC.
Mineola, New York

This Dover Platinum DVD includes all of the images included in the book. You can:

- Print out the images at poster size
- Create art, crafts, and web projects
- Play the images on a DVD player

To Print:

There is no installation necessary to print out the images on the Platinum DVD. Each image has been saved in JPEG format in three different sizes. Within the Images folder on the DVD, you will find three additional folders:

- Poster Size folder: the images within this folder have been designed for use on wide-bed printers and have been saved at 300 dpi, with a 15" short dimension.

- Screensaver Hi-res folder: these images can be used as screensavers—refer to the instructions included in the folder. They are also useful for printing high-resolution images at a smaller size for projects such as cards, brochures, or iron-on-transfers. The images have been saved at 300 dpi, with an 8" short dimension.

- JPG folder: these images are for Internet or on-screen use and have been saved at 72 dpi, with an 8" short dimension.

The images within these folders are identical, except for size. Every image has a unique file name in the following format: xxx.JPG. The first 3 digits of the file name, before the period, correspond to the number printed under the image of the book. The last 3 letters of the file name, "JPG," refer to the file format. So, 001.JPG would be the first file in the folder.

To Create:

The images can be used in a wide range of word processing and graphic software applications. Just insert the Platinum DVD into your computer and call the images into your favorite software. Please refer to the software's documentation for further instructions.

Also included on the DVD is Dover Design Manager, a simple graphics-editing program for Windows that will allow you to view, print, crop, and rotate the images.

To Play:

- DVD Player

You can play the Platinum DVD just as you would any other DVD. After you place the DVD in your player, a continuous slideshow will begin automatically.

- Personal Computer

If your personal computer is equipped with a DVD player, you can play the Platinum DVD just as you would any DVD.

For technical support, contact:
Telephone: 1 (617) 249-0245
Fax: 1 (617) 249-0245
Email: dover@artimaging.com
Internet: **http://www.dovertechsupport.com**
The fastest way to receive technical support is via email or the Internet.

Bibliographical Note

120 Great Paintings of the American West Platinum DVD and Book is a new selection of images, first published by Dover Publications, Inc., in 2008.

Dover Electronic Clip Art®

International Standard Book Number
ISBN-13: 978-0-486-99898-5
ISBN-10: 0-486-99898-3

Manufactured in the United States of America
Dover Publications, Inc., 31 East 2nd Street, Mineola, N.Y. 11501

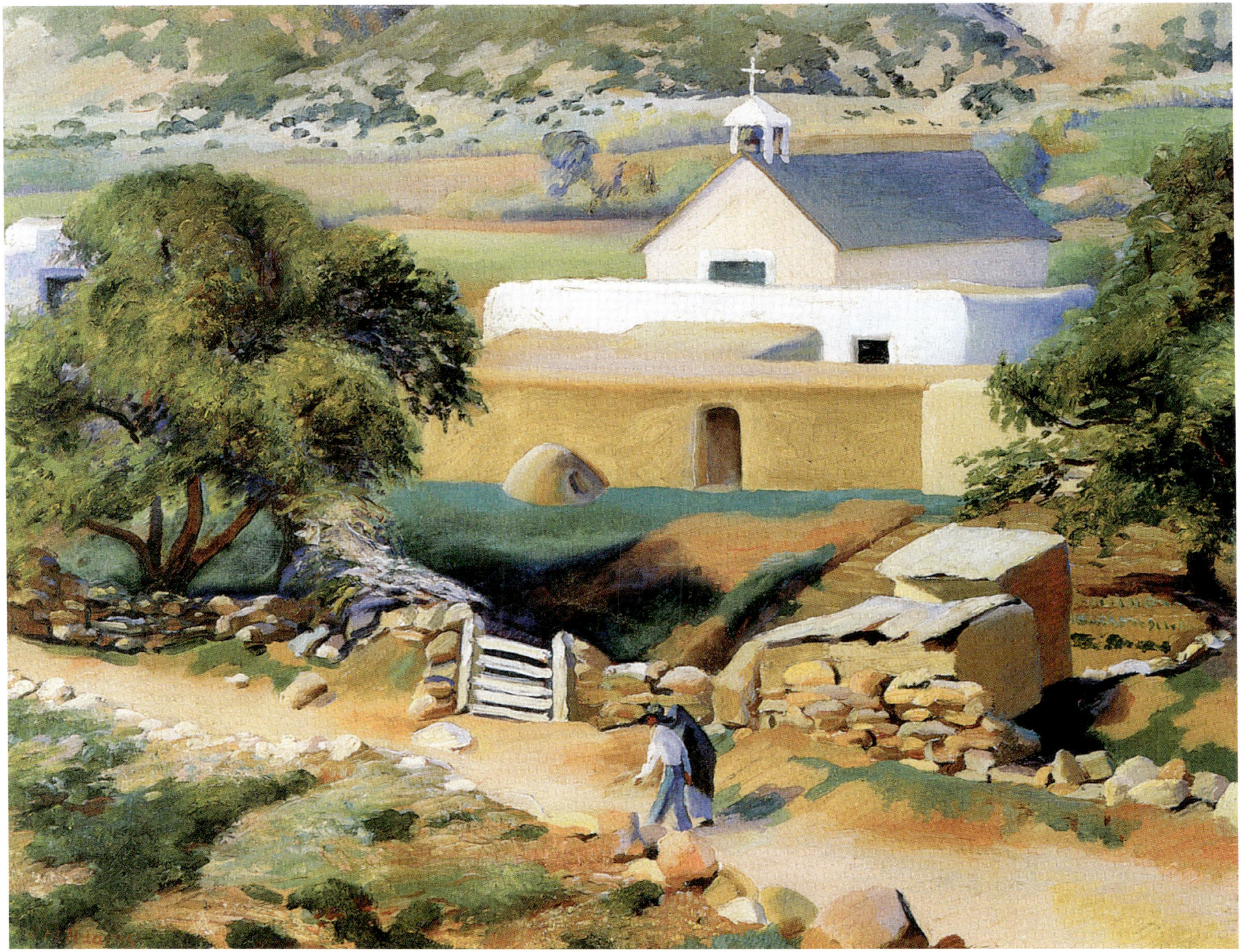

001. KENNETH MILLER ADAMS (1897–1966)
The Mission Church, before 1925
Oil on canvas. 20½ x 25 in. (52 x 63.5 cm)

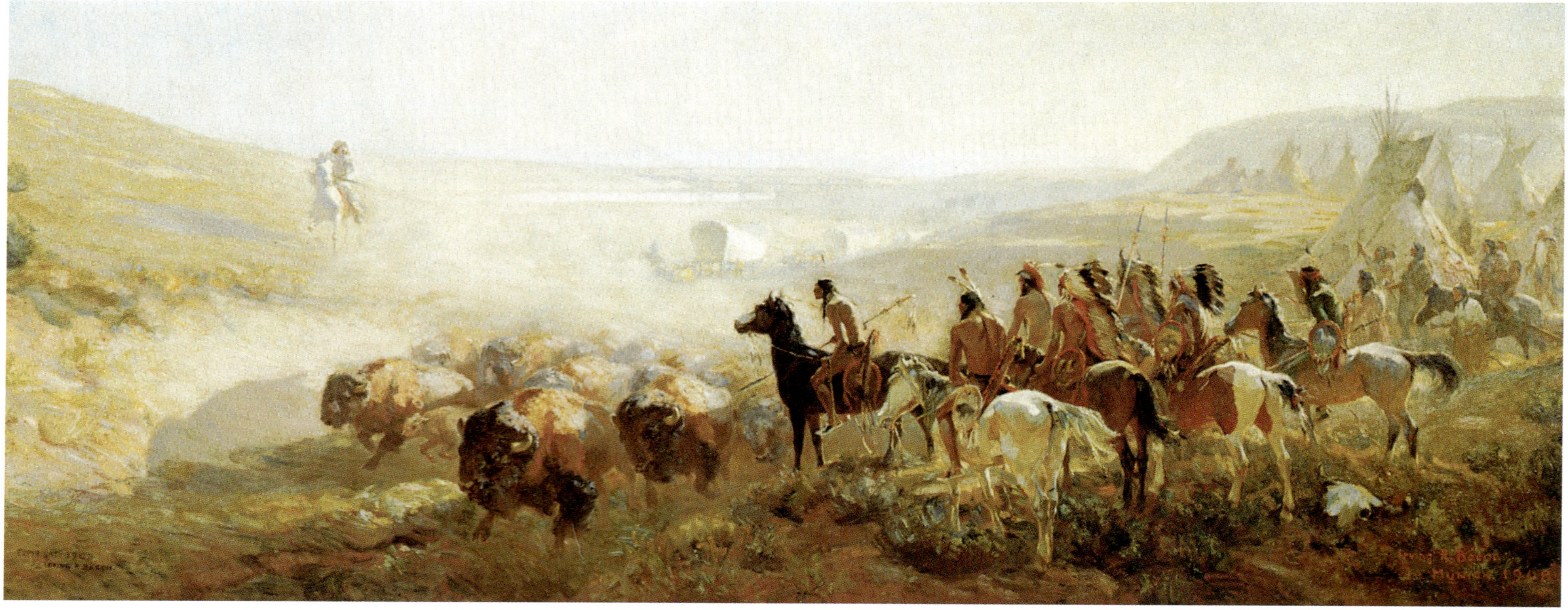

002. IRVING R. BACON (1875–1962)
The Conquest of the Prairie, 1908
Oil on canvas. 47¼ x 118½ in. (120 x 301 cm)

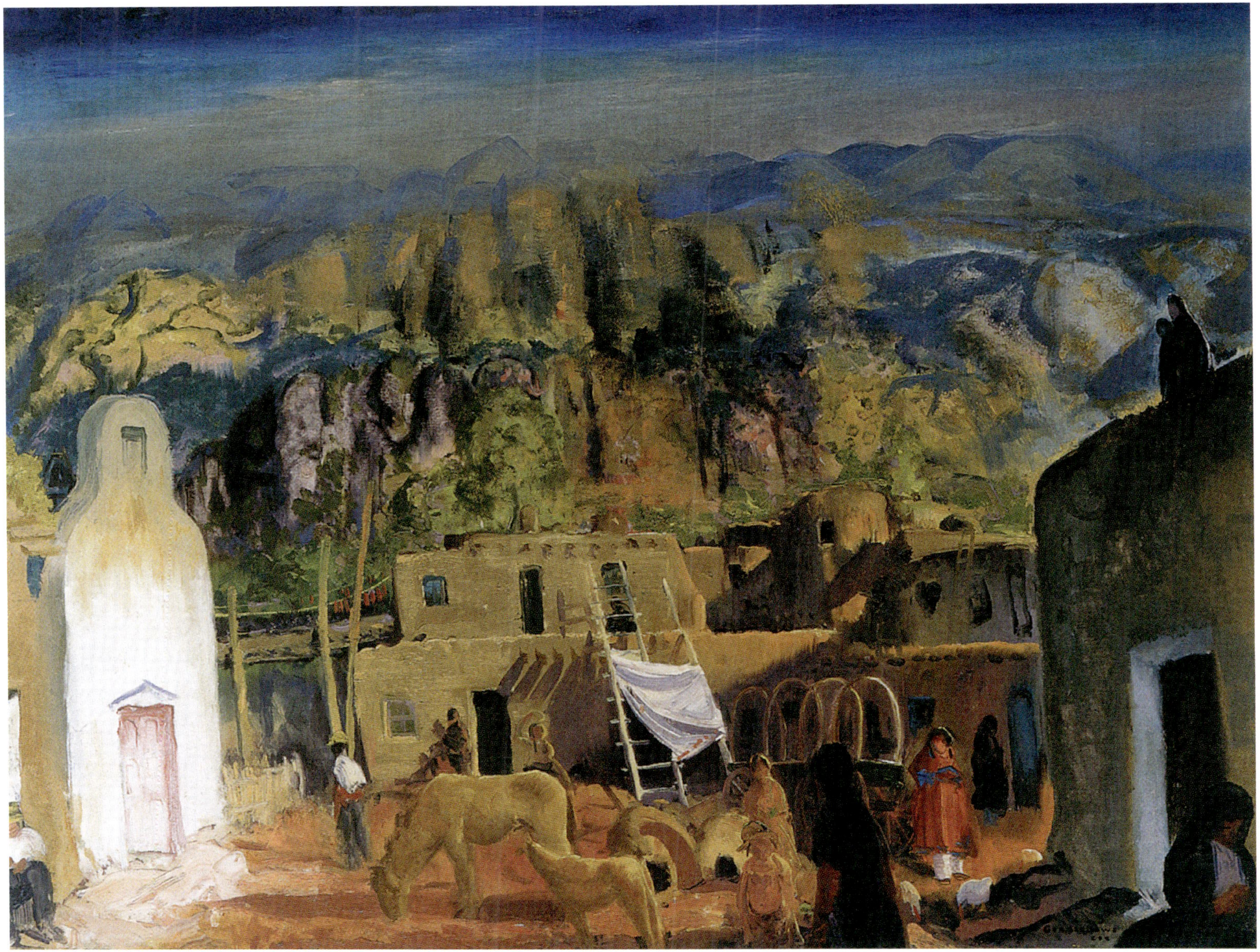

003. GEORGE BELLOWS (1882–1925)
Pueblo, Tesuque, Number One, 1917
Oil on canvas. 34 x 44¼ in. (86.4 x 112.4 cm)

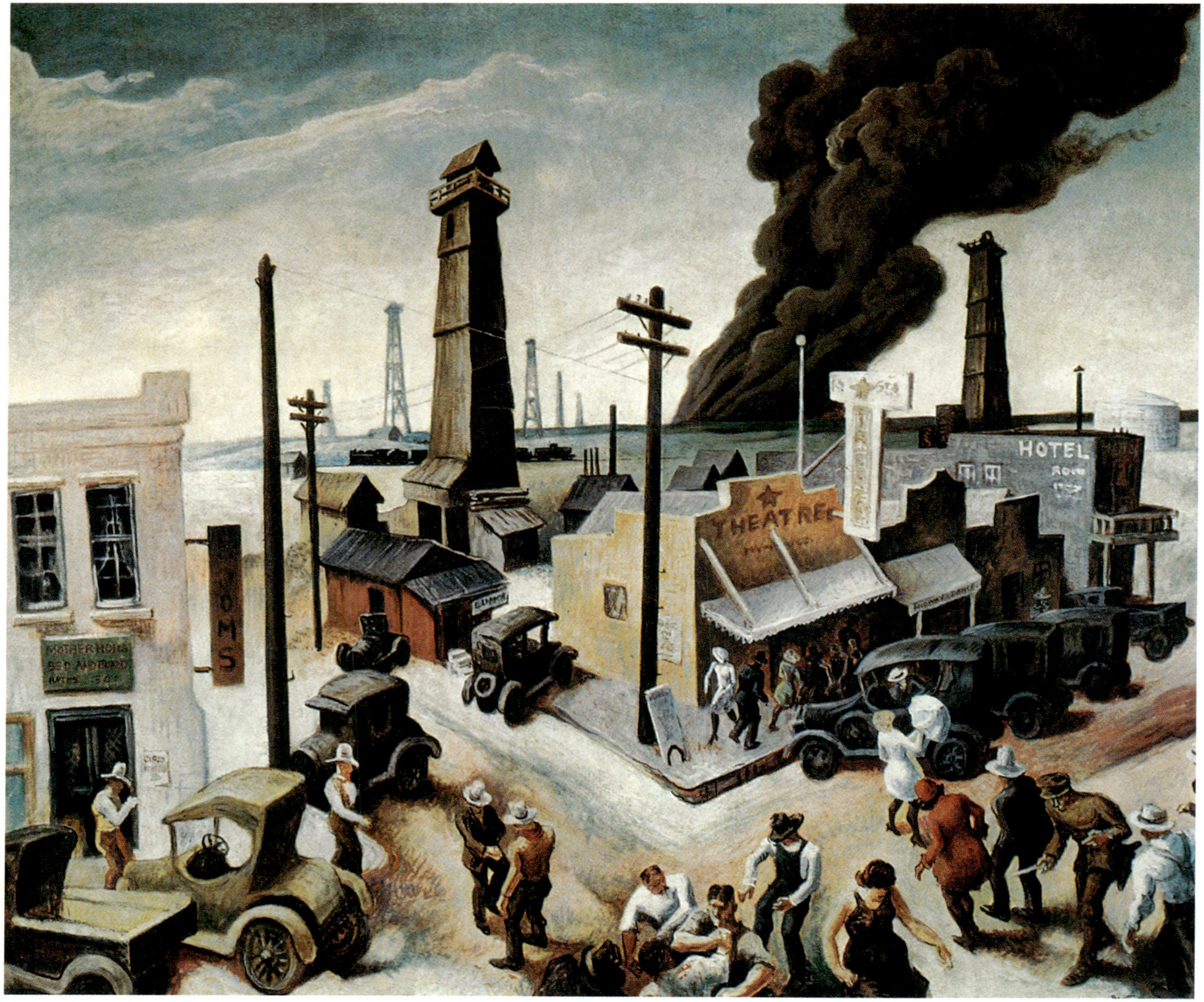

004. THOMAS HART BENTON (1889–1975)
Boomtown, 1928
Oil on canvas. 45 x 54 in. (114.3 x 137.2 cm)

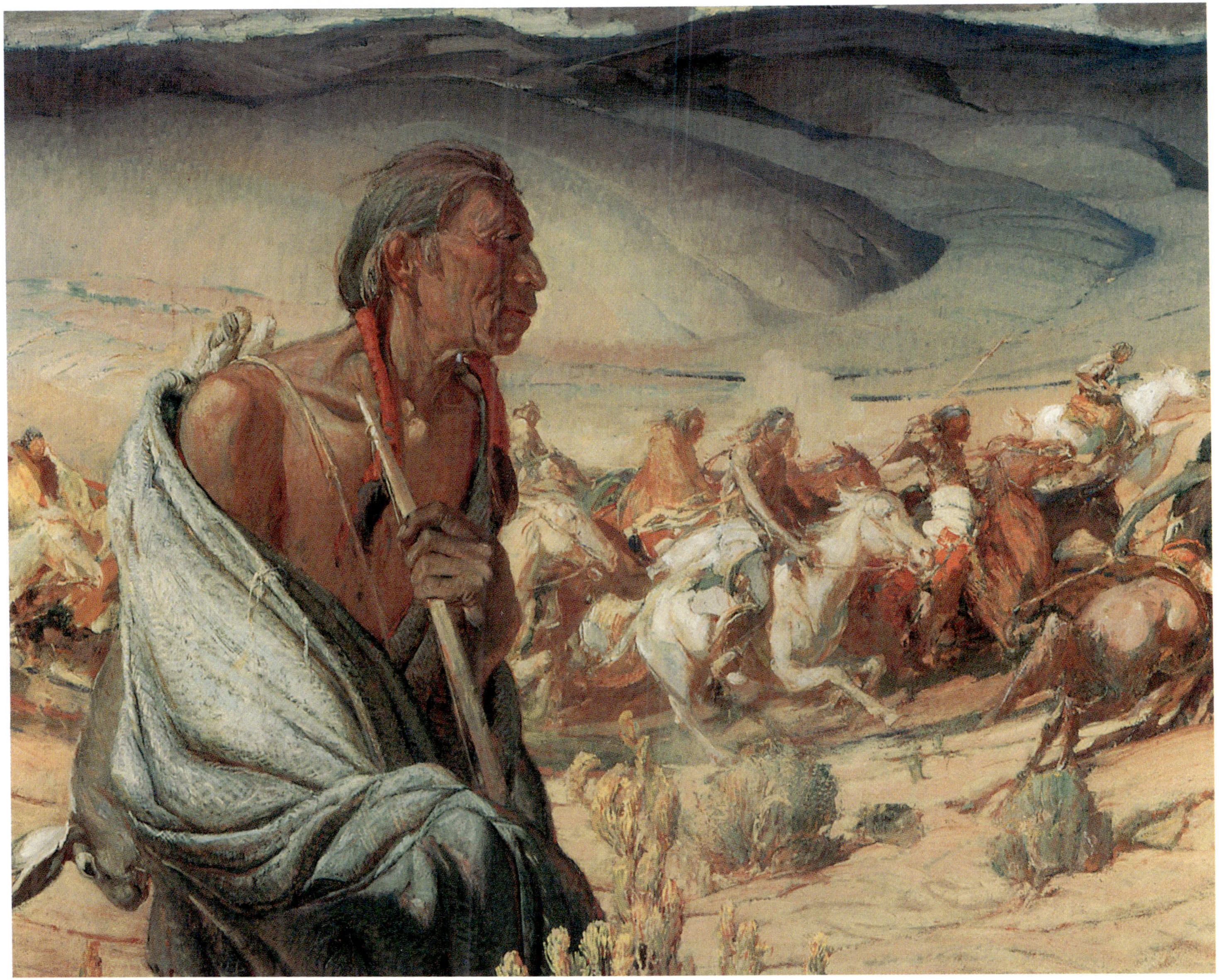

005. OSCAR E. BERNINGHAUS (1874–1952)
Too Old for the Rabbit Hunt, 1927
Oil on canvas. 35 x 40 in. (88.9 x 101.6 cm)

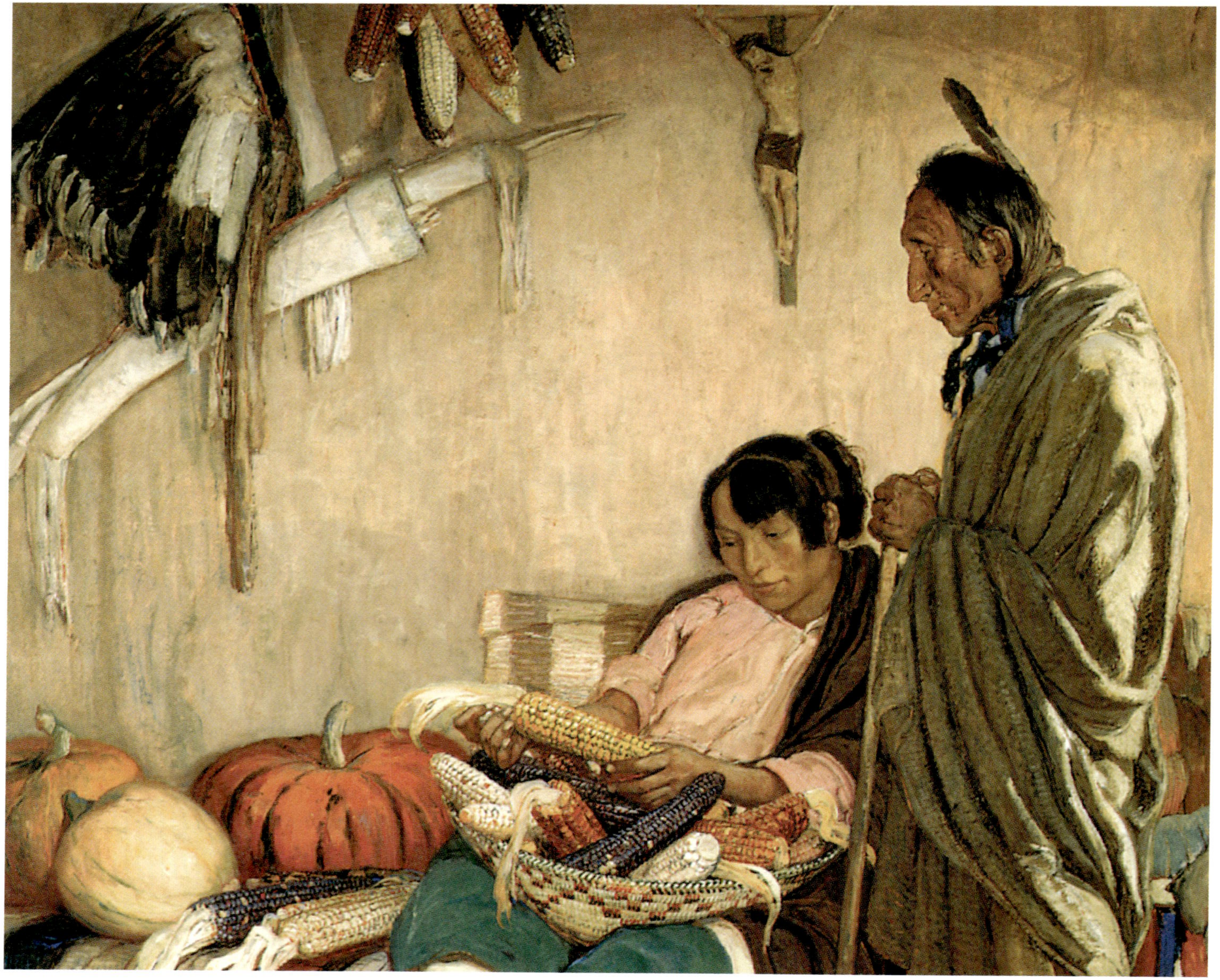

006. OSCAR E. BERNINGHAUS (1874–1952)
Peace and Plenty, 1925
Oil on canvas. 35 x 39½ in. (88.9 x 100.3 cm)

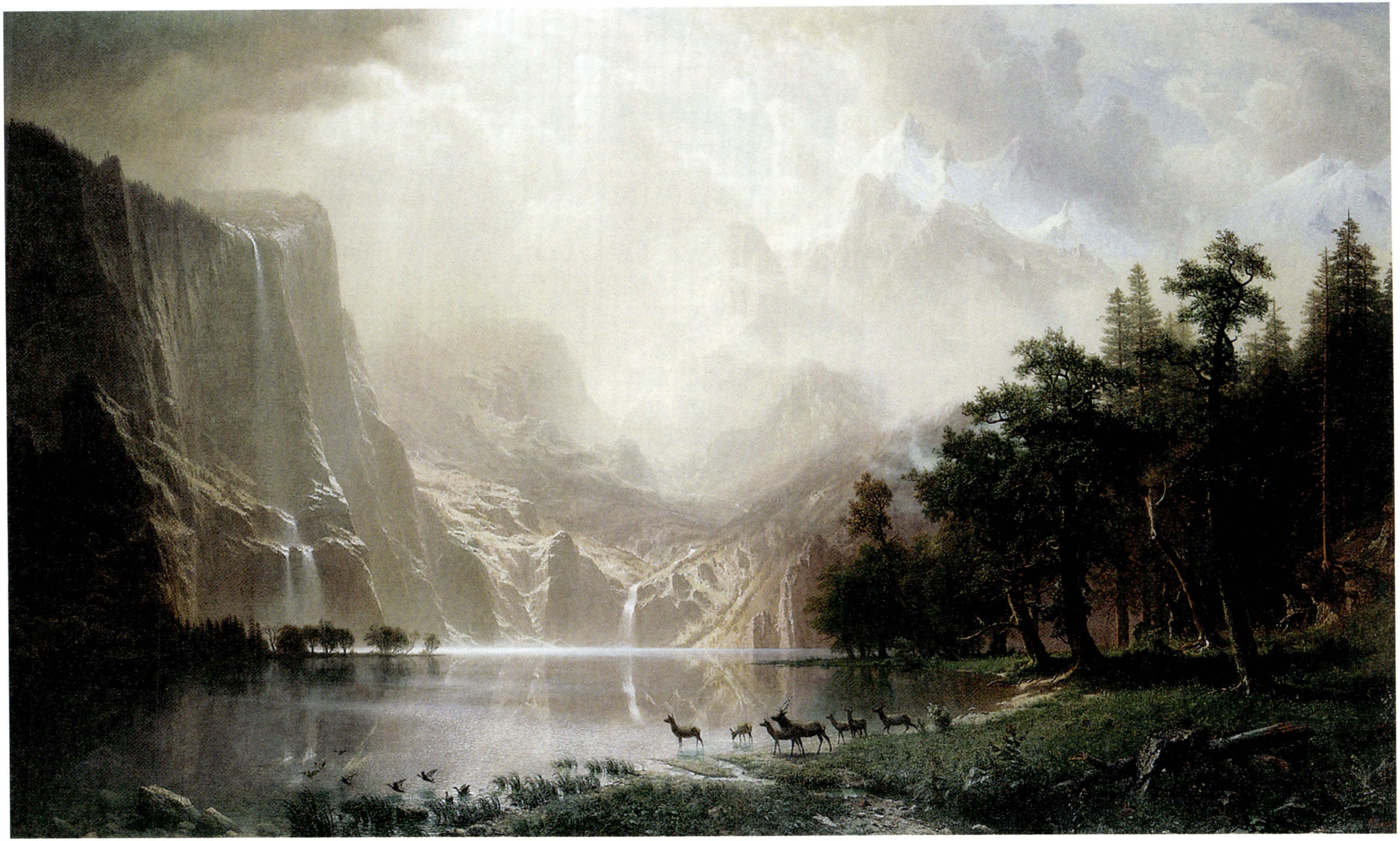

007. ALBERT BIERSTADT (1830–1902)
Among the Sierra Nevada Mountains, California, 1868
Oil on canvas. 72 x 120 in. (182.9 x 304.8 cm)

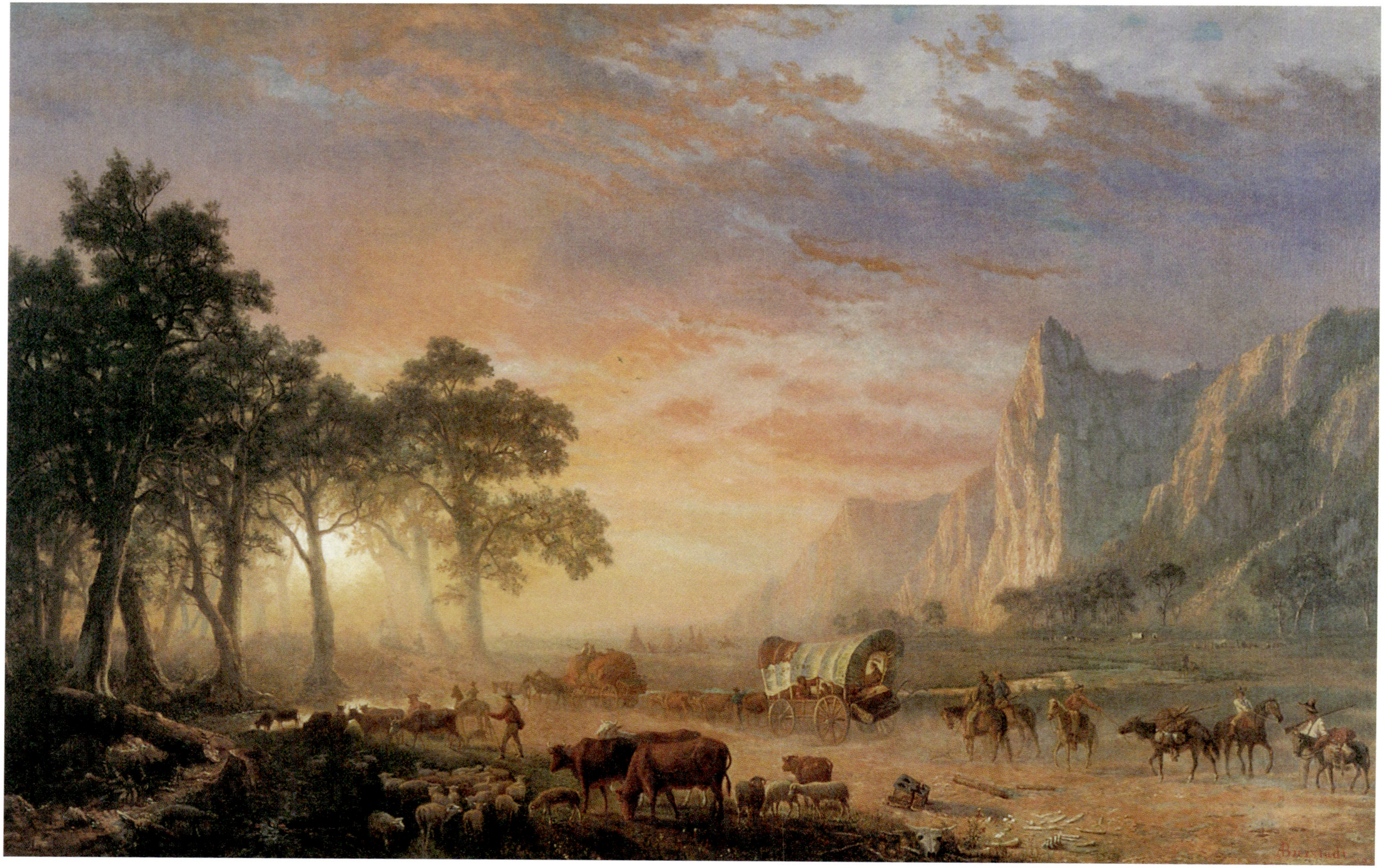

008. ALBERT BIERSTADT (1830–1902)
The Oregon Trail, 1869
Oil on canvas. 31 x 49 in. (78.7 x 125.7 cm)

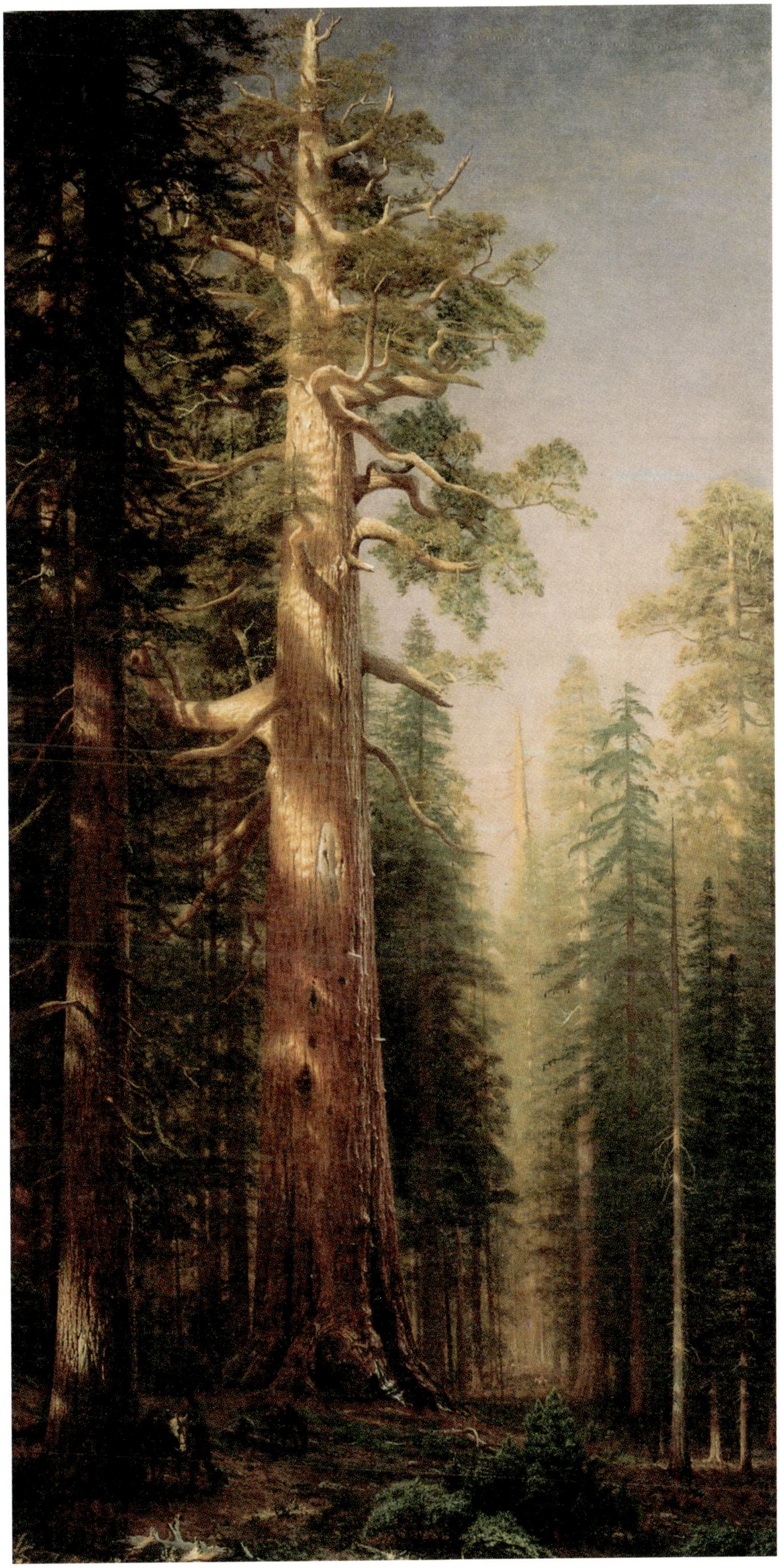

009. ALBERT BIERSTADT (1830–1902)
The Great Trees, Mariposa Grove, California, 1876
Oil on canvas. 118⅜ x 59¼ in. (300.1 x 150.5 cm)

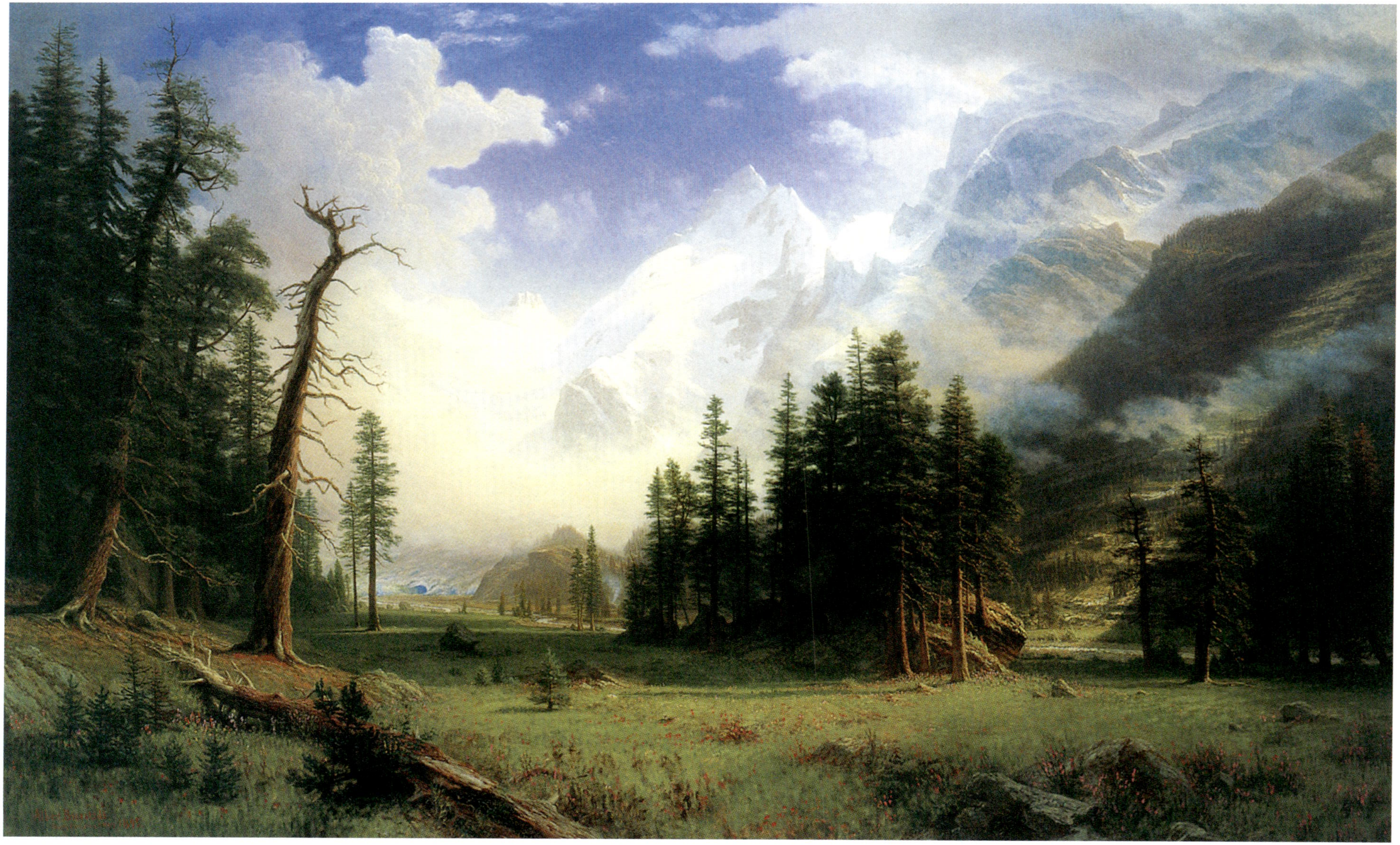

010. ALBERT BIERSTADT (1830–1902)
Mountain Landscape, 1895
Oil on canvas. 72 x 120 in. (182.9 x 304.8 cm)

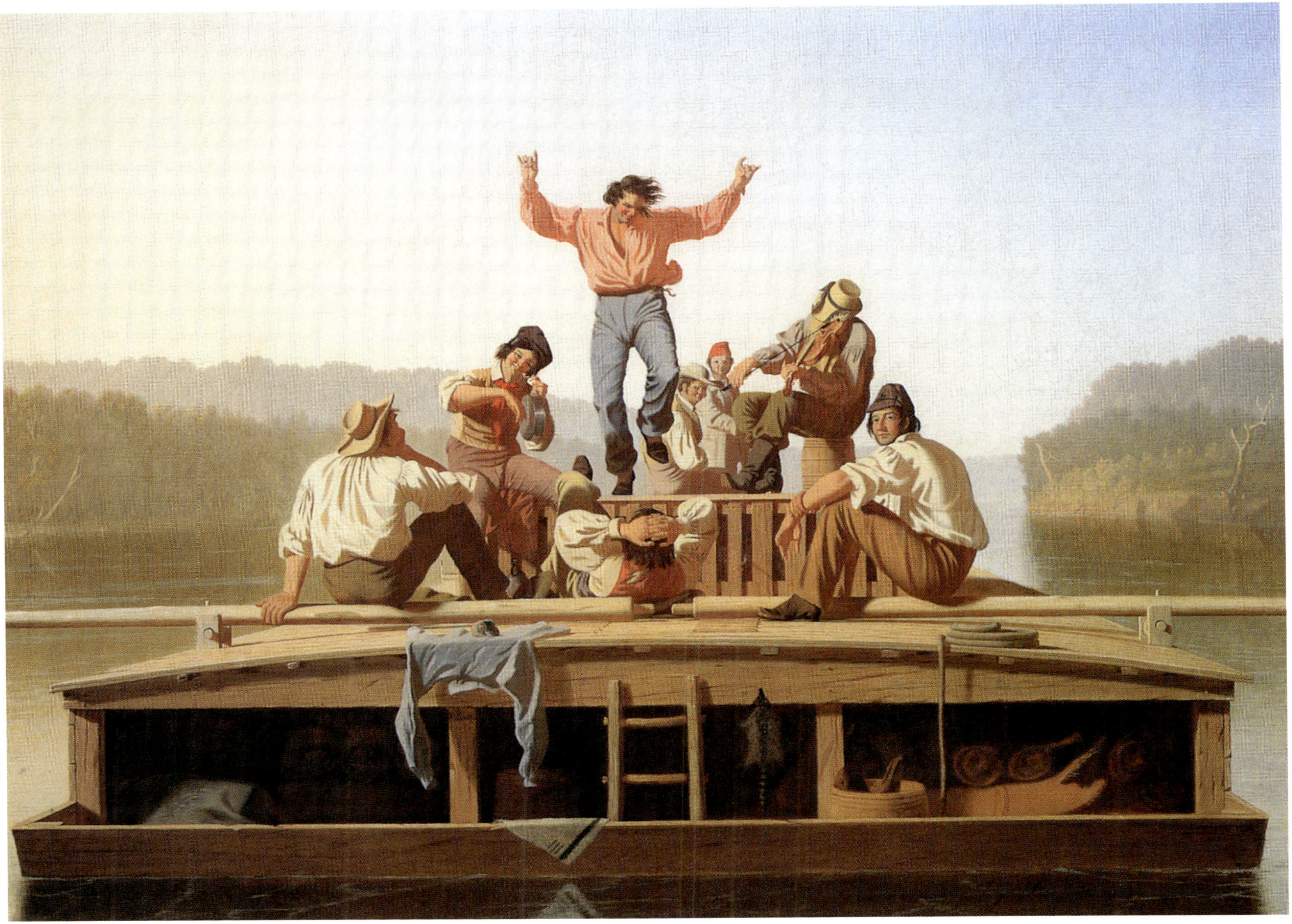

011. GEORGE CALEB BINGHAM (1811–1879)
The Jolly Flatboatmen, 1846
Oil on canvas.

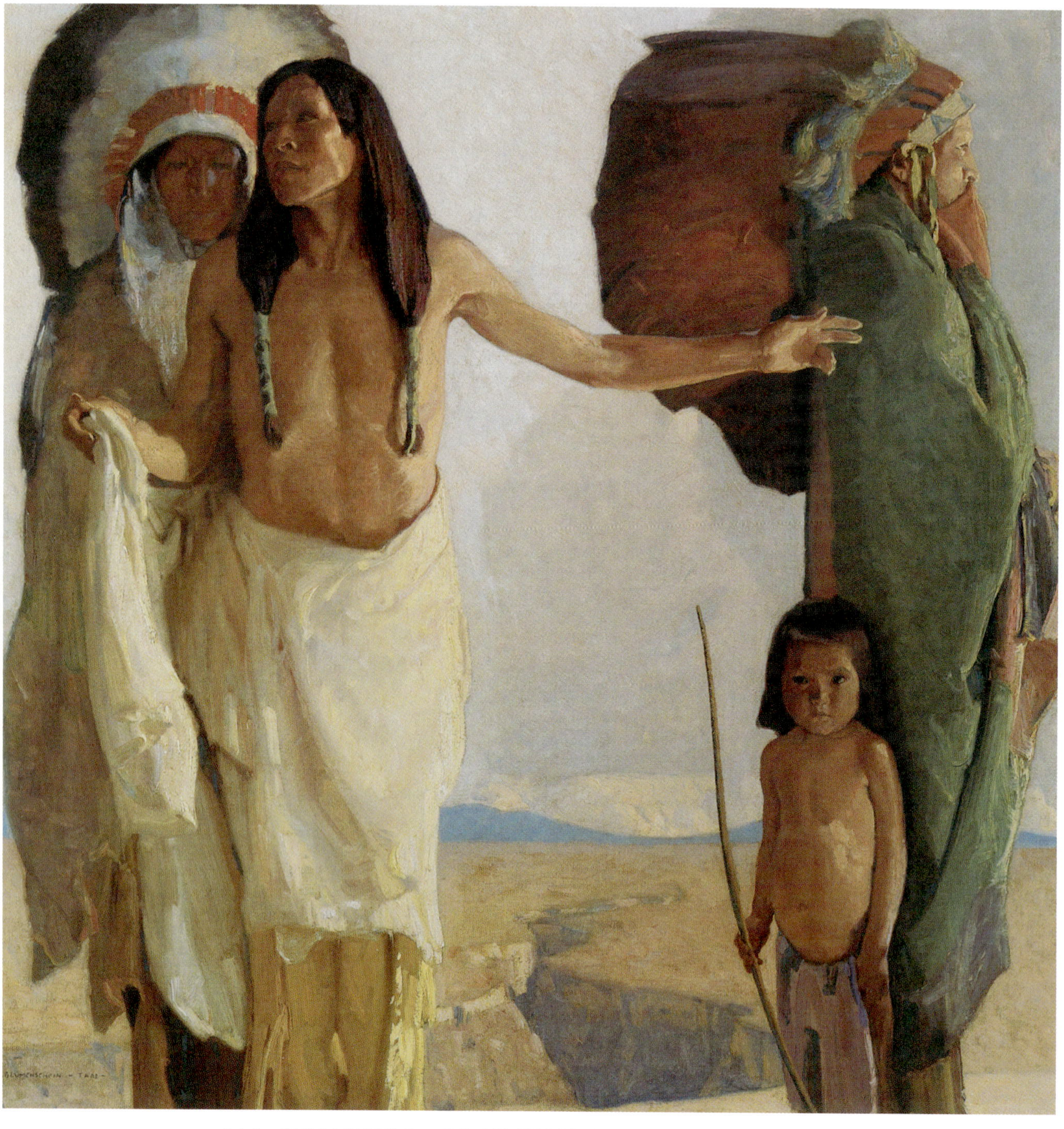

012. ERNEST L. BLUMENSCHEIN (1874–1960)
The Peacemaker, 1913
Oil on canvas. 44¼ x 45 in. (112.4 x 114.3 cm)

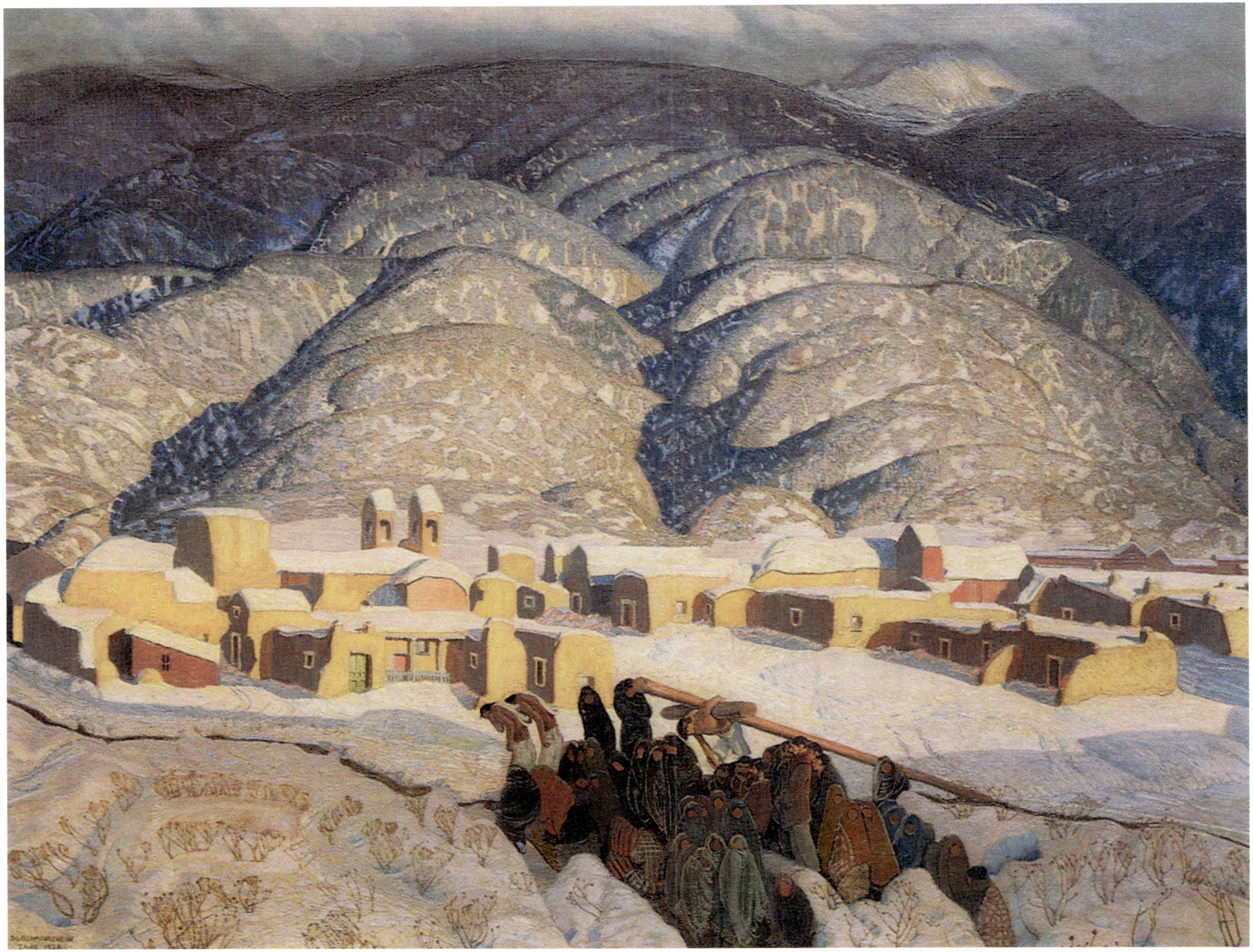

013. ERNEST L. BLUMENSCHEIN (1874–1960)
Sangre de Cristo Mountains, 1925
Oil on canvas. 50 x 60 in. (127 x 152.4 cm)

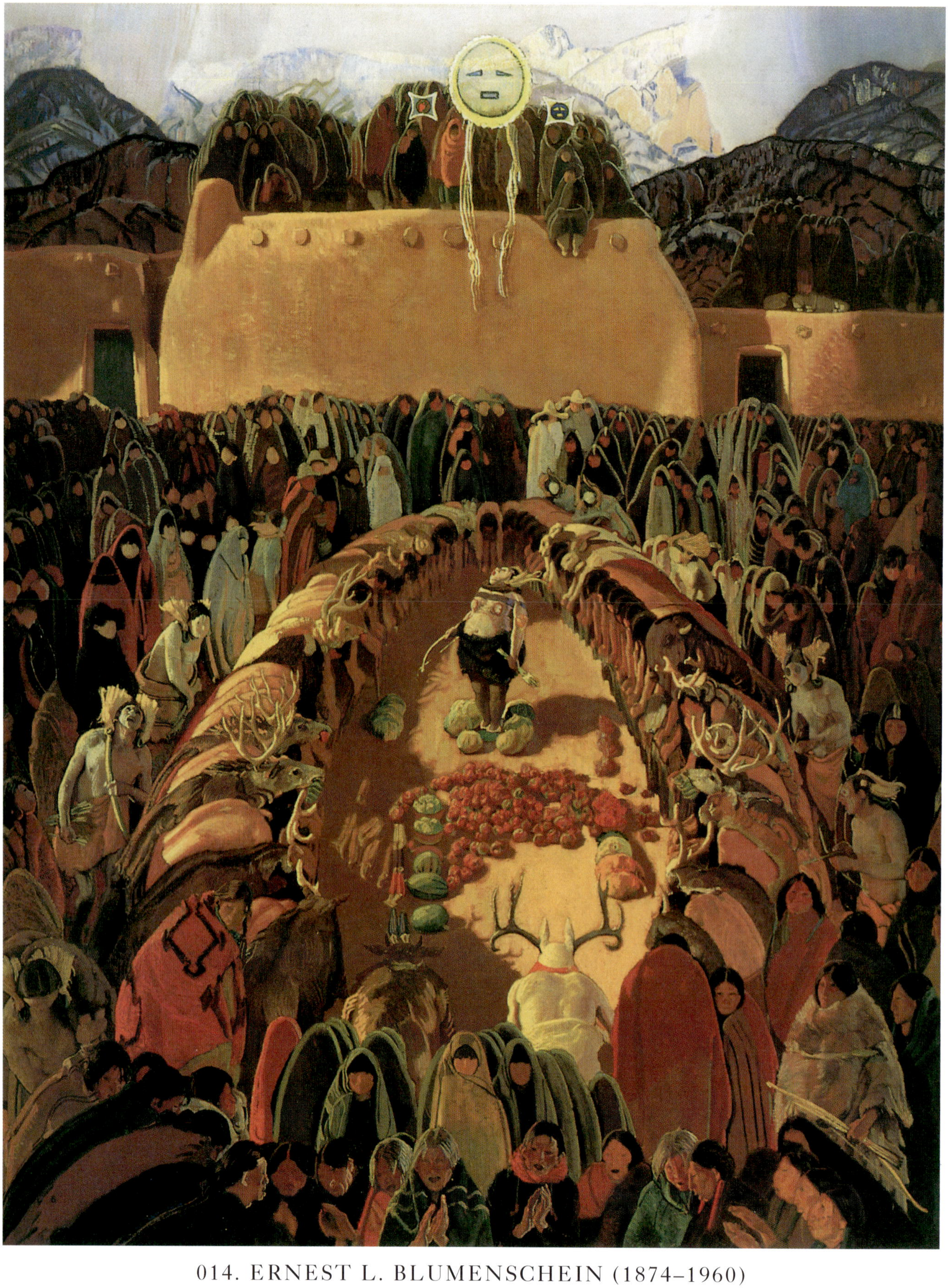

014. ERNEST L. BLUMENSCHEIN (1874–1960)
Moon, Morning Star, and Evening Star, 1922
Oil on canvas. 50 x 40 in. (127 x 101.6 cm)

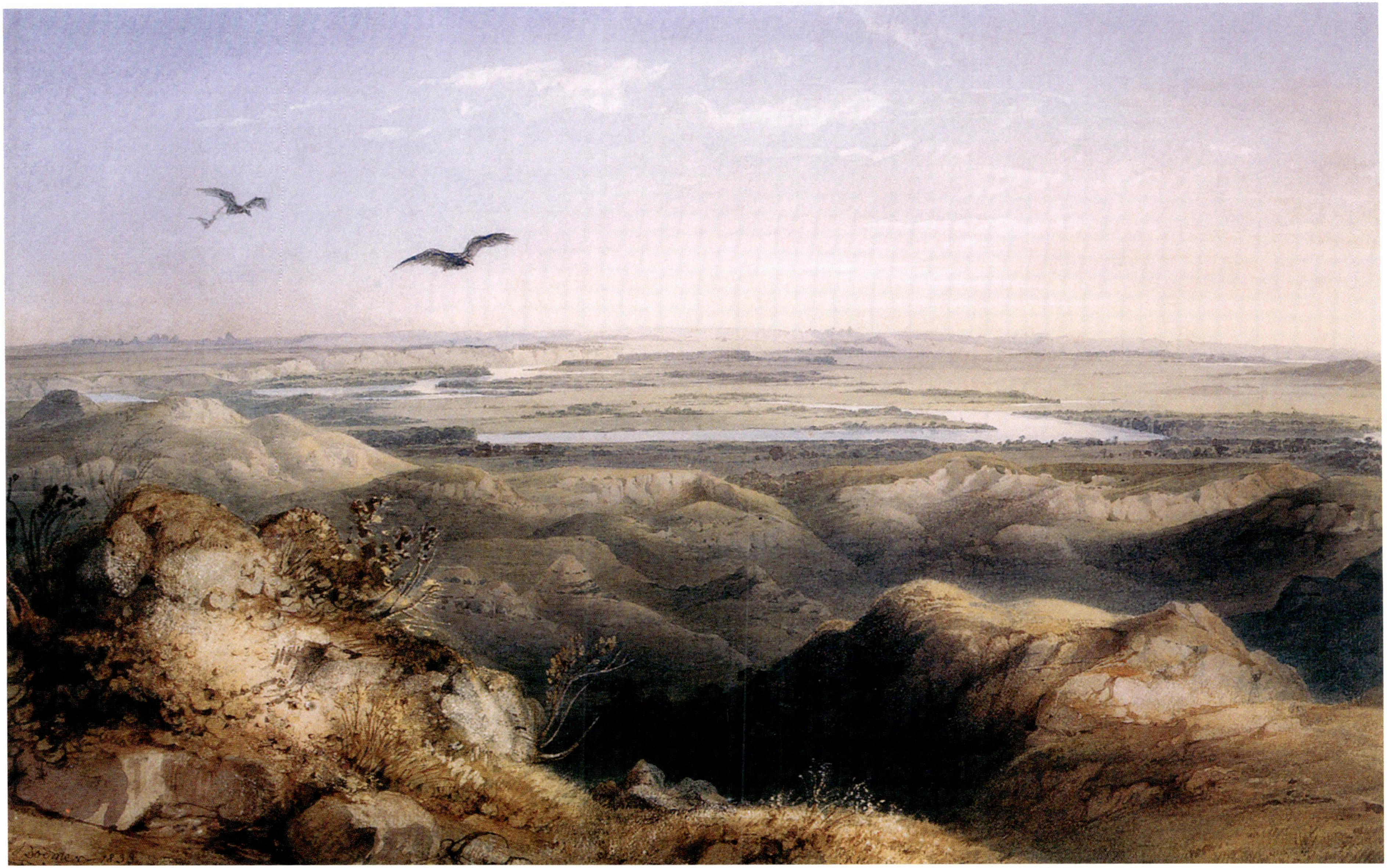

015. KARL BODMER (1809–1893)
Junction of the Yellowstone and the Missouri, 1833
Watercolor on paper.

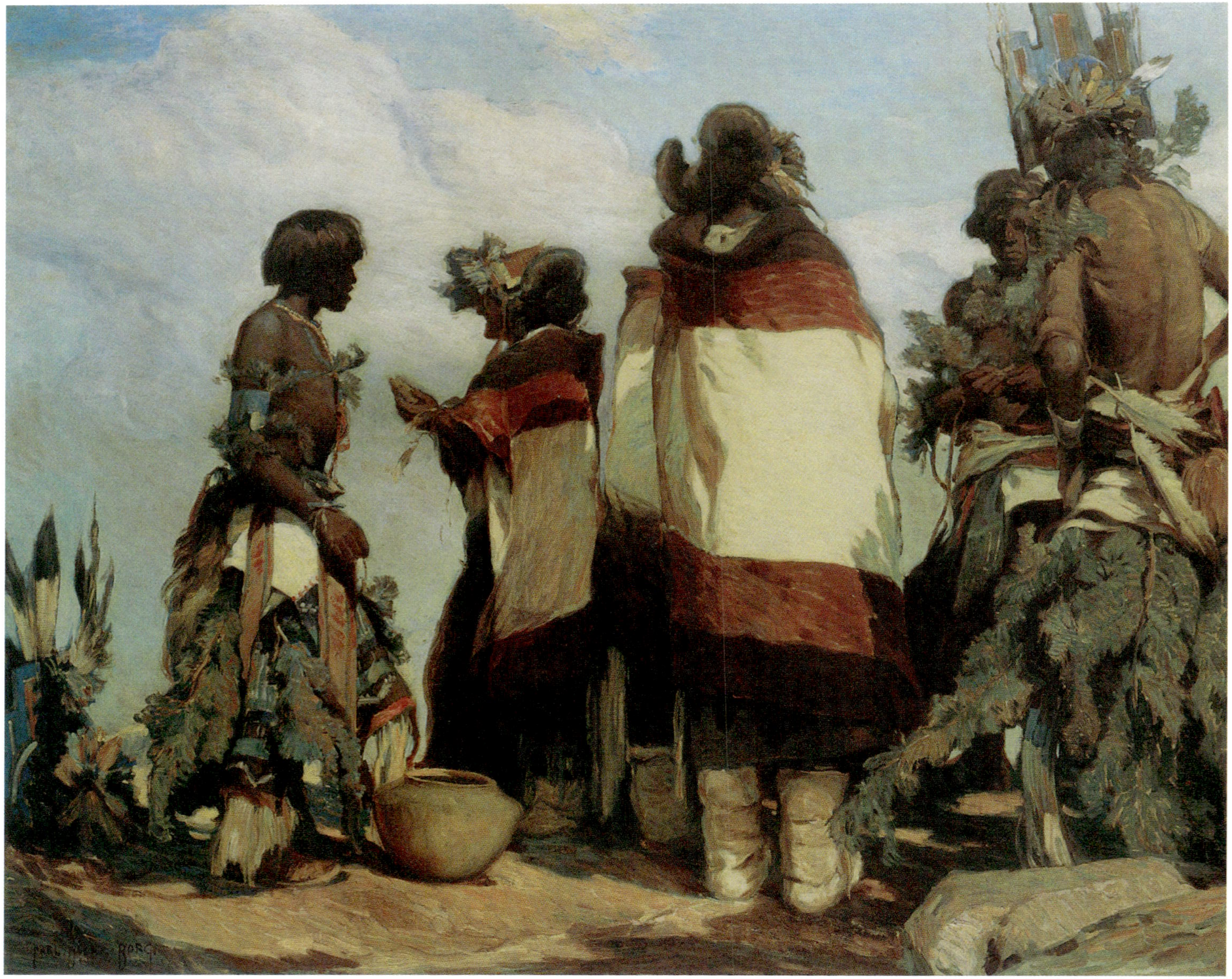

016. CARL OSCAR BORG (1879–1947)
The Niman Kachinas, 1926
Oil on canvas. 44⅛ x 54¼ in. (112.1 x 137.8 cm)

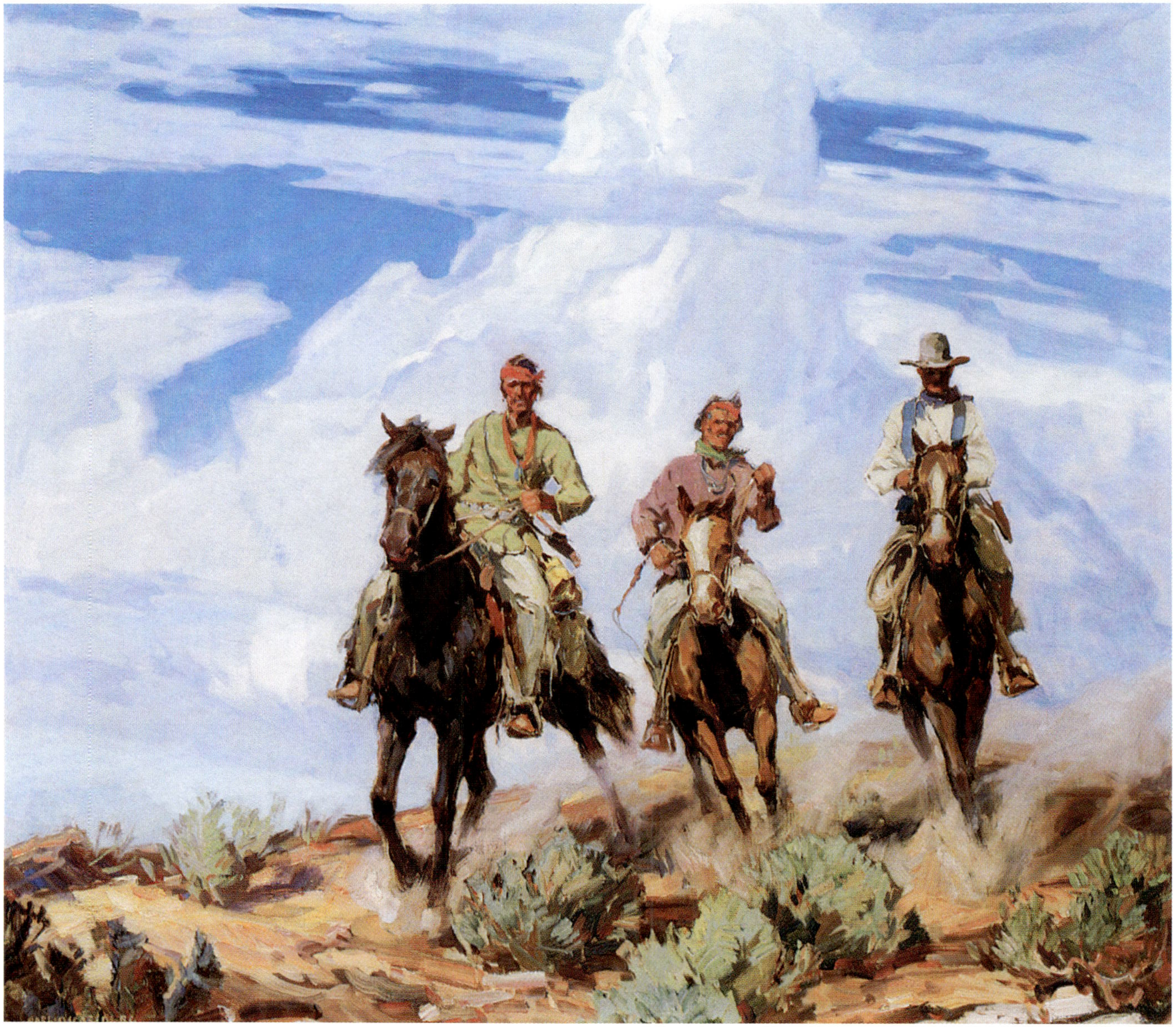

017. CARL OSCAR BORG (1879–1947)
Sons of the Desert, c. 1925
Oil on canvas. 38 x 40½ in. (96.5 x 102.9 cm)

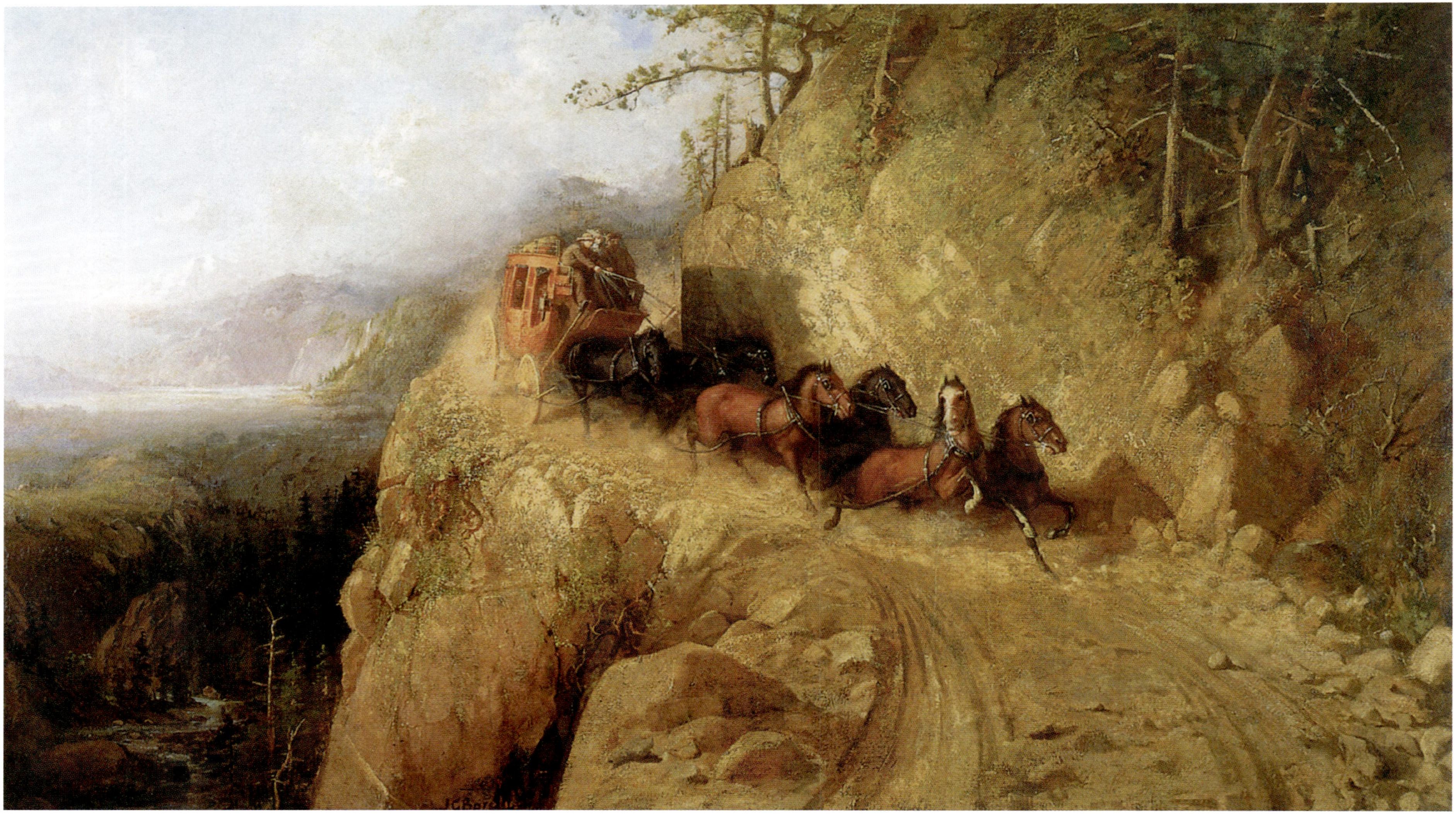

018. GUTZON BORGLUM (1867–1941)
Staging in California, 1889
Oil on canvas. 60 x 108 in. (152.4 x 274.3 cm)

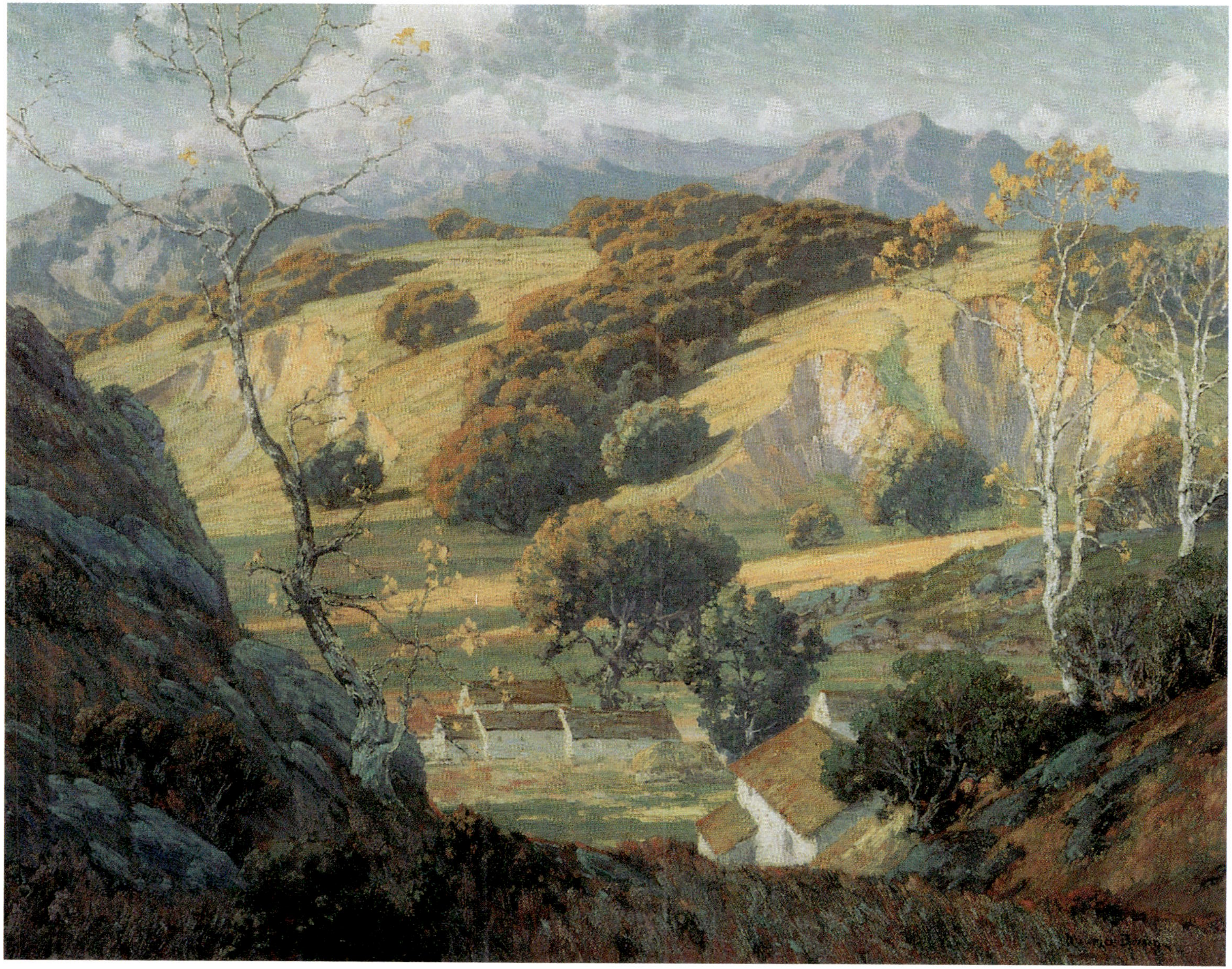

019. MAURICE BRAUN (1877–1941)
California Valley Farm, c. 1920
Oil on canvas. 40 x 50 in. (101.5 x 127 cm)

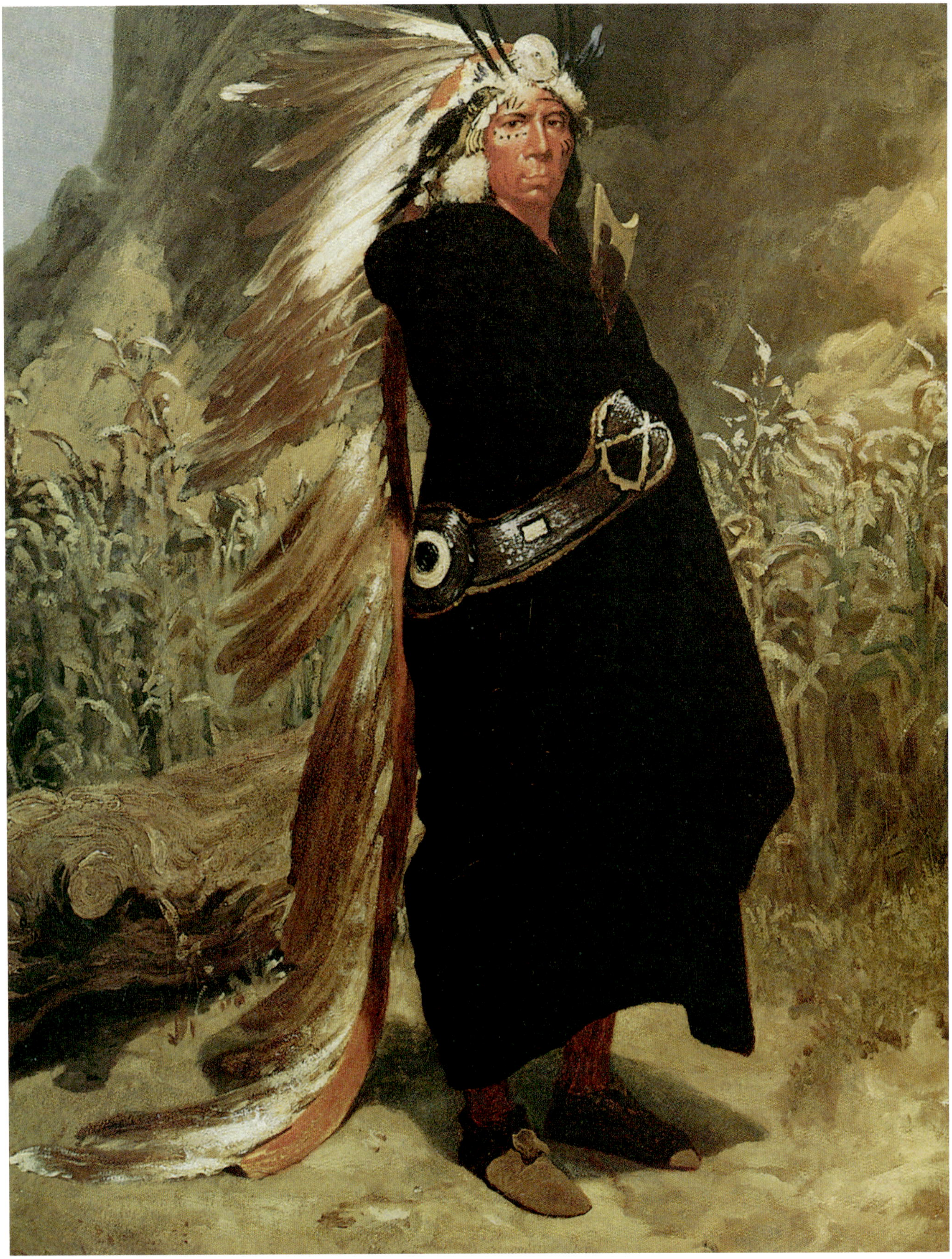

020. VALENTINE BROMLEY (1848–1877)
Portrait of an Indian Chief, 1875
Oil on canvas. 23 x 19 in. (58.4 x 48.2 cm)

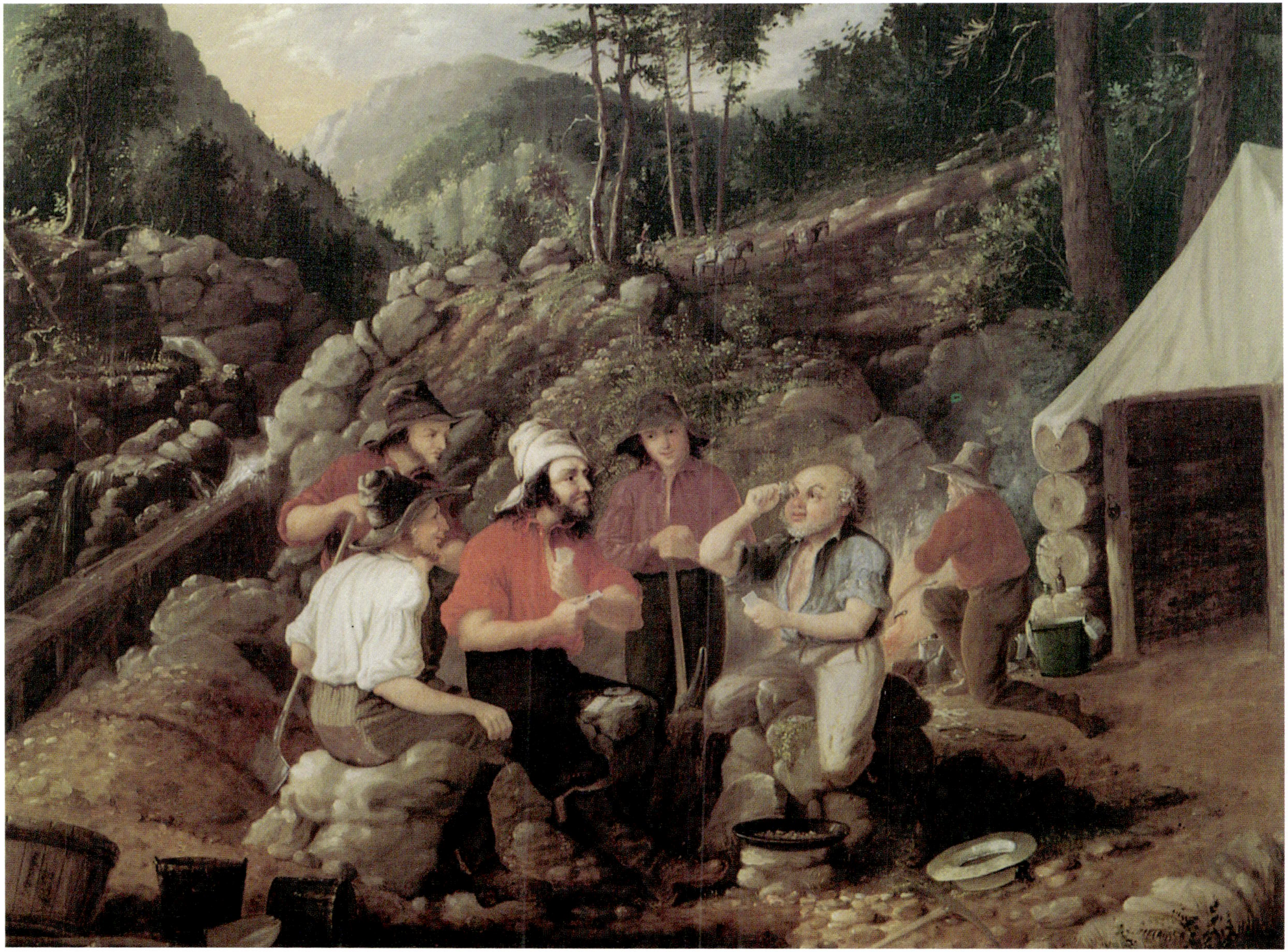

021. ALBERTUS DEL ORIENT BROWERE (1814–1887)
Goldminers, 1858
Oil on canvas. 29 x 36 in. (73.7 x 91.5 cm)

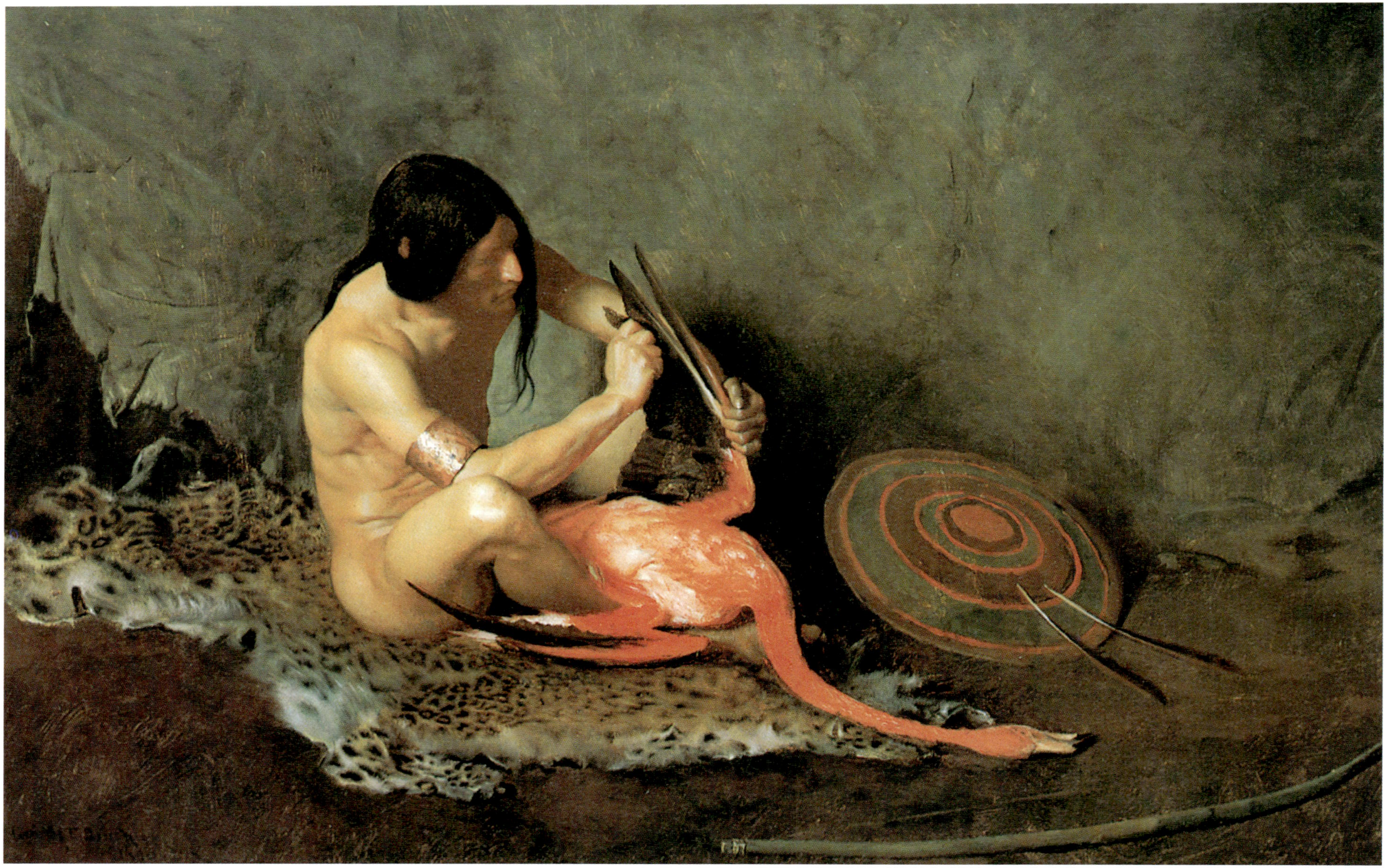

022. GEORGE DE FOREST BRUSH (1855–1941)
The Shield Maker, 1890
Oil on canvas. 11 x 16 in. (27.9 x 40.6 cm)

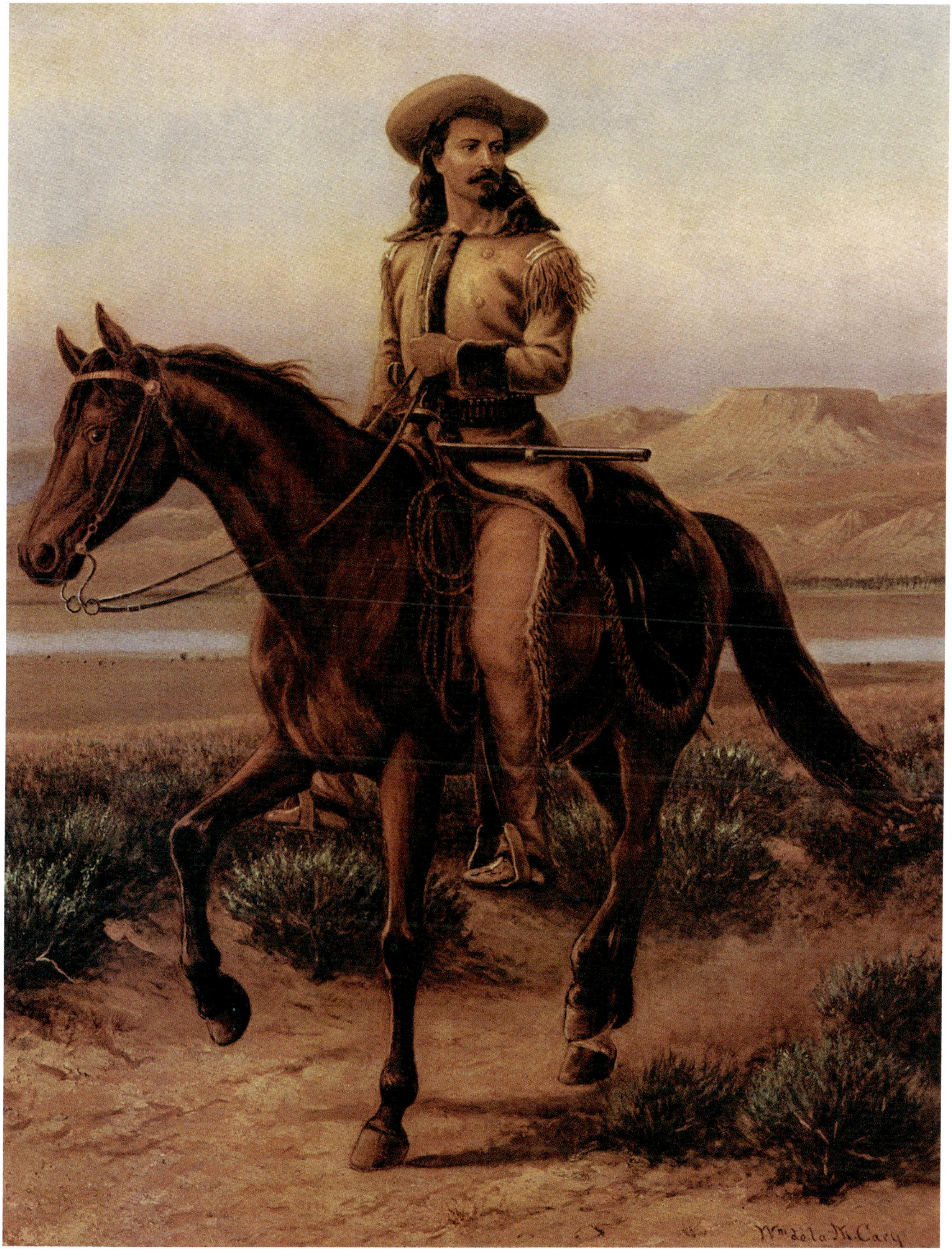

023. WILLIAM CARY (1840–1922)
Buffalo Bill on Charlie, n.d.
Oil on canvas. 52 x 40¼ in. (132.1 x 102.2 cm)

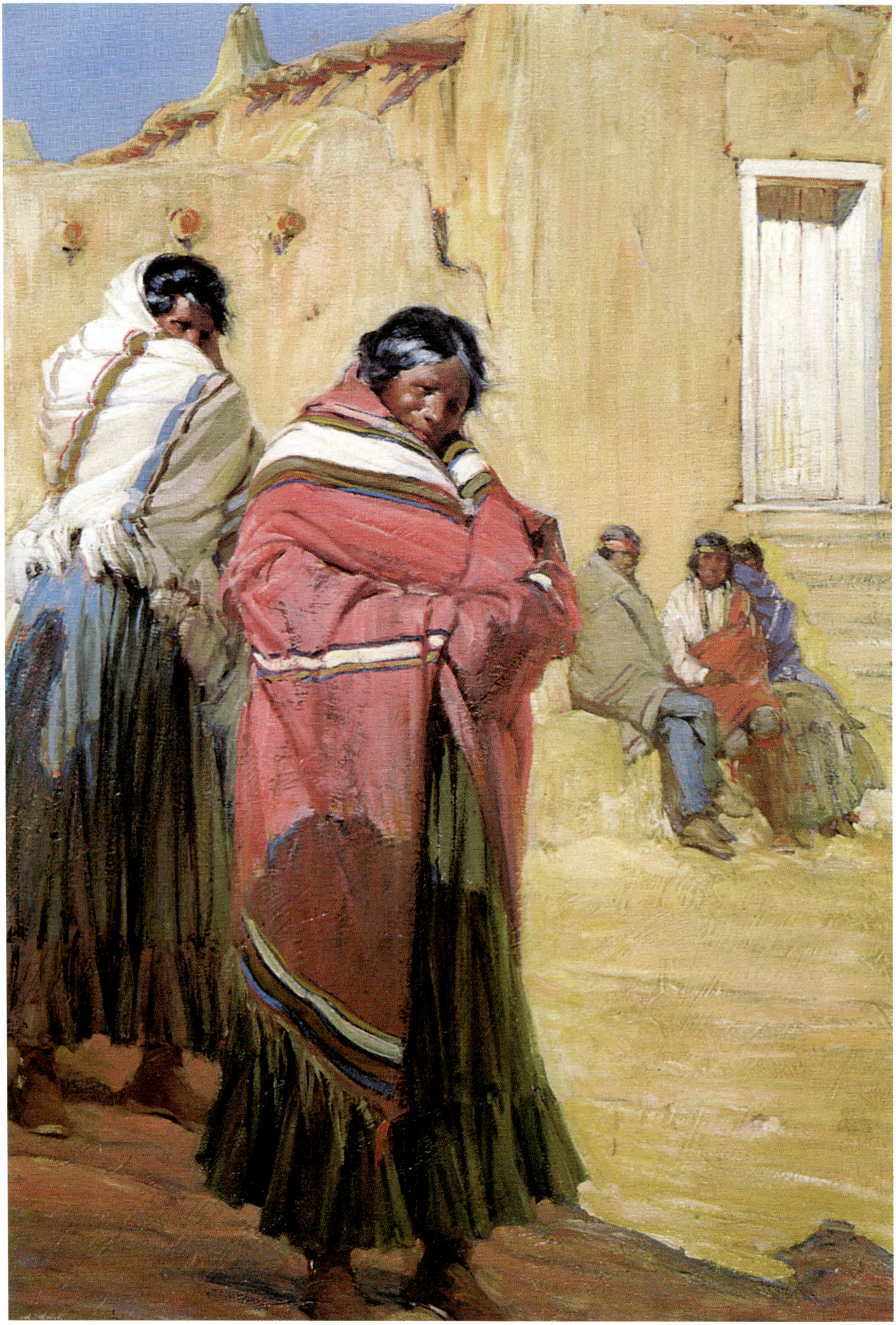

024. GERALD CASSIDY (1879–1934)
Indians Outside Taos Pueblo, n.d.
Oil on canvas. 44 x 30 in. (111.8 x 76.2 cm)

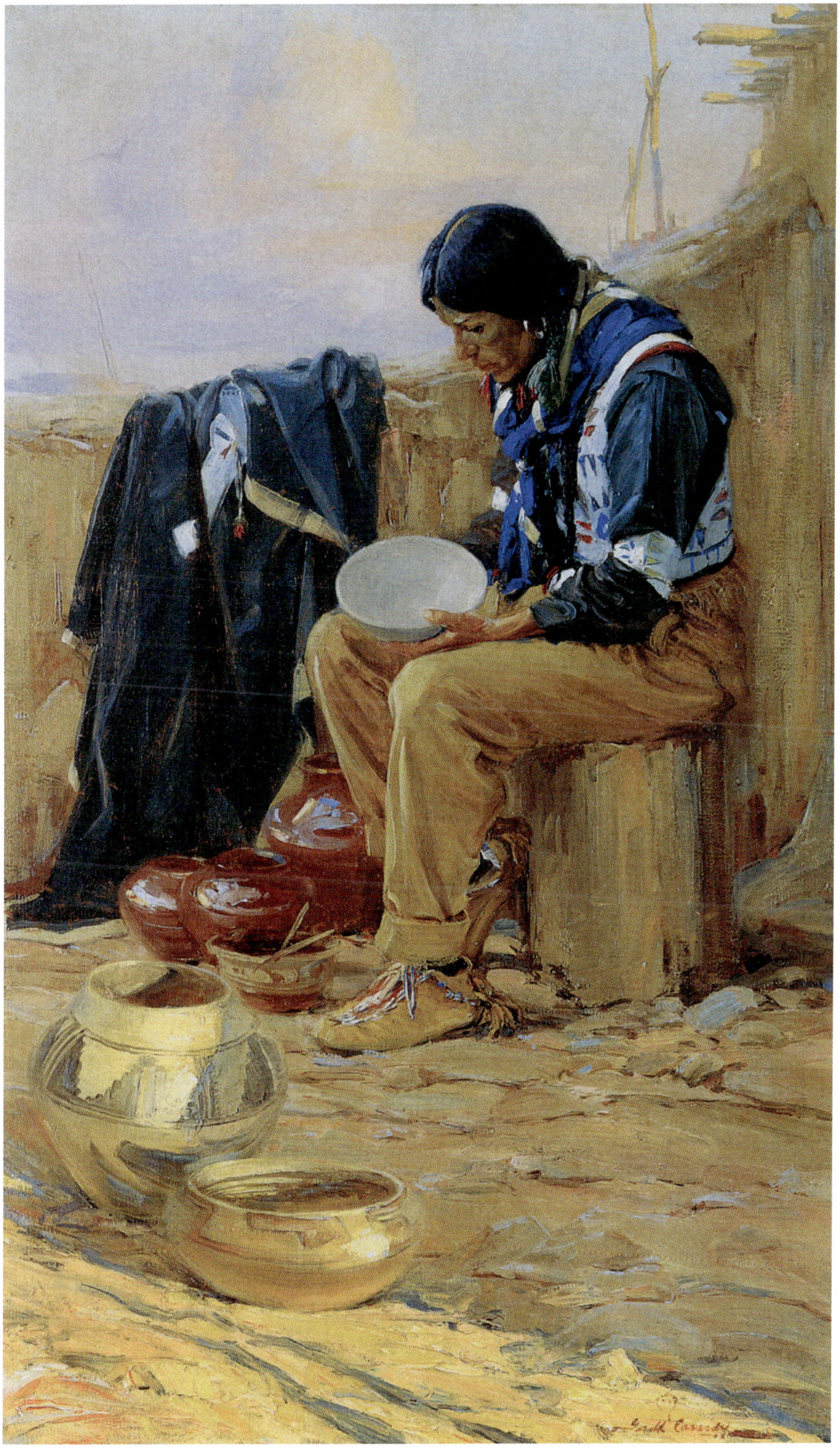

025. GERALD CASSIDY (1879–1934)
The Pottery Maker, 1912–17
Oil on canvas. 46 x 28 in. (116.8 x 71.1 cm)

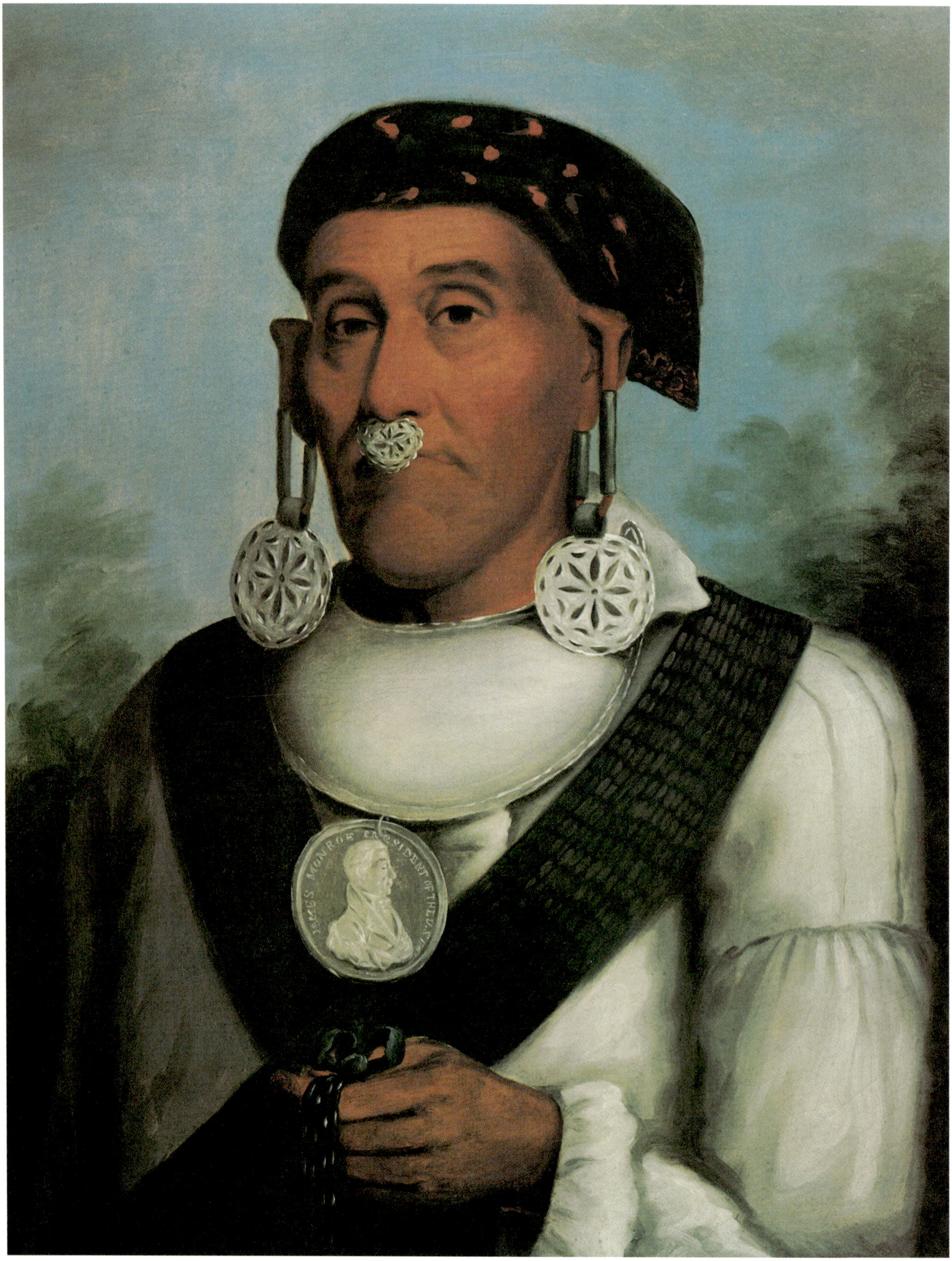

026. GEORGE CATLIN (1796–1872)
George Lowrey, n.d.
Oil. 26 x 22½ in. (66 x 57.1 cm)

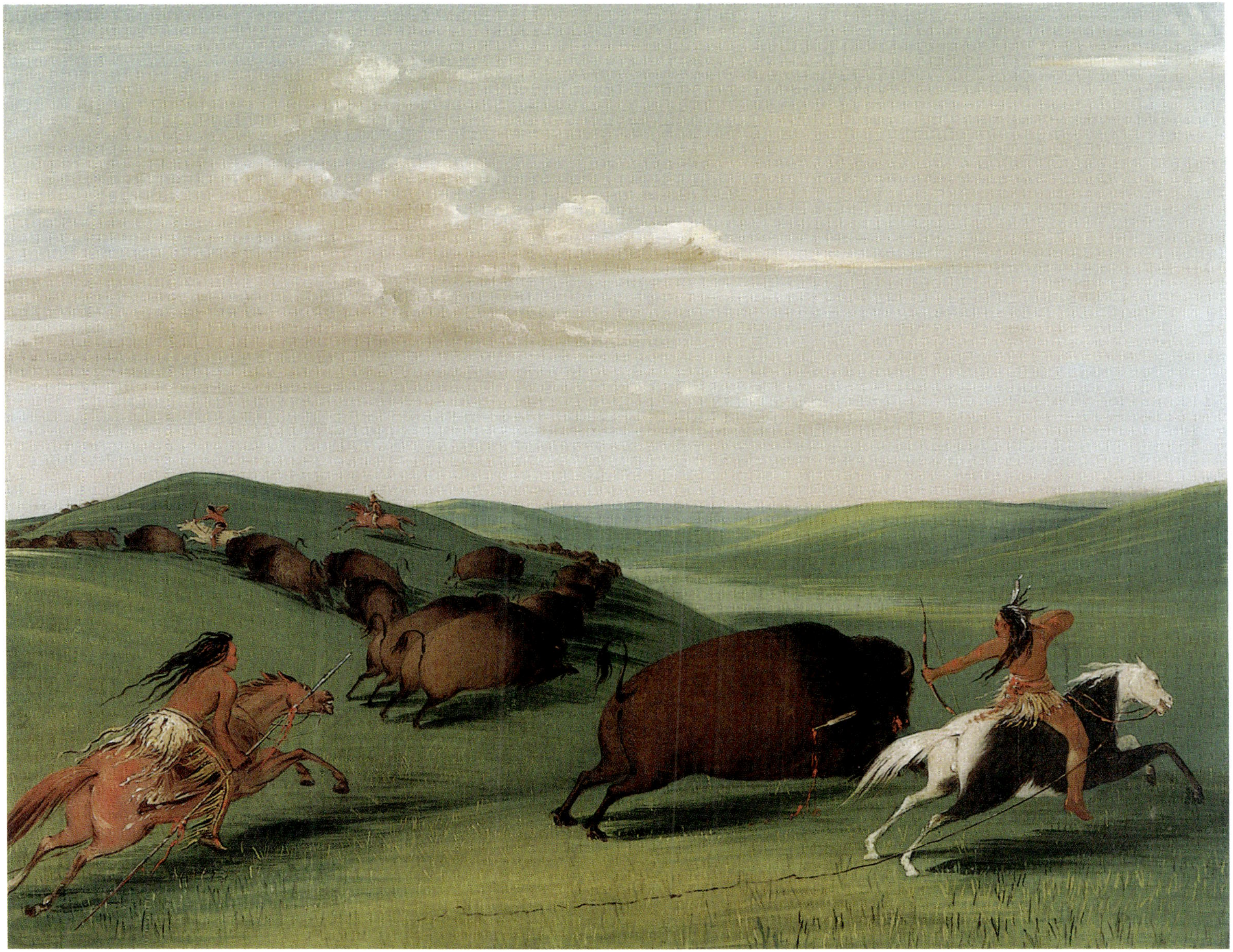

027. GEORGE CATLIN (1796–1872)
Buffalo Chase with Bows and Lances, 1832–33
Oil on canvas. 24 x 29 in. (61 x 73.7 cm)

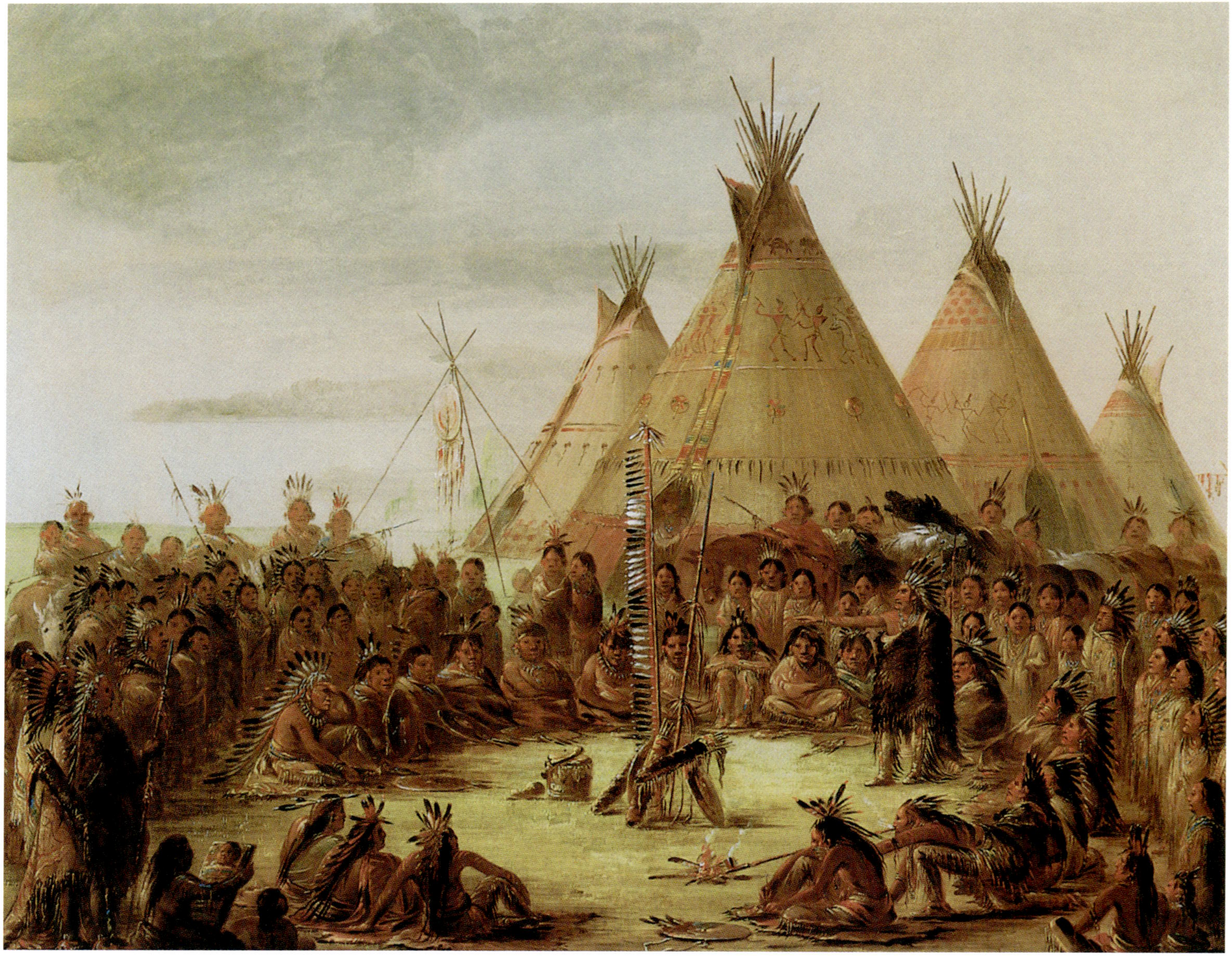

028. GEORGE CATLIN (1796–1872)
Sioux War Council, c. 1848
Oil on canvas. 25¾ x 32 in. (65.4 x 81.3 cm)

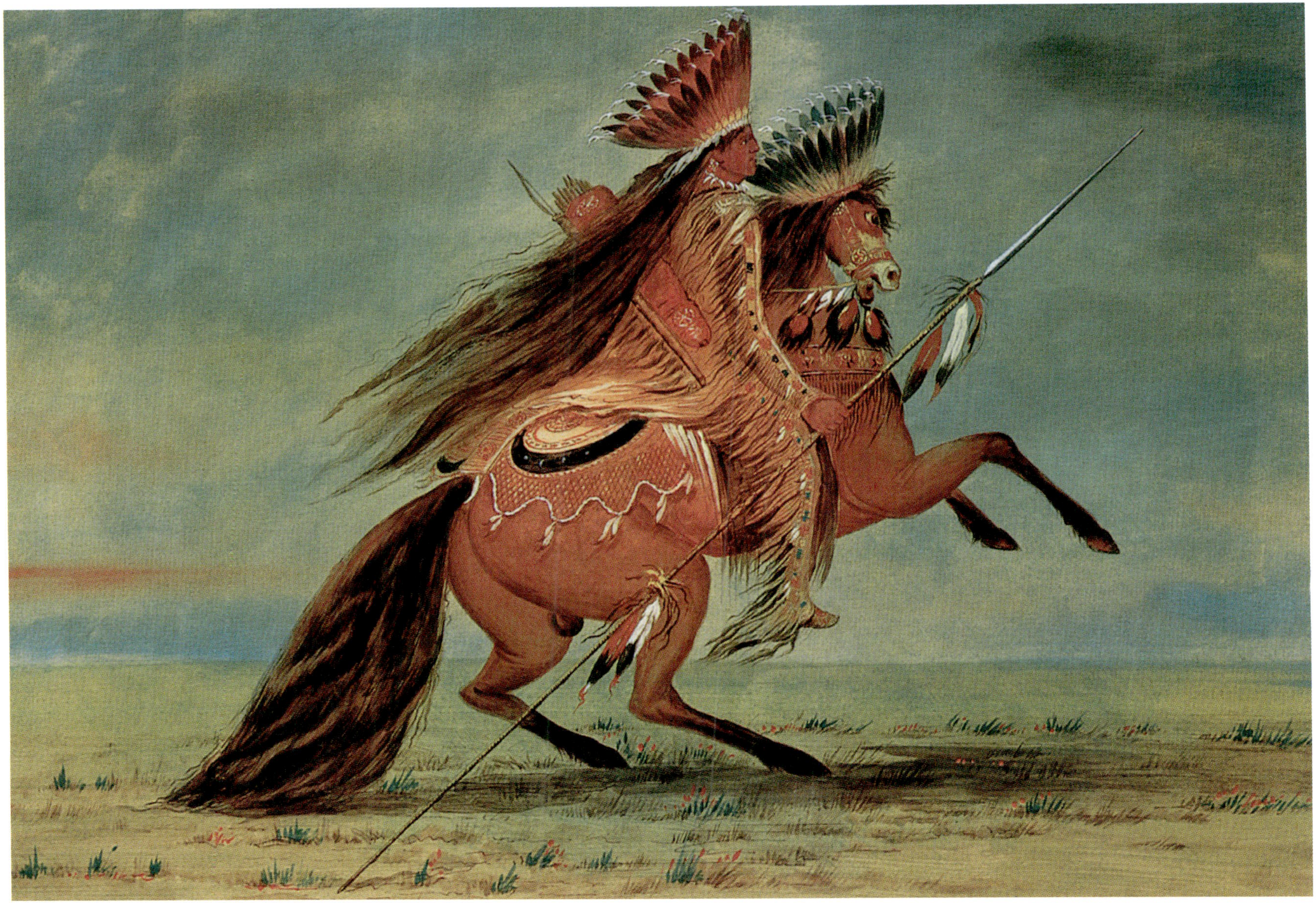

029. GEORGE CATLIN (1796–1872)
Crow Chief, c. 1850
Oil on board. 15⅞ x 21⅝ in. (40.3 x 54.9 cm)

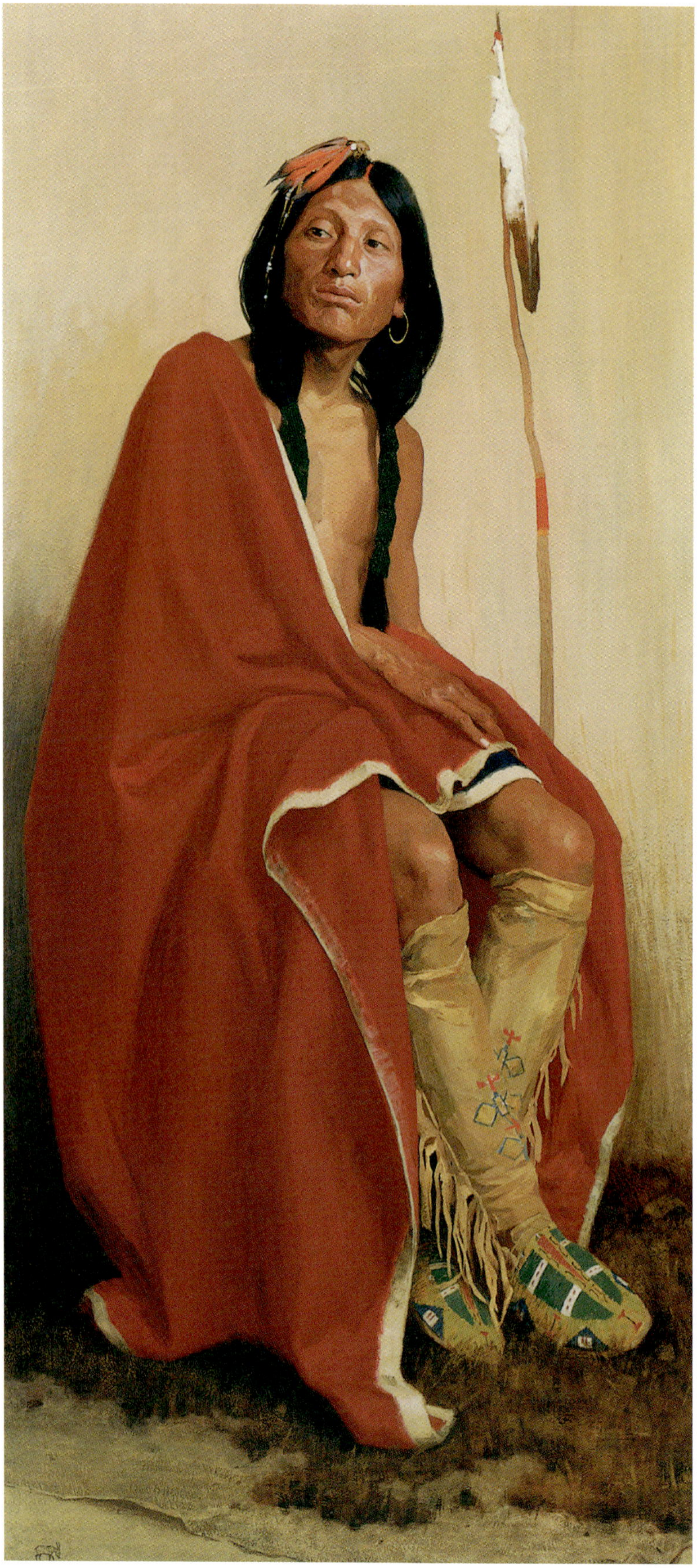

030. EANGER IRVING COUSE (1866–1936)
Elk-Foot of the Taos Tribe, 1909
Oil on canvas. 78¼ x 36⅜ in. (198.8 x 92.4 cm)

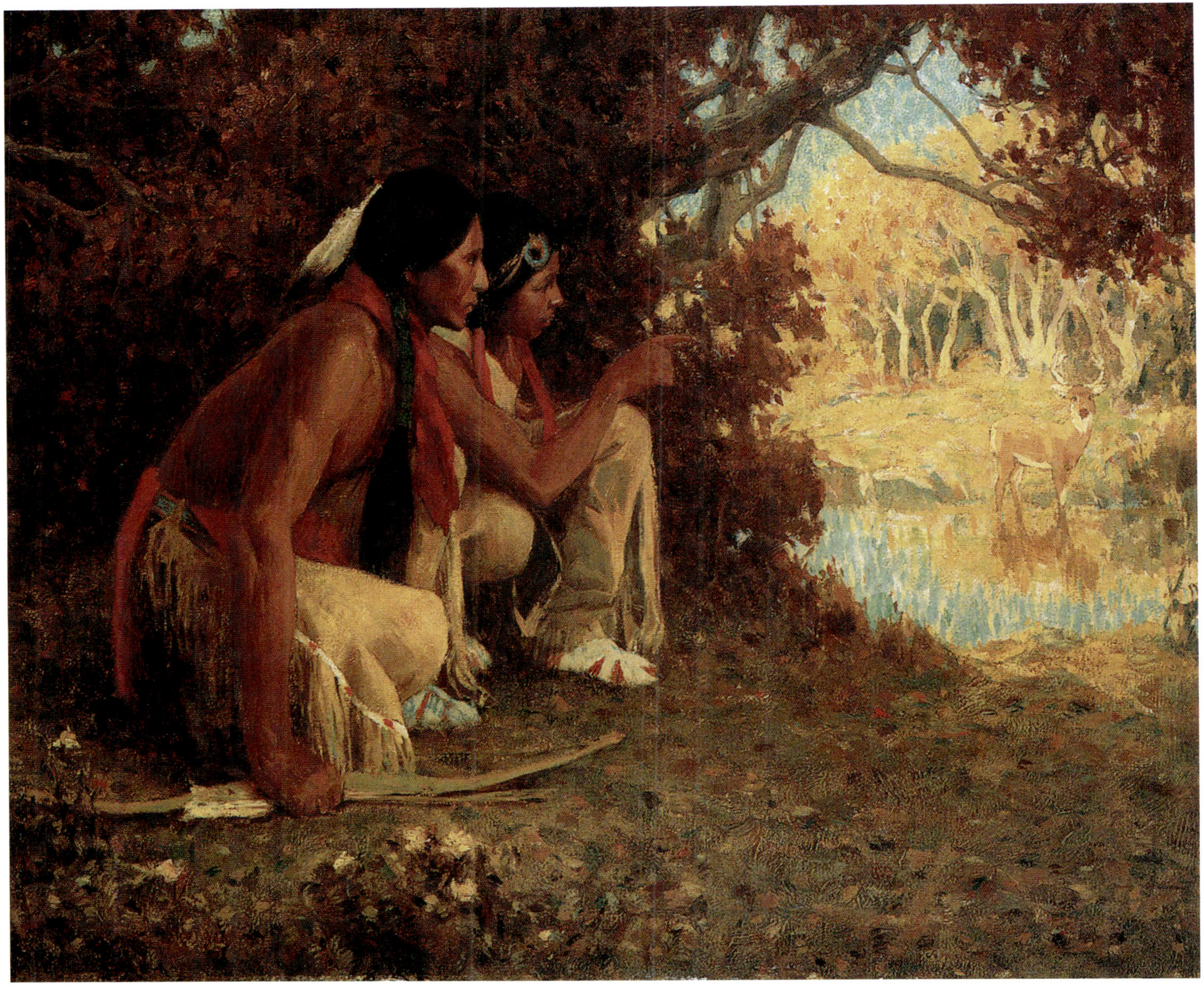

031. EANGER IRVING COUSE (1866–1936)
Hunting for Deer, 1909
Oil on canvas. 24 x 29 in. (61 x 73.7 cm)

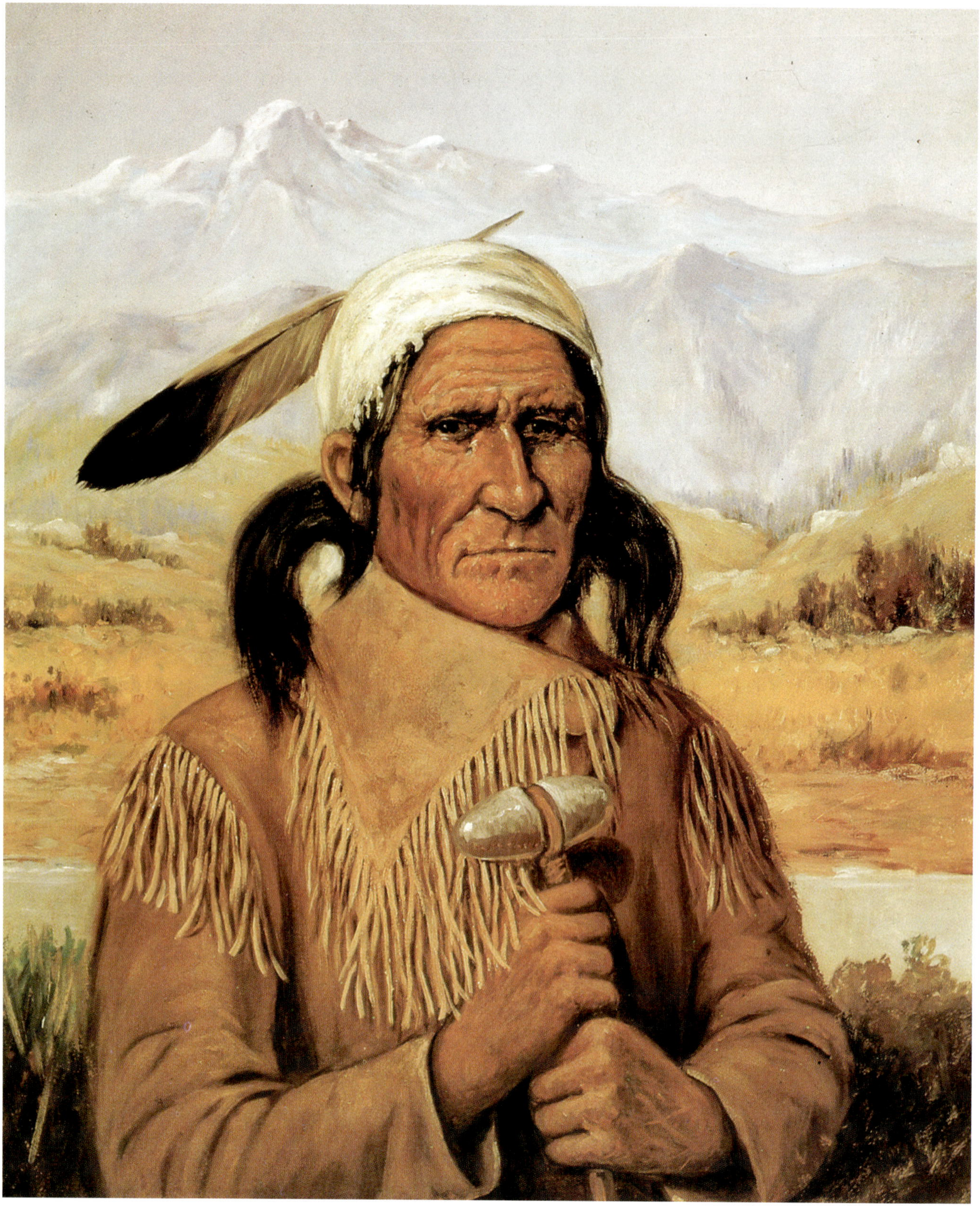

032. HENRY CROSS (1837–1918)
Geronimo, c. 1900
Oil on canvas. 30¼ x 25⅛ in. (76.8 x 63.8 cm)

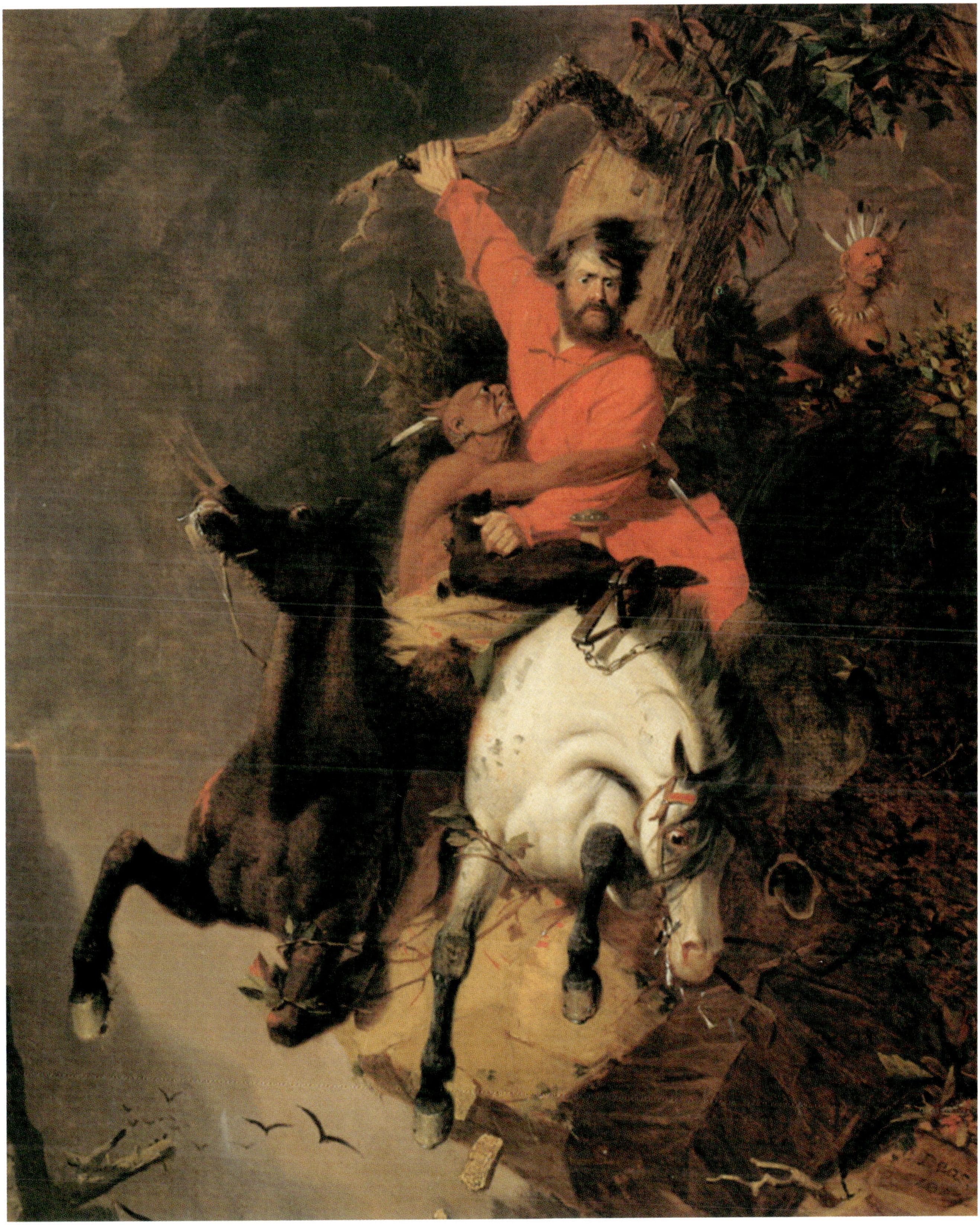

033. CHARLES DEAS (1818–1867)
The Death Struggle, c. 1845–47
Oil on canvas.

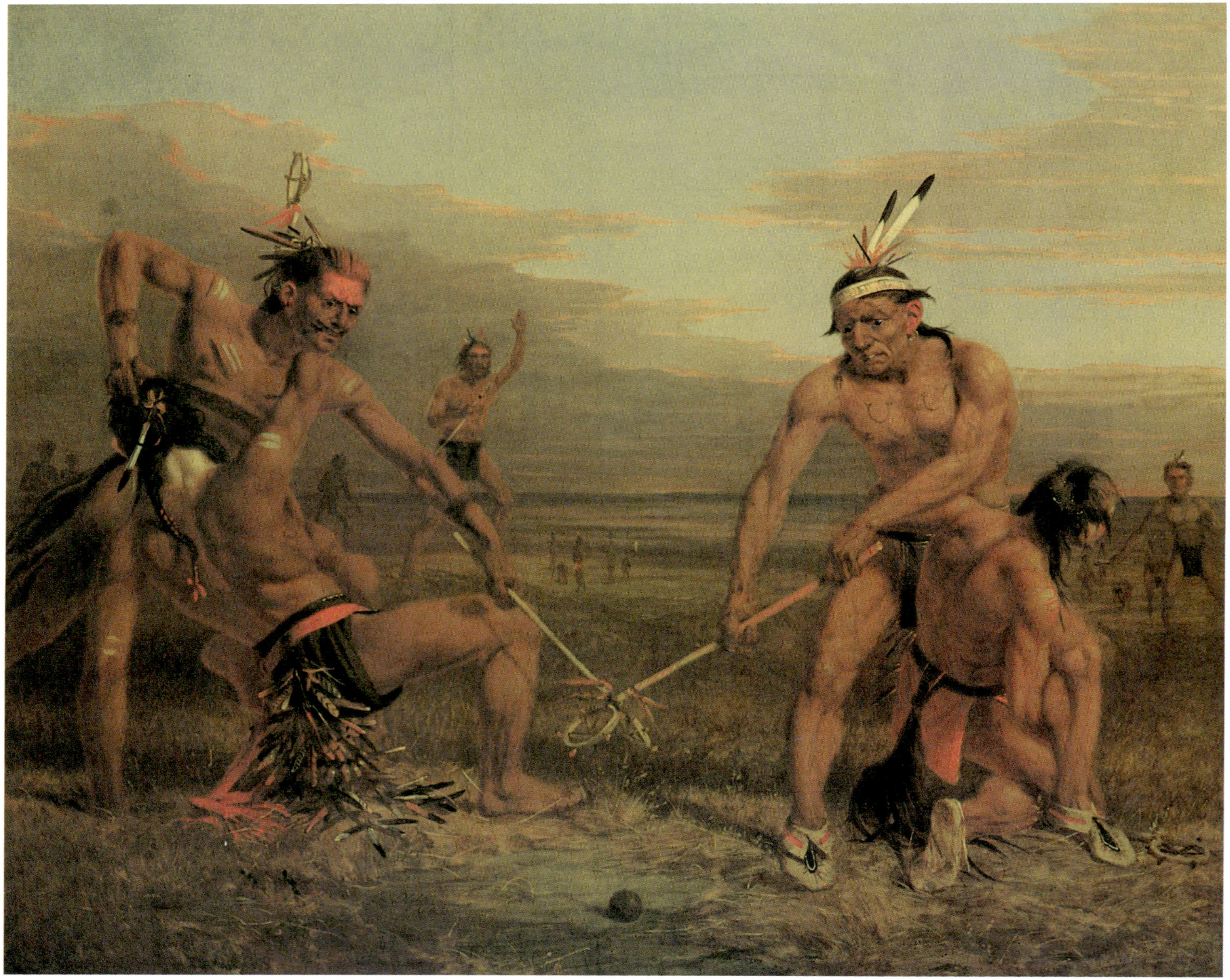

034. CHARLES DEAS (1818–1867)
Indian Ball Game, 1843
Oil. 29 x 37 in. (73.7 x 94 cm)

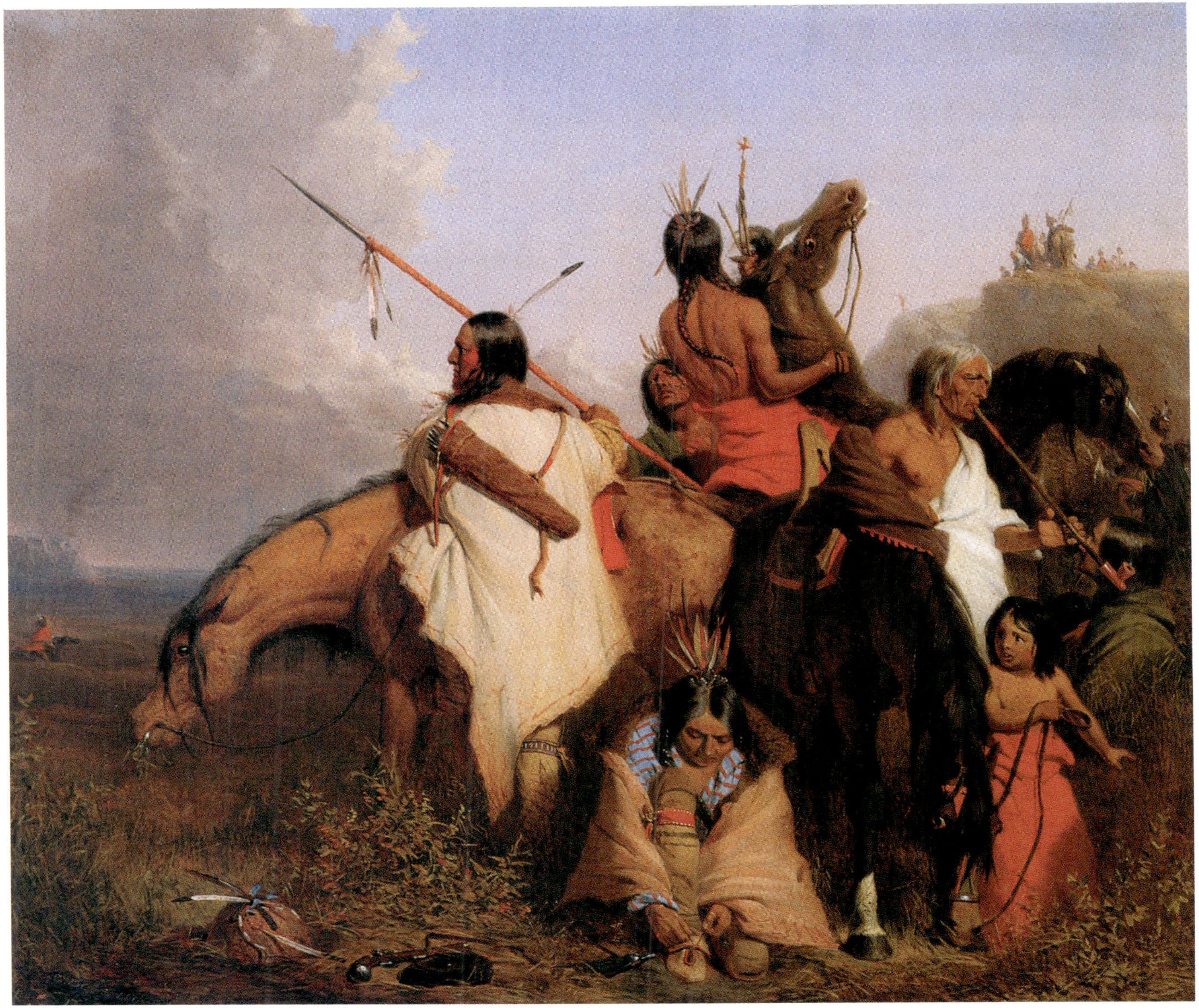

035. CHARLES DEAS (1818–1867)
A Group of Sioux, 1845
Oil on canvas.

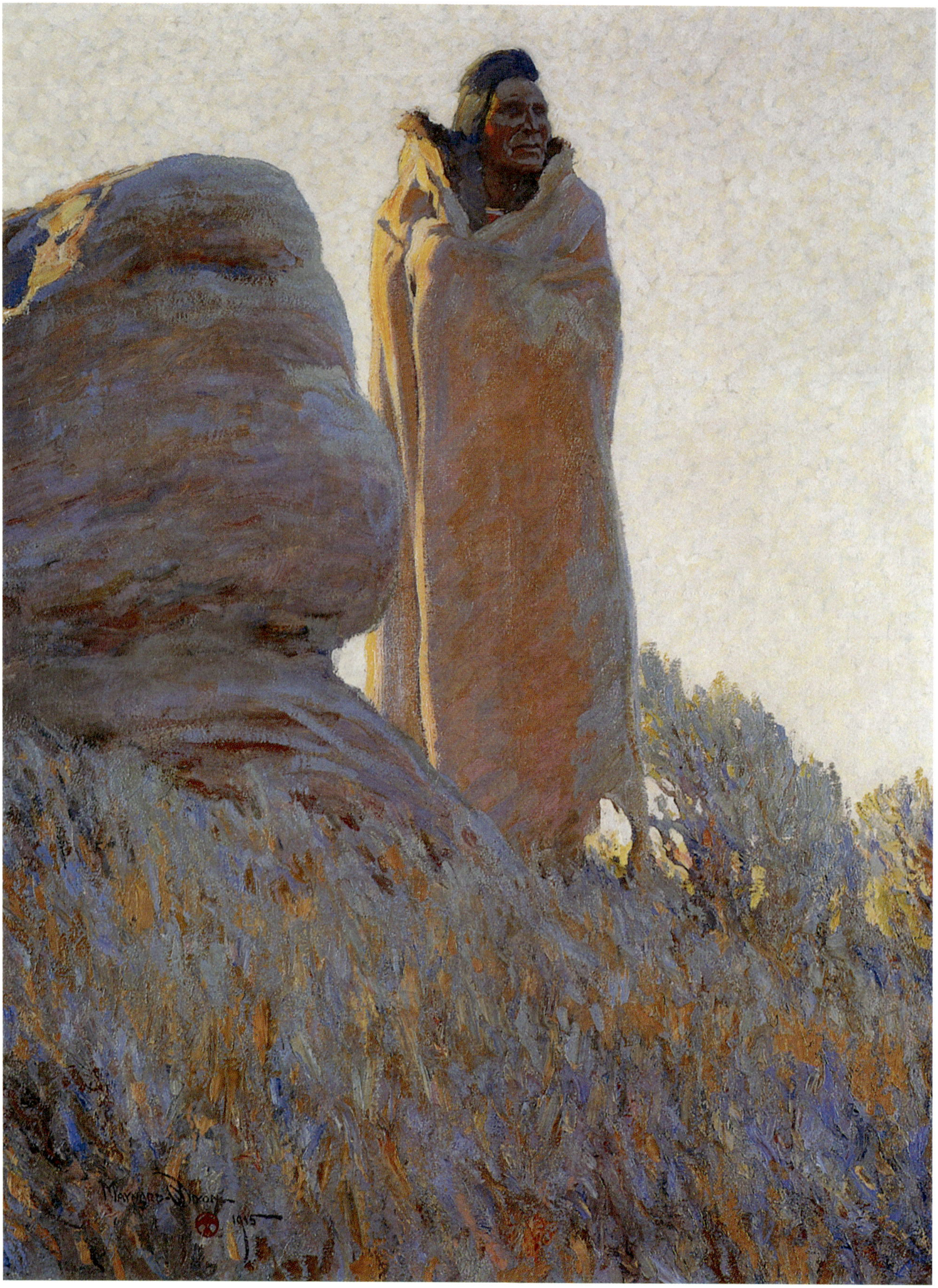

036. MAYNARD DIXON (1875–1946)
The Medicine Robe, 1915
Oil on canvas. 40 x 30 in. (101.6 x 76.2 cm)

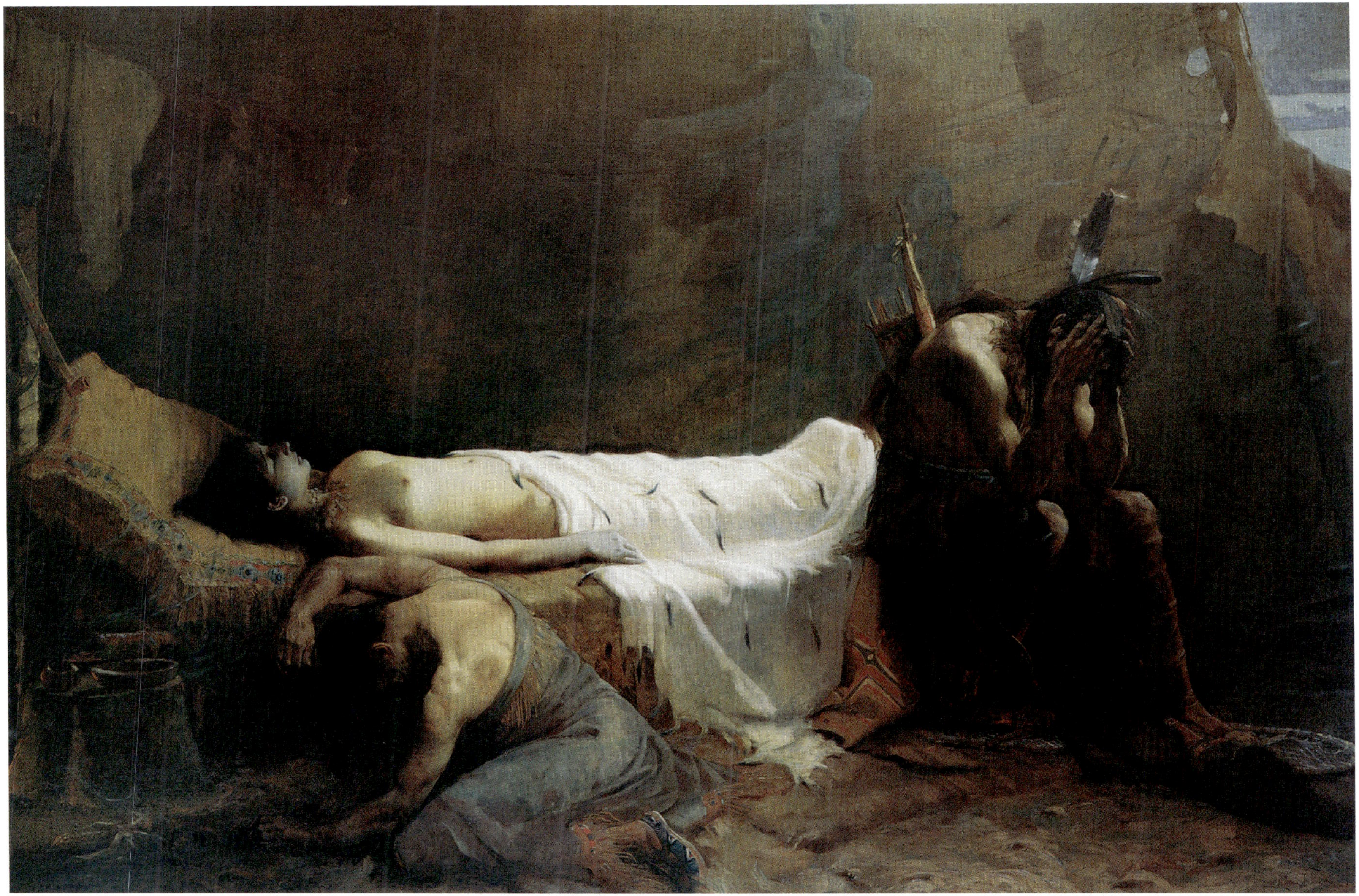

037. WILLIAM DE LEFTWICH DODGE (1867–1935)
The Death of Minnehaha, 1885
Oil on canvas. 80 x 120¼ in. (203.2 x 305.4 cm)

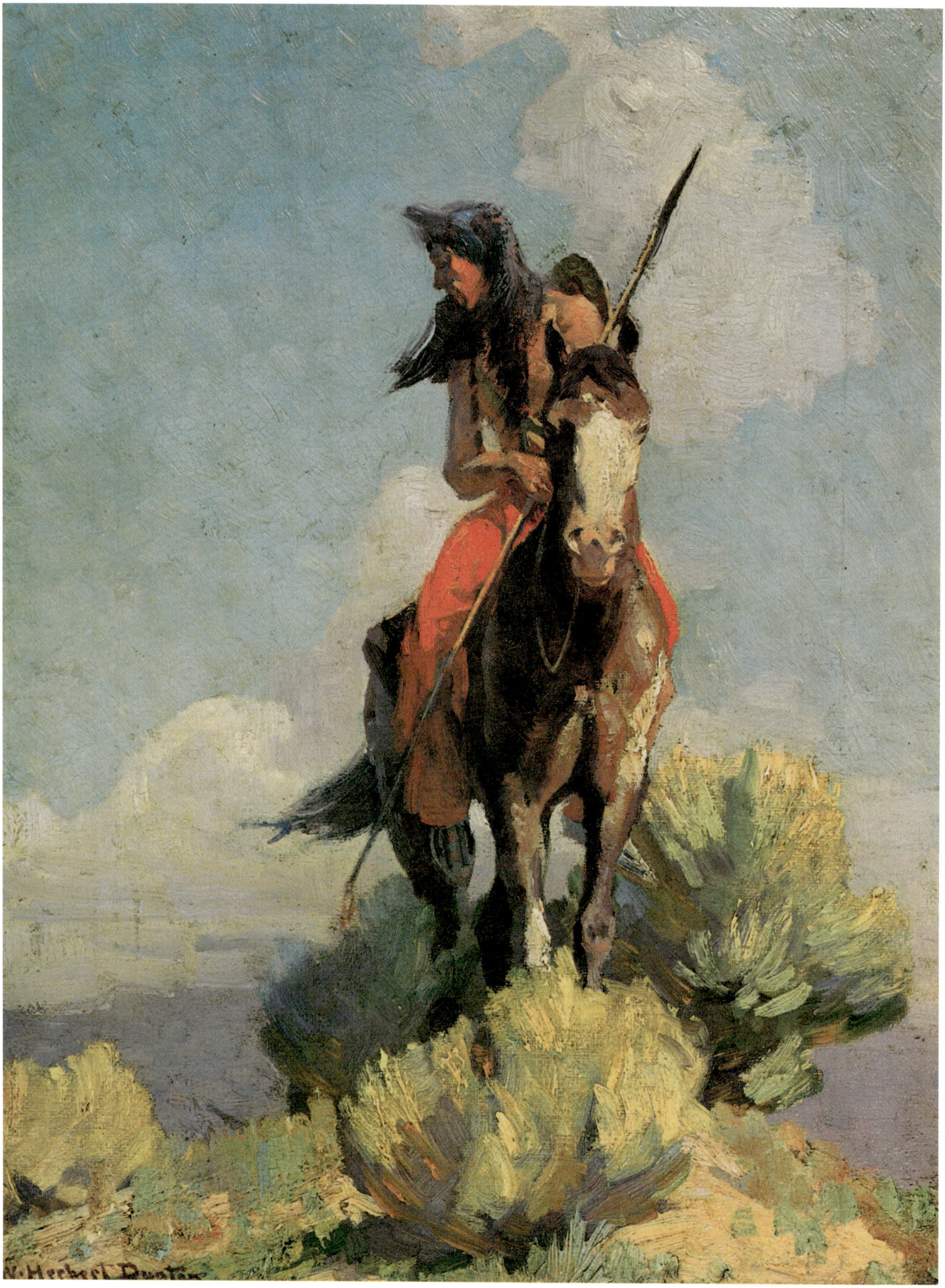

038. WILLIAM HERBERT DUNTON (1878–1936)
Crow Outlier, c. 1896.
Oil. 16⅛ x 12⅛ in. (41 x 30.8 cm)

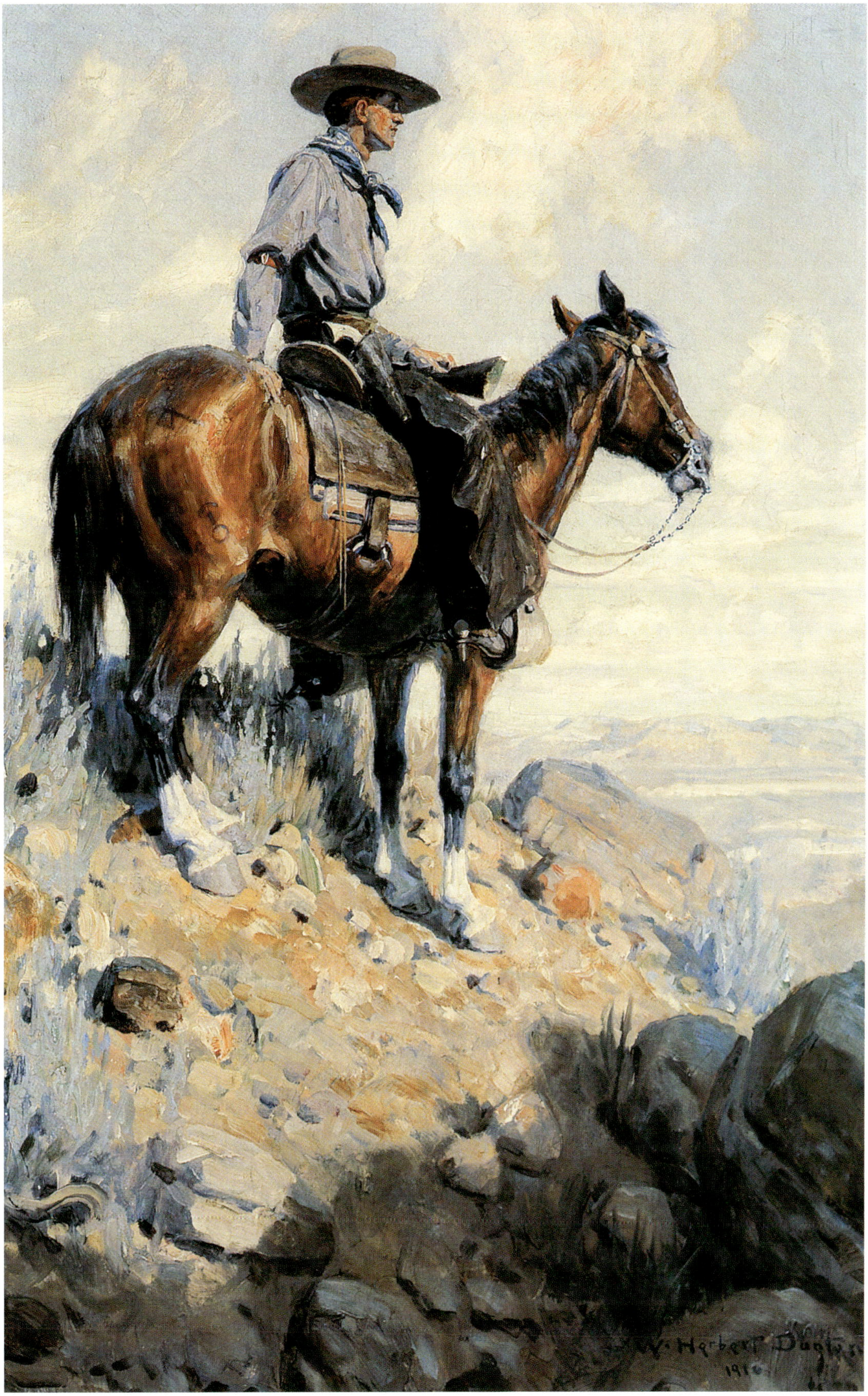

039. WILLIAM HERBERT DUNTON (1878–1936)
Sentinel of the Plains, 1906
Oil on canvas. 39 x 26 in. (99 x 66 cm)

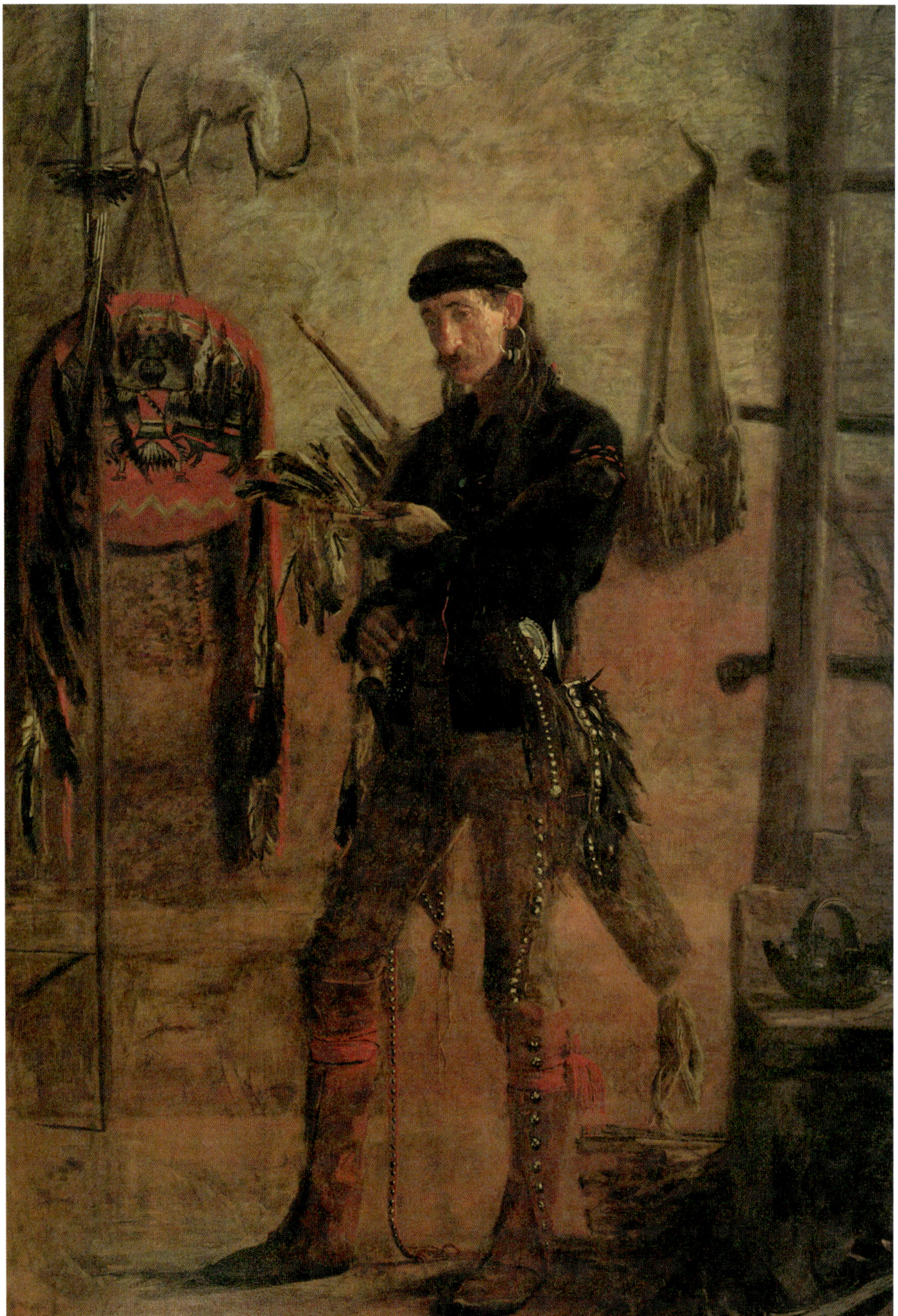

040. THOMAS EAKINS (1844–1916)
Frank Hamilton Cushing, n.d.
Oil. 47 x 45 in. (119.4 x 114.3 cm)

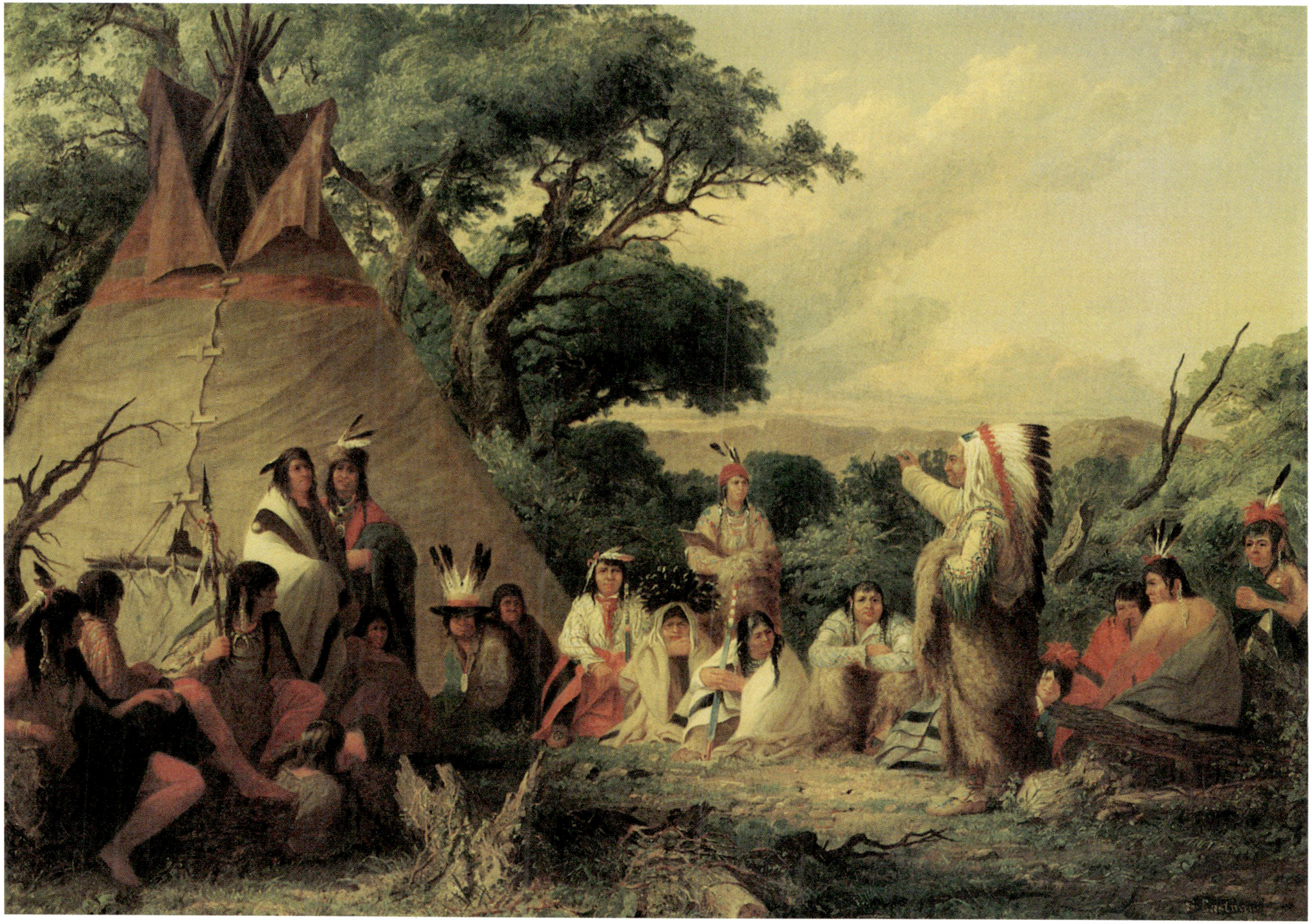

041. SETH EASTMAN (1808–1875)
The Indian Council, 1852
Oil. 26 x 35 in. (66 x 88.9 cm)

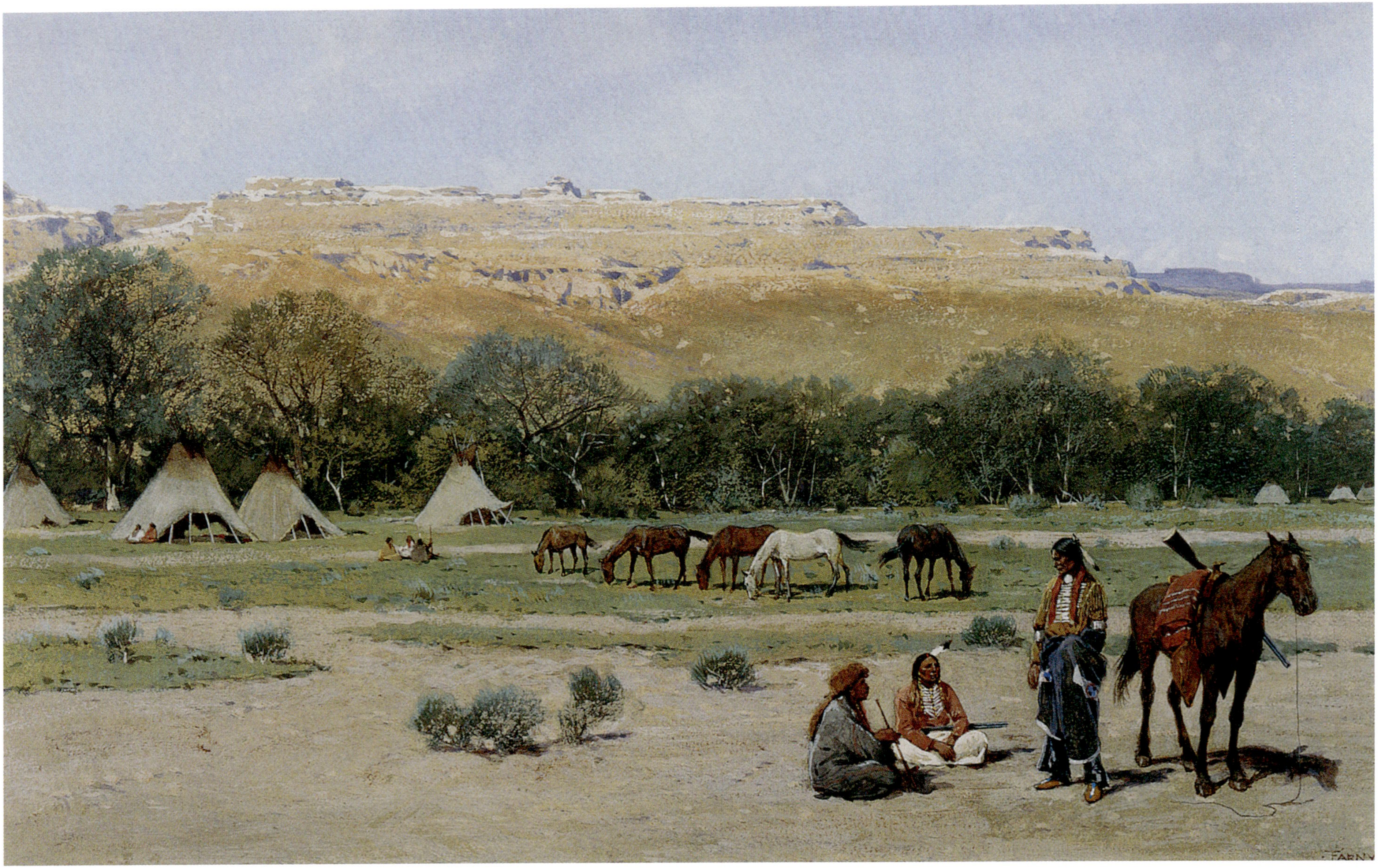

042. HENRY FARNY (1847–1916)
Indian Encampment, 1901
Gouache on paper. 9½ x 14 in. (24.1 x 35.6 cm)

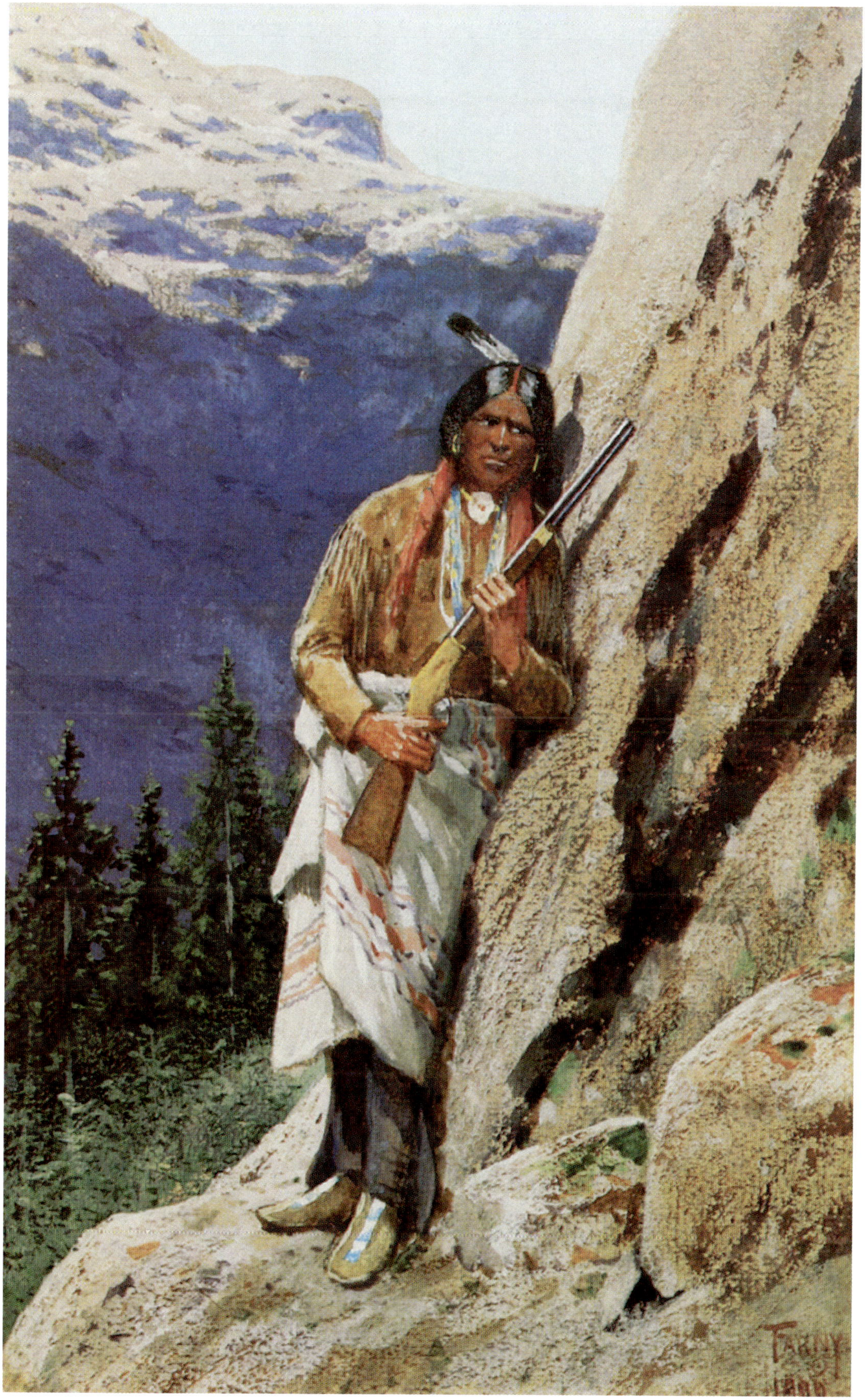

043. HENRY FARNY (1847–1916)
The Hunter, 1900
Gouache. 8⅜ x 5⅛ in. (21.1 x 13 cm)

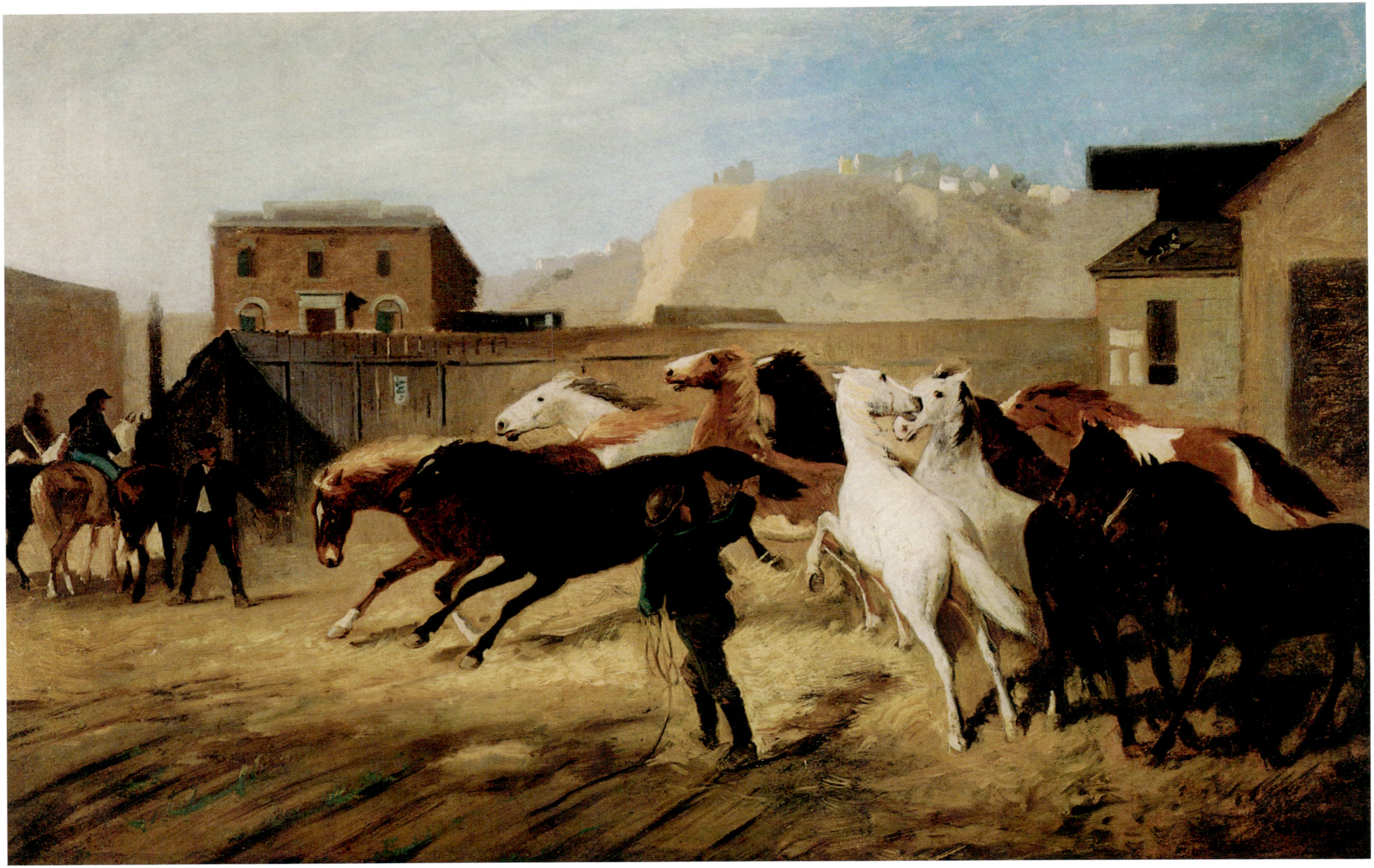

044. WILLIAM HAHN (1829–1887)
Vallejo Street Wharf—Arrival of Government Horses (The Government Corral), n.d.
Oil on canvas. 18¼ x 28¼ in. (46.4 x 71.8 cm)

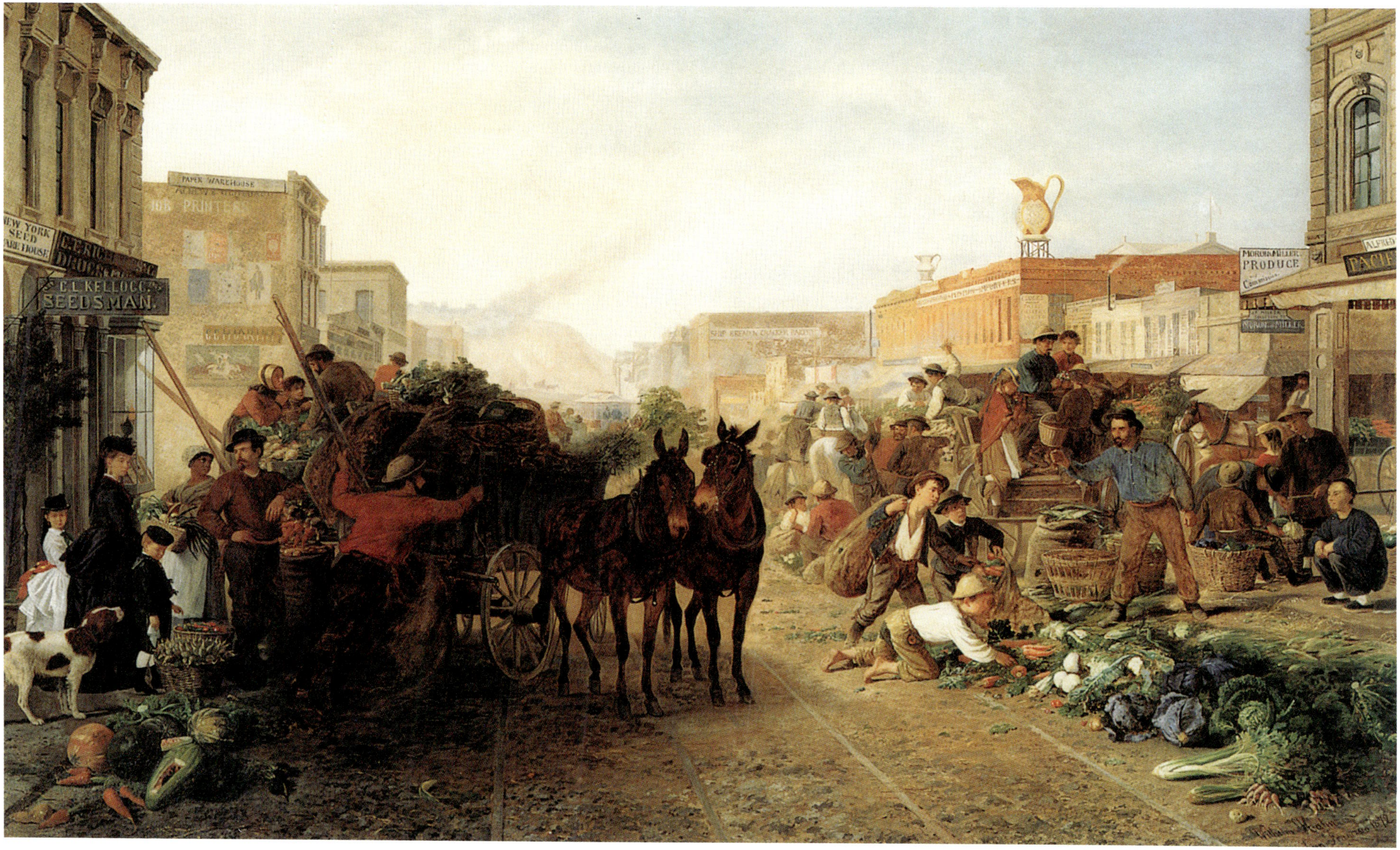

045. WILLIAM HAHN (1829–1887)
Market Scene, Sansome Street, San Francisco, 1872
Oil on canvas. 60 x 96 in. (152.5 x 244 cm)

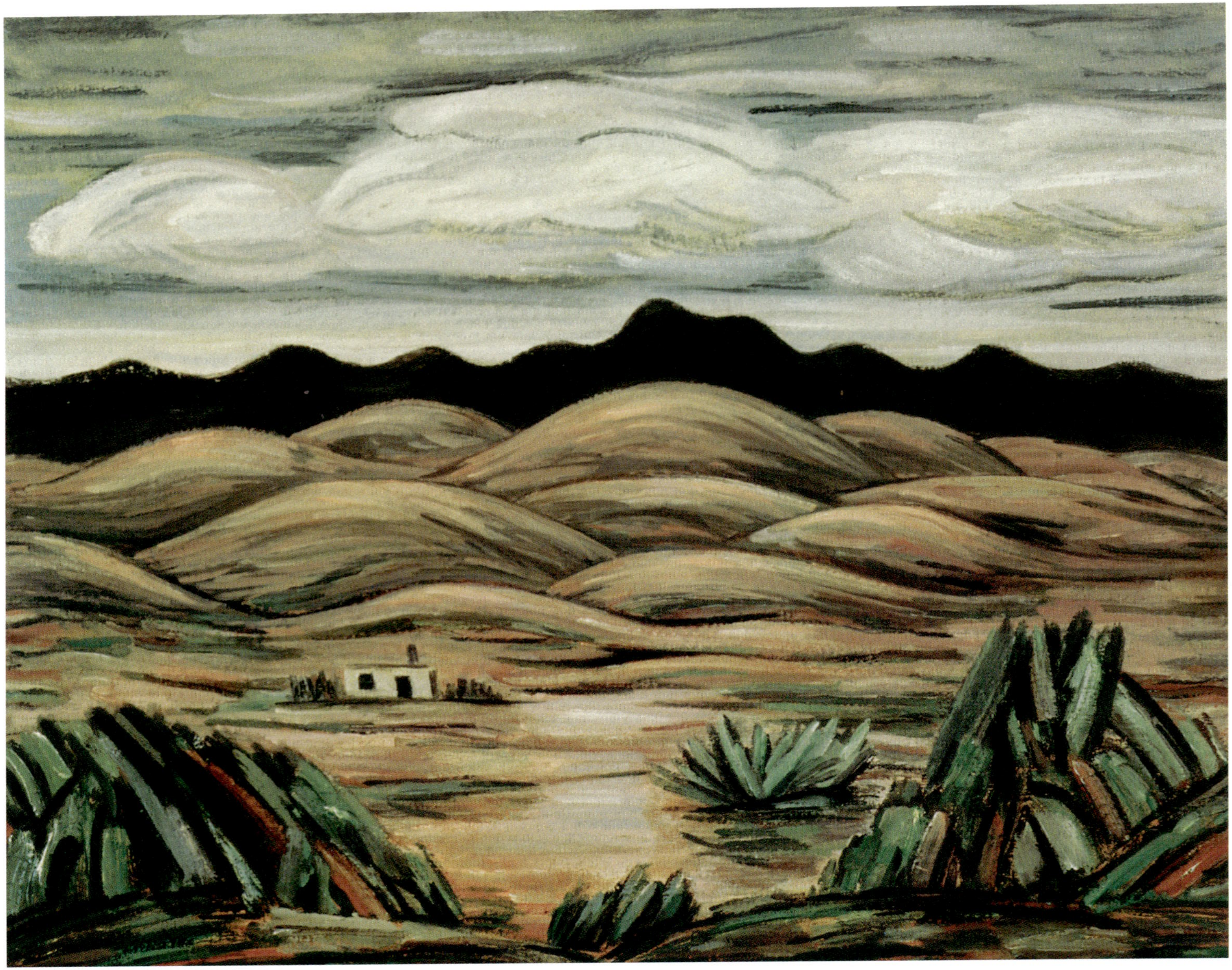

046. MARSDEN HARTLEY (1877–1943)
Desert Scene, 1911
Oil. 15 x 21⅛ in. (38.1 x 53.7 cm)

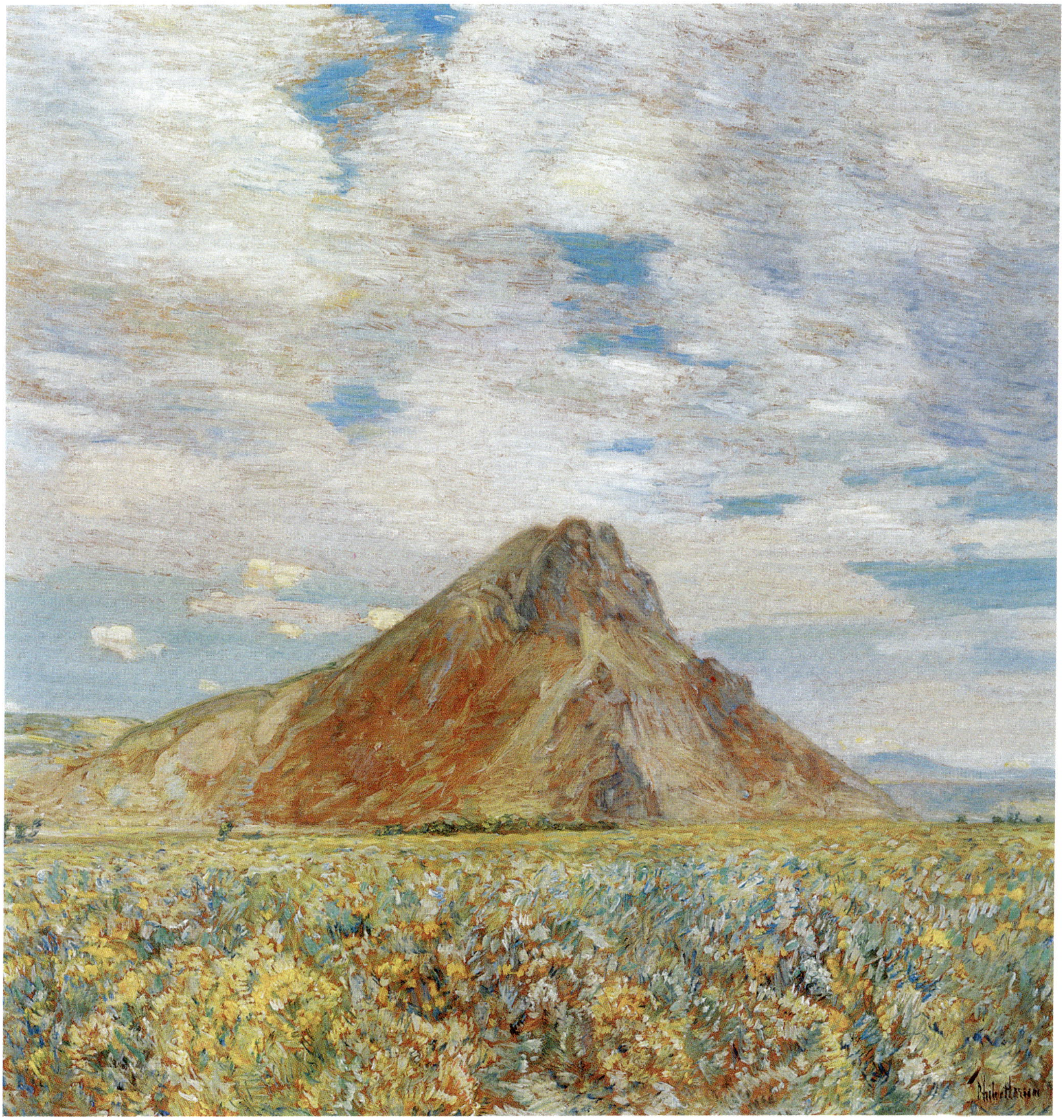

047. CHILDE HASSAM (1859–1935)
Sand Springs Butte, 1904
Oil on canvas. 30 x 30 in. (76.2 x 76.2 cm)

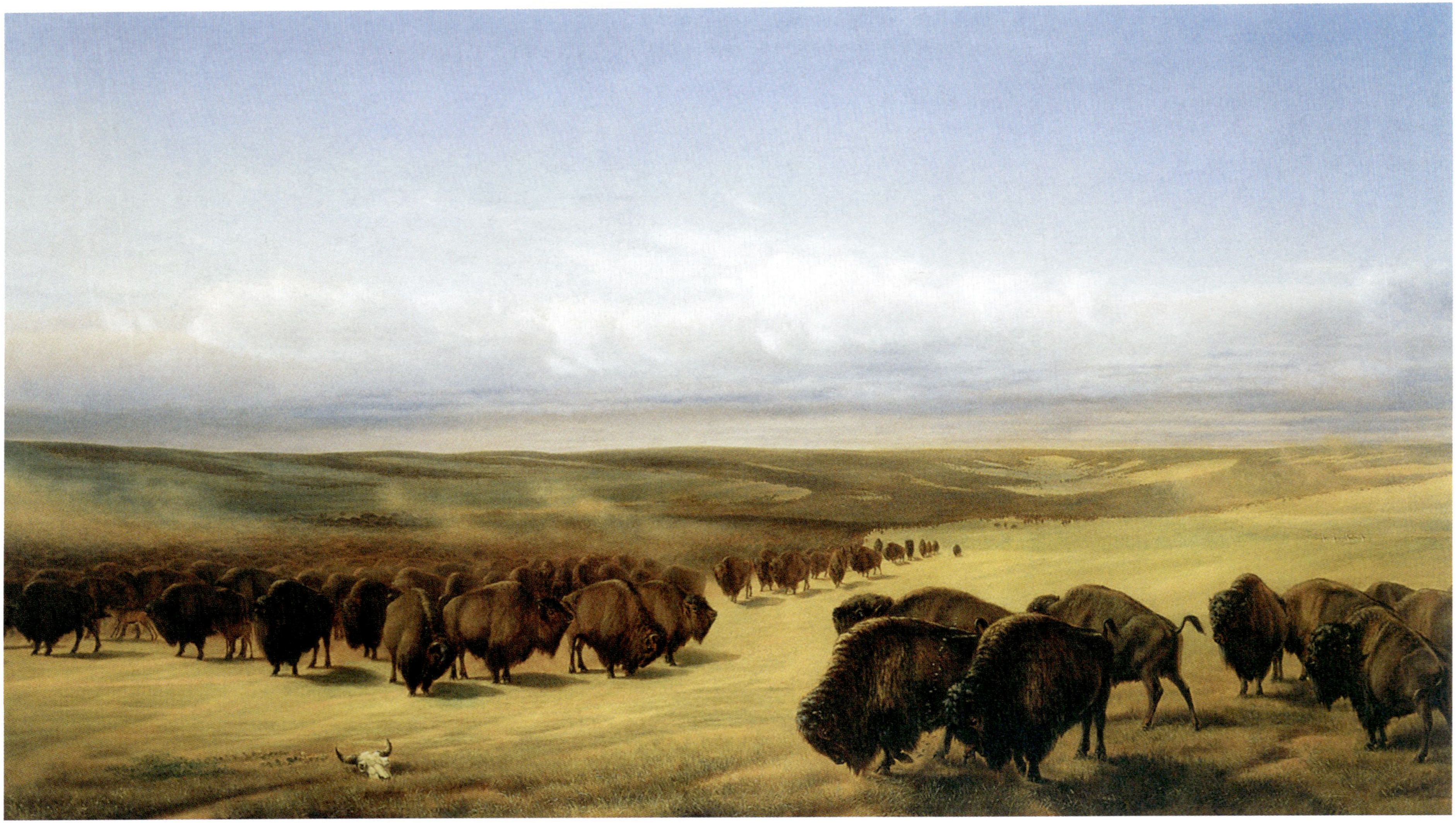

048. WILLIAM JACOB HAYS (1830–1875)
The Gathering of the Herds, 1866
Oil on canvas. 42 x 75⅝ in. (106.7 x 192.1 cm)

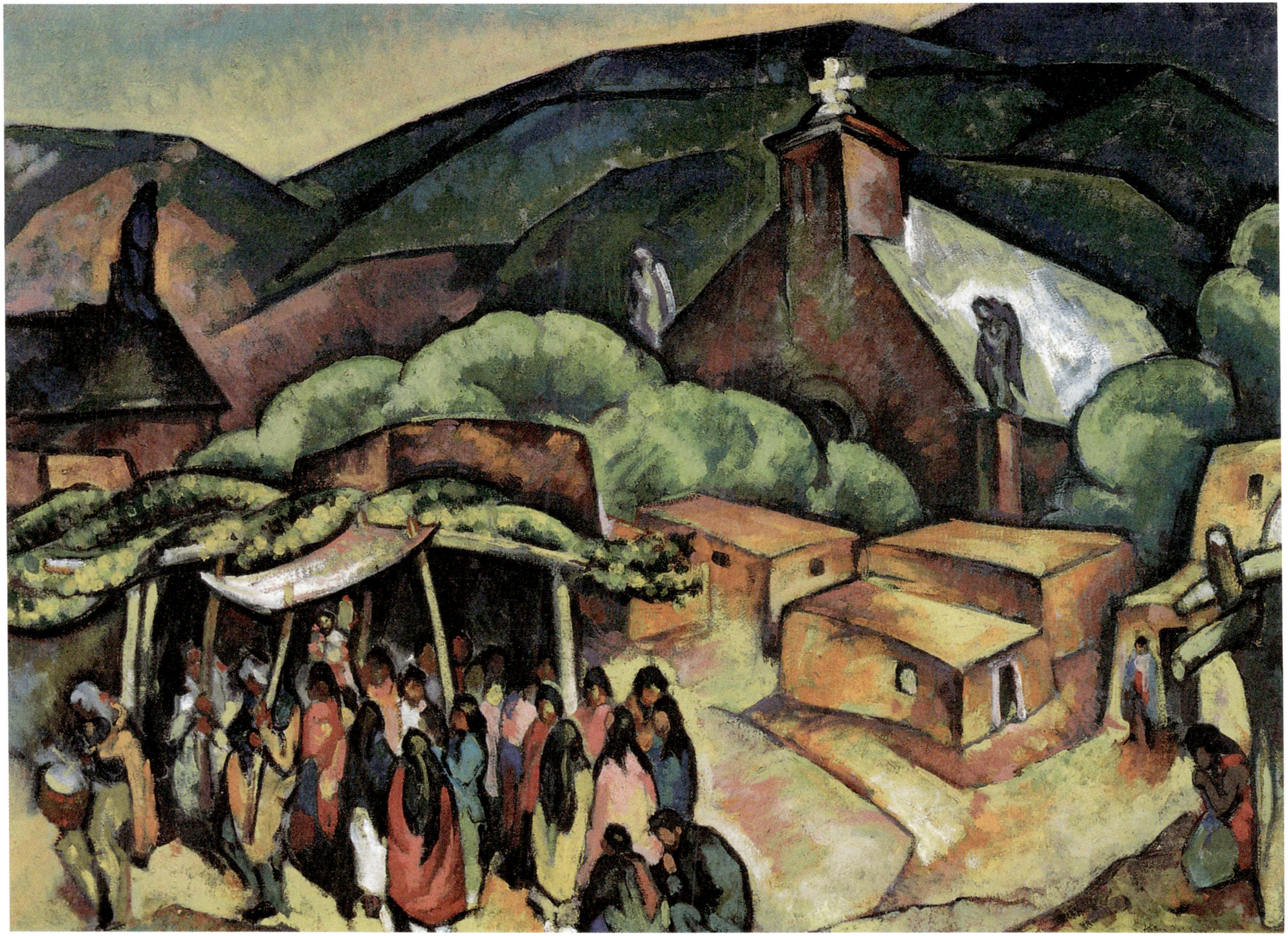

049. WILLIAM PENHALLOW HENDERSON (1877–1943)
Feast Day: San Juan Pueblo, c. 1921
Oil. 22 x 30 in. (55.9 x 76.2 cm)

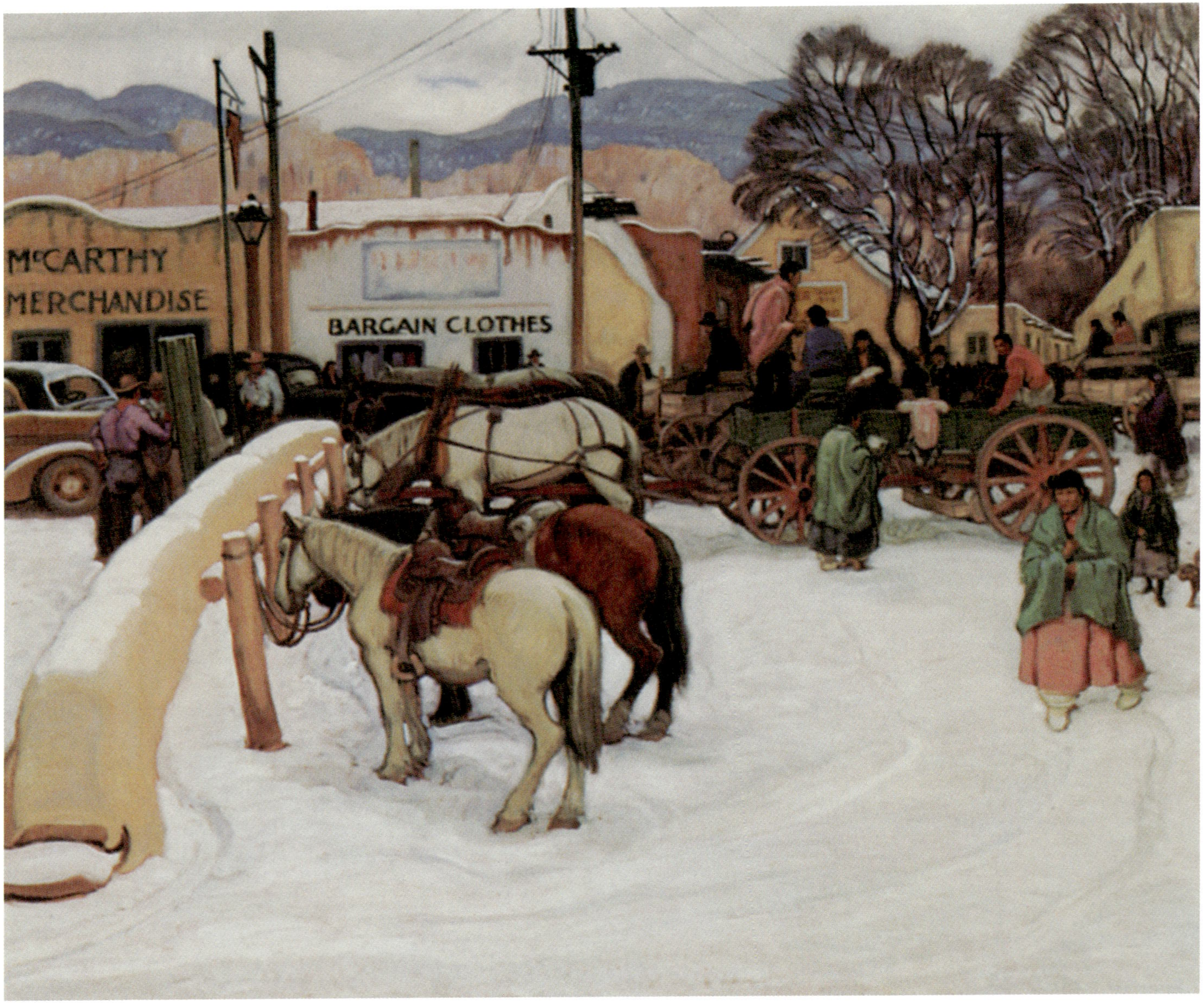

050. E. MARTIN HENNINGS (1886–1956)
Taos Plaza, Winter 1921
Oil on canvas. 34 x 40 in. (86.3 x 101.6 cm)

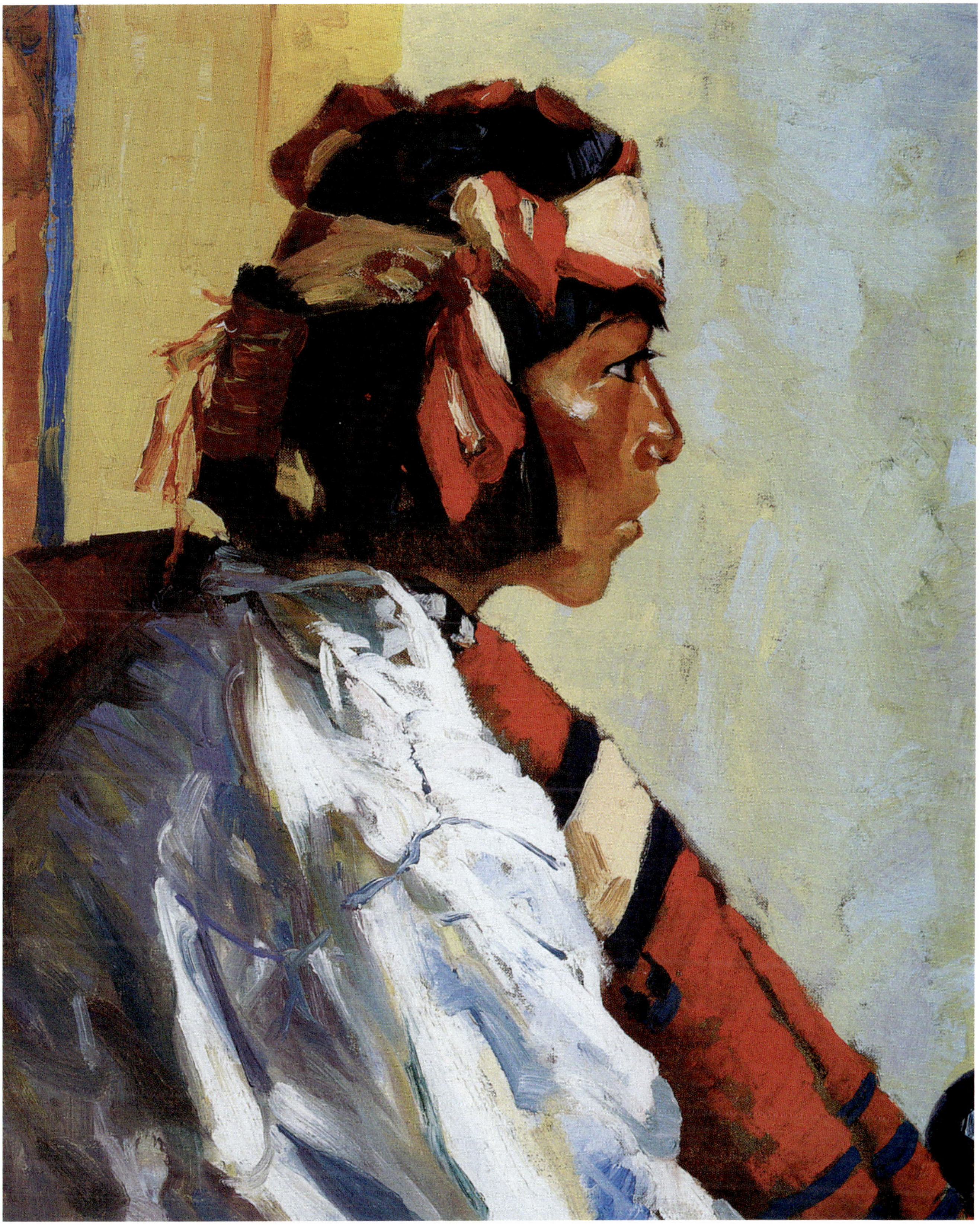

051. ROBERT HENRI (1865–1929)
Miguel of Tesuque, 1917
Oil on canvas. 24⅛ x 20¼ in. (61.3 x 51.4 cm)

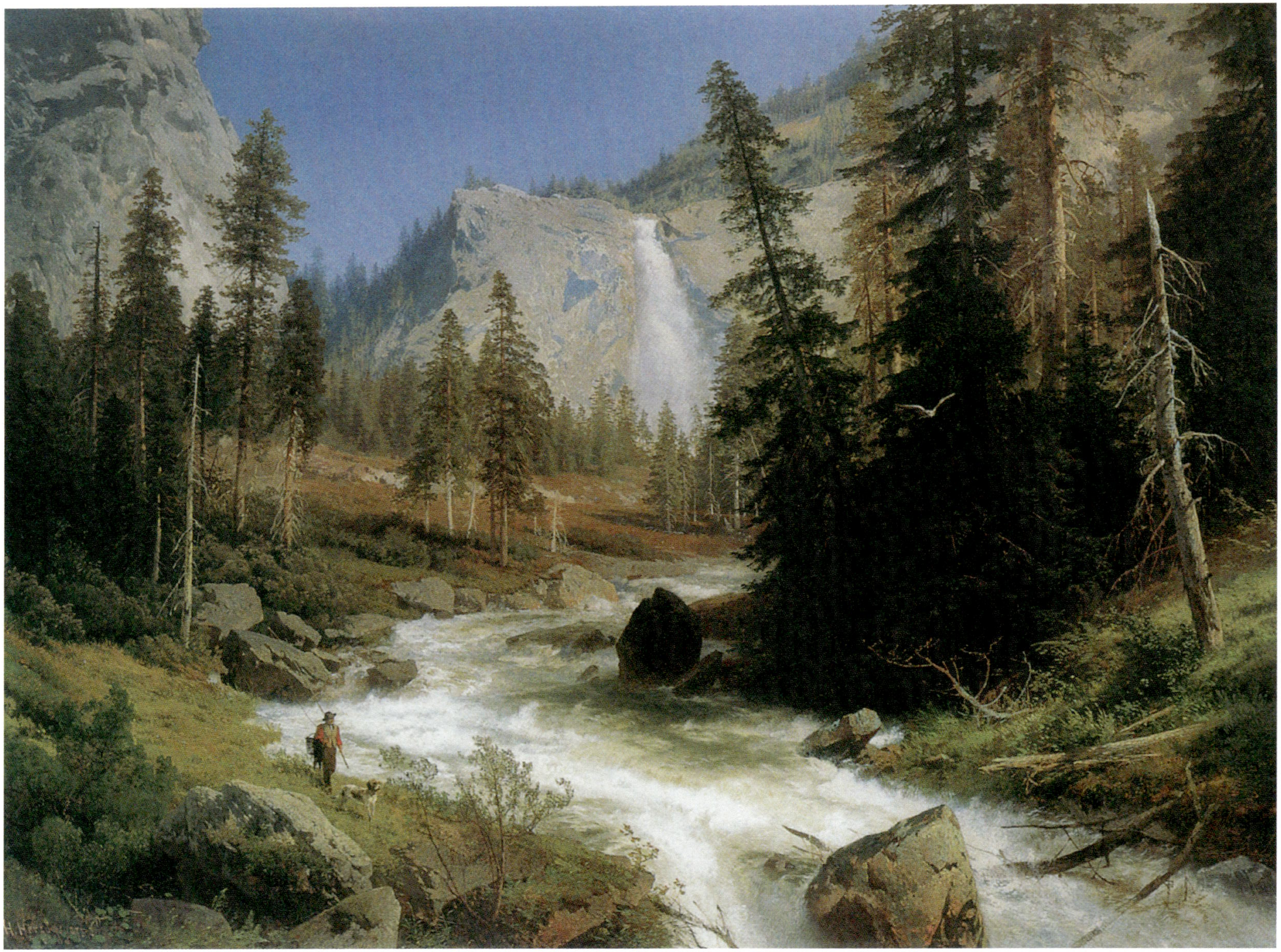

052. HERMAN HERZOG (1831–1932)
Nevada Fall, Yosemite, 1875
Oil on canvas. 33½ x 44½ in. (85.1 x 113 cm)

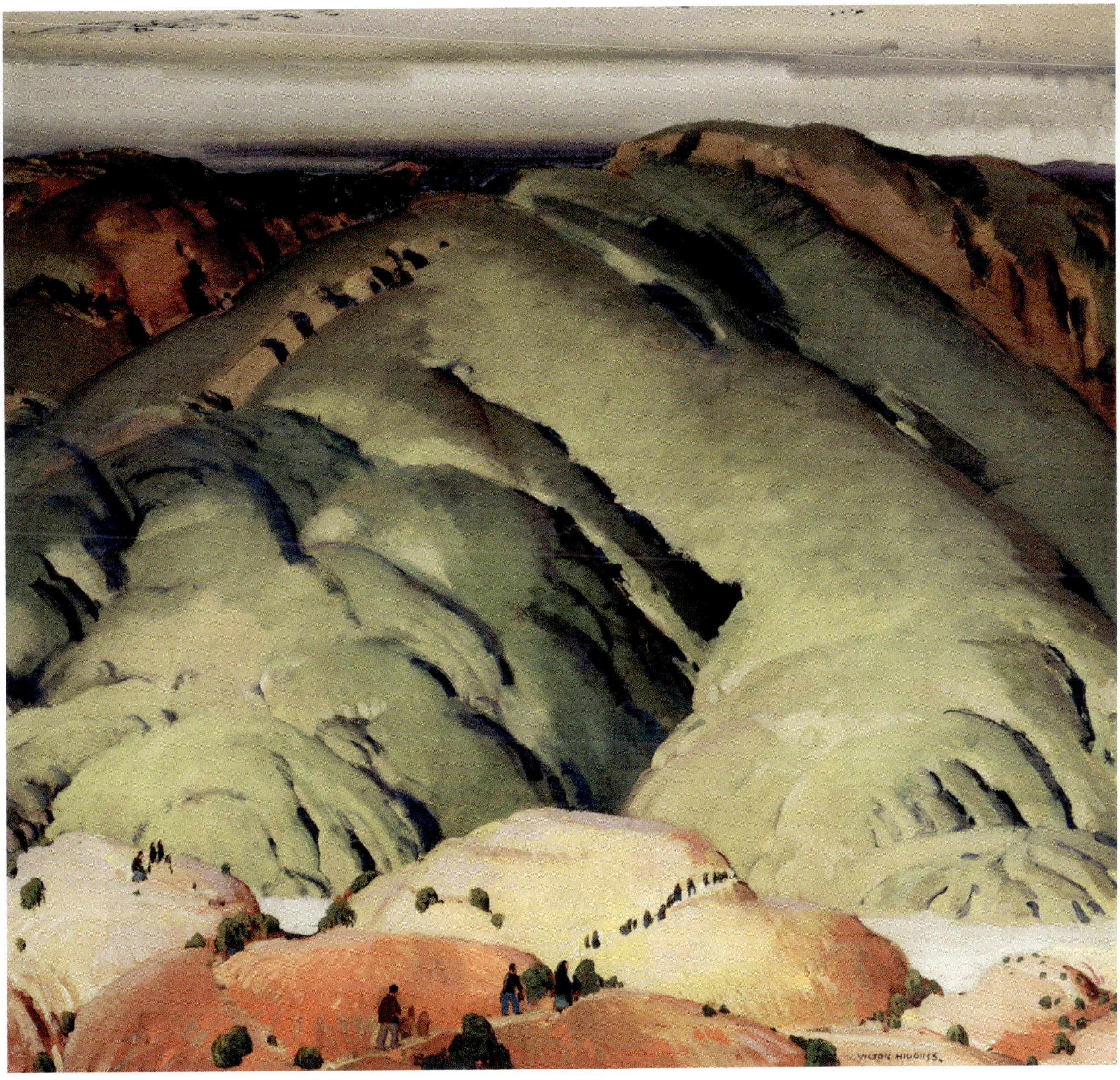

053. VICTOR HIGGINS (1884–1949)
Mountain Forms #2, c. 1925–27
Oil on canvas. 40½ x 43 in. (102.9 x 109.2 cm)

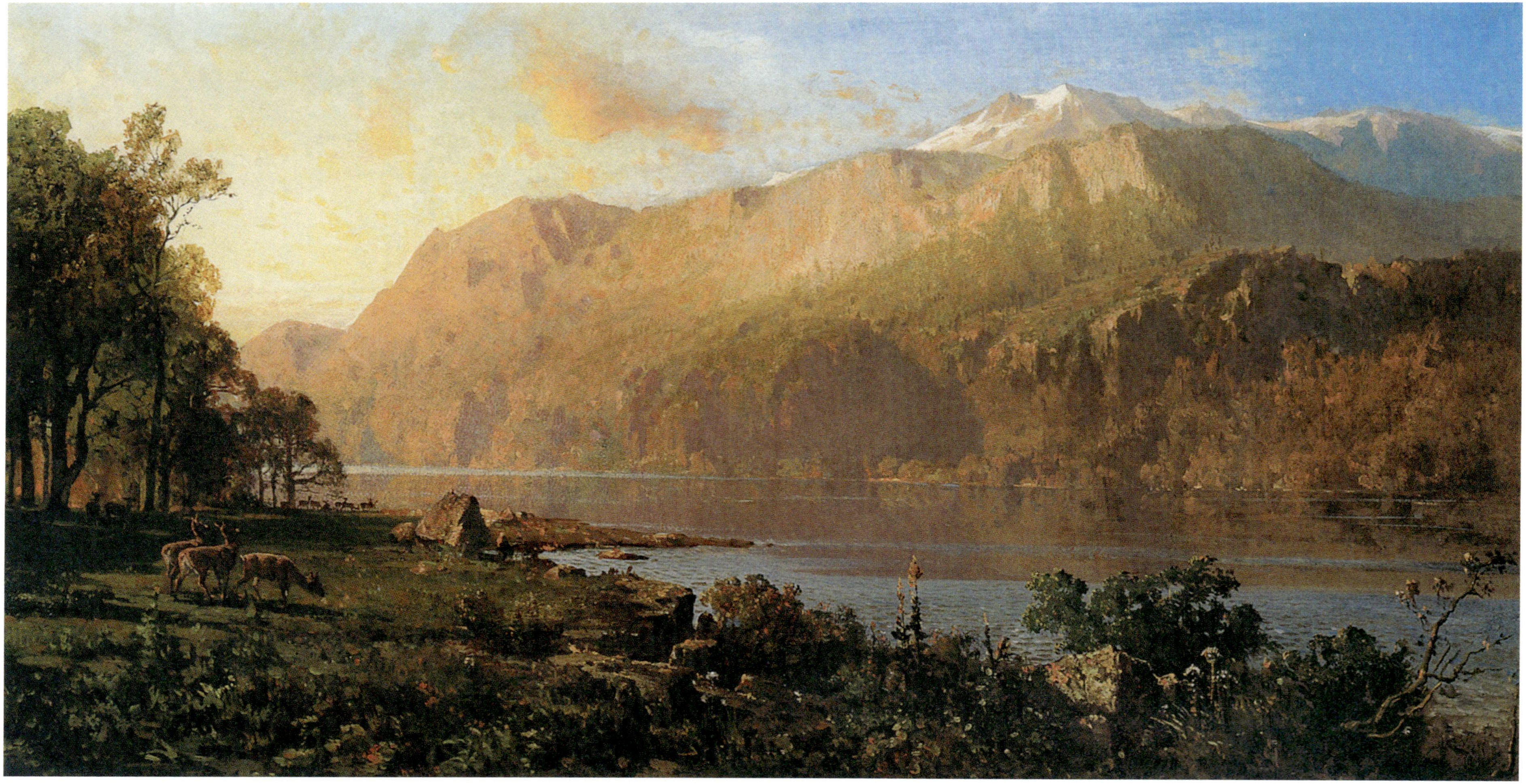

054. THOMAS HILL (1829–1908)
Emerald Lake near Tahoe, 1880–1900
Oil on canvas. 17¾ x 33½ in. (45.09 x 85.09 cm)

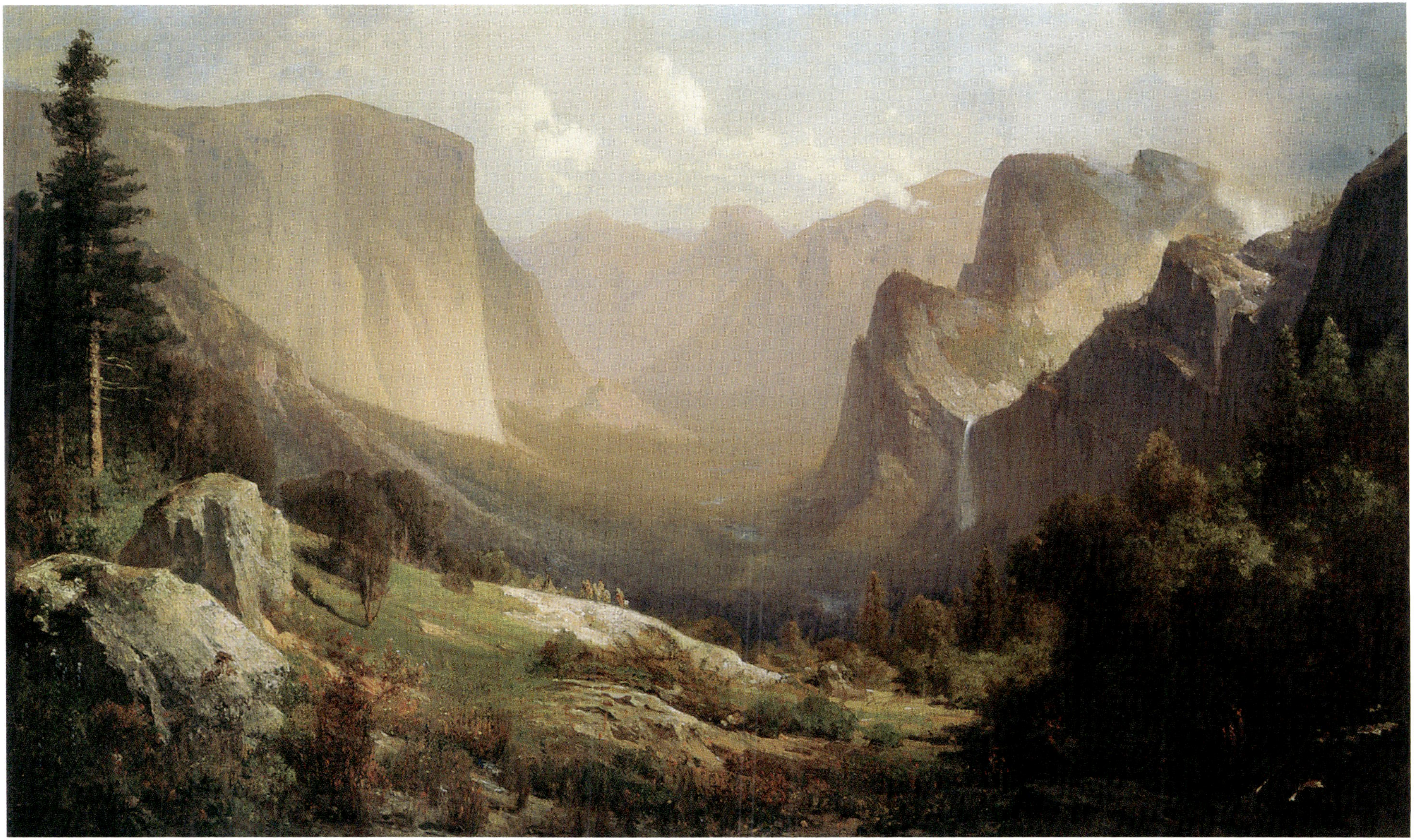

055. THOMAS HILL (1829–1908)
View of Yosemite Valley, 1871
Oil on canvas. 30 x 48 in. (76.2 x 121.9 cm)

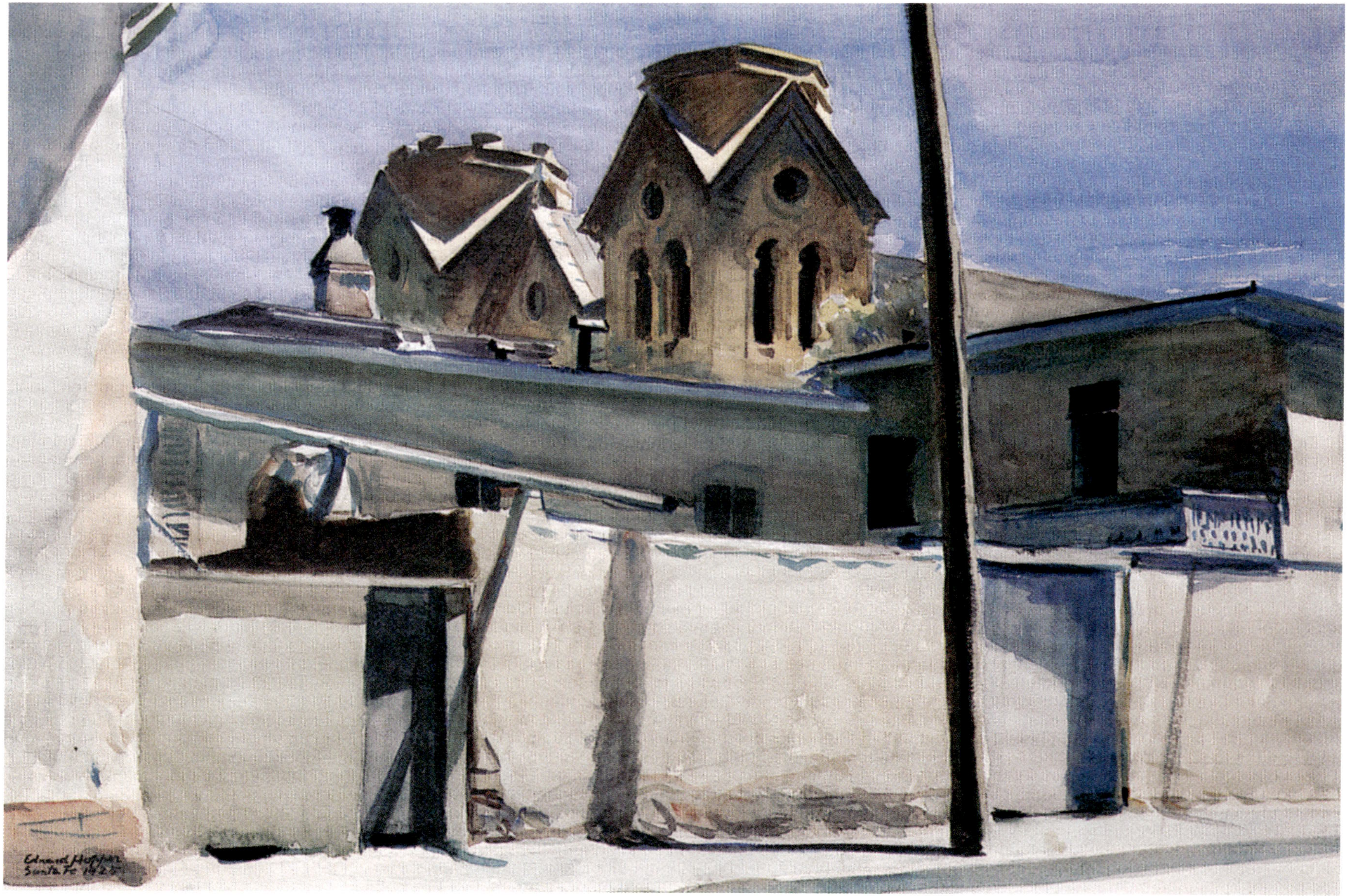

056. EDWARD HOPPER (1882–1967)
St. Francis's Towers, Santa Fe, 1925
Watercolor on paper. 13½ x 19½ in. (34.3 x 49.5 cm)

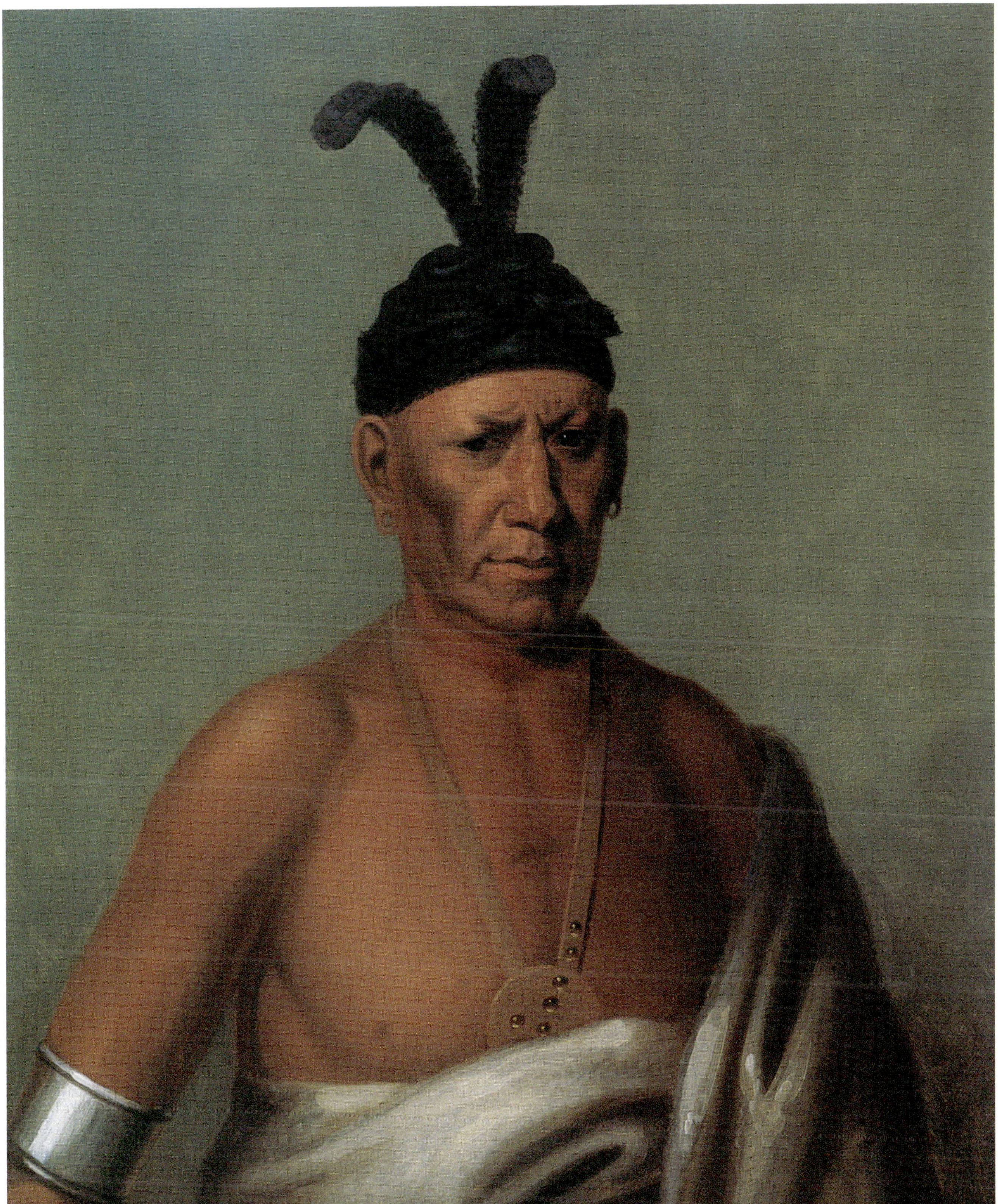

057. HENRY INMAN (1801–1846)
Crouching Eagle (after a work by Charles Bird King), c. 1833
Oil on canvas. 30½ x 25½ in. (77.5 x 64.8 cm)

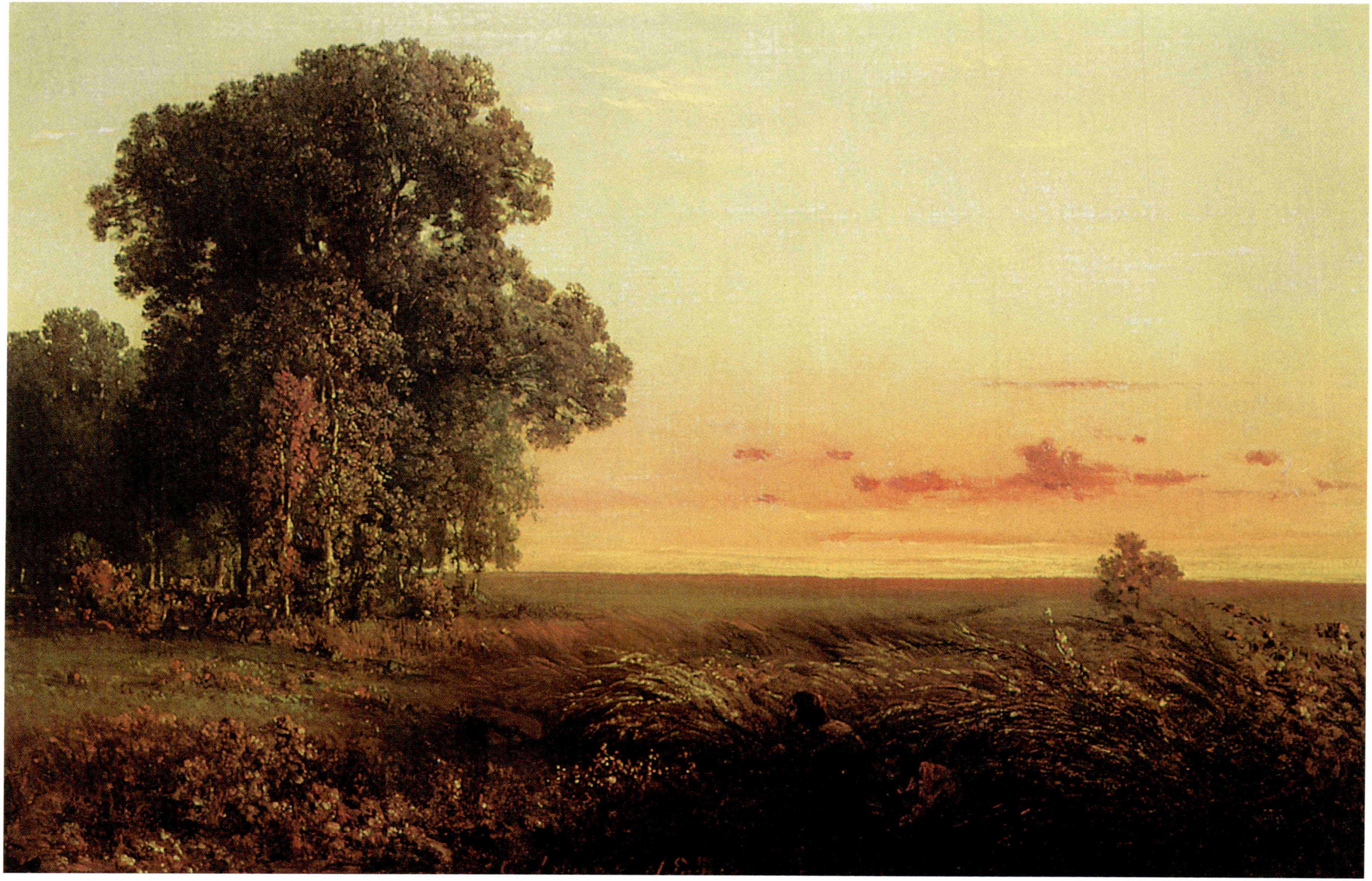

058. GEORGE INNESS (1825–1894)
Afterglow on the Prairie, 1856
Oil on canvas. 14 x 21 in. (35.5 x 53.4 cm)

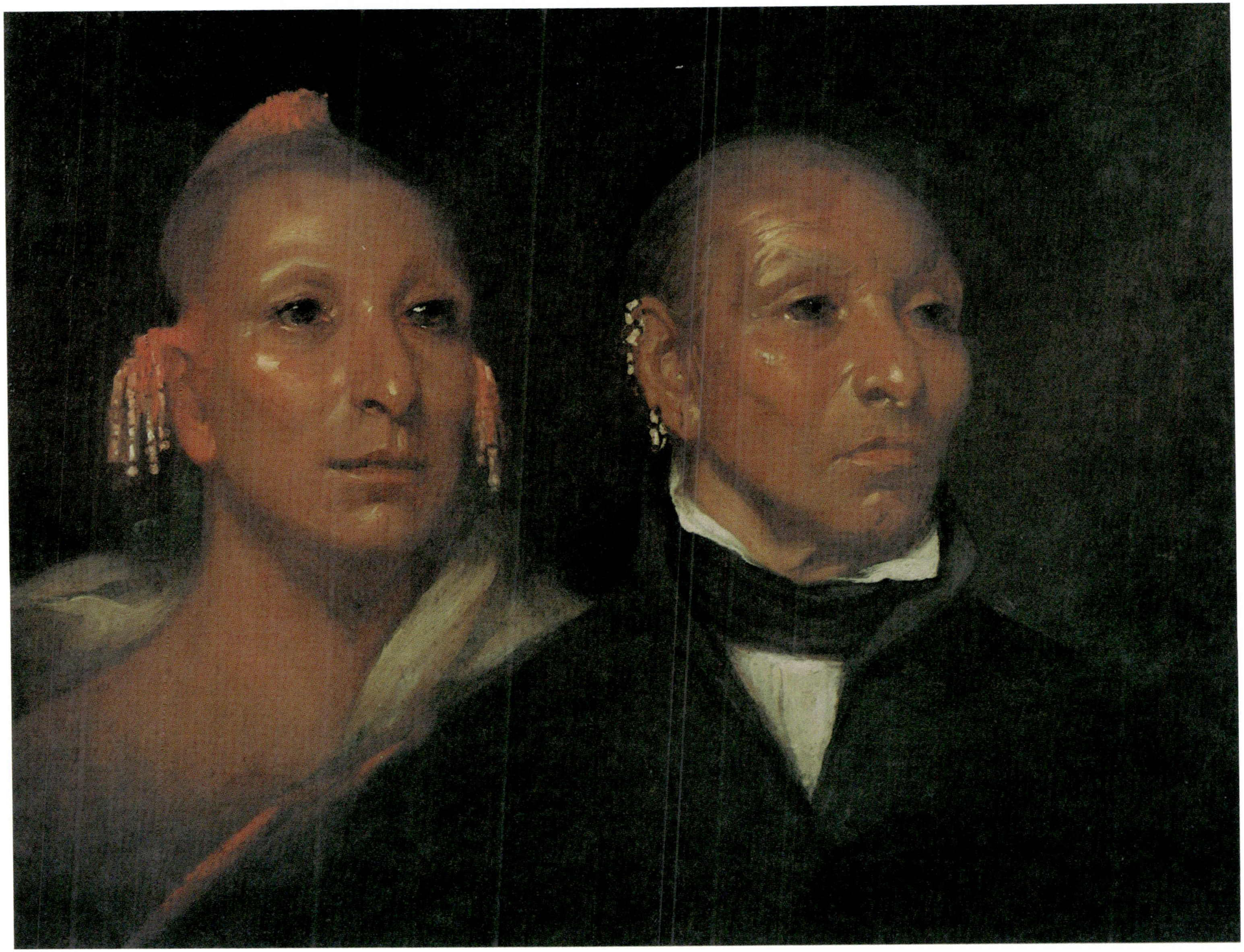

059. JOHN WESLEY JARVIS (1780–1840)
Black Hawk and His Son, Whirling Thunder, 1833
Oil. 23½ x 30 in. (59.7 x 76.2 cm)

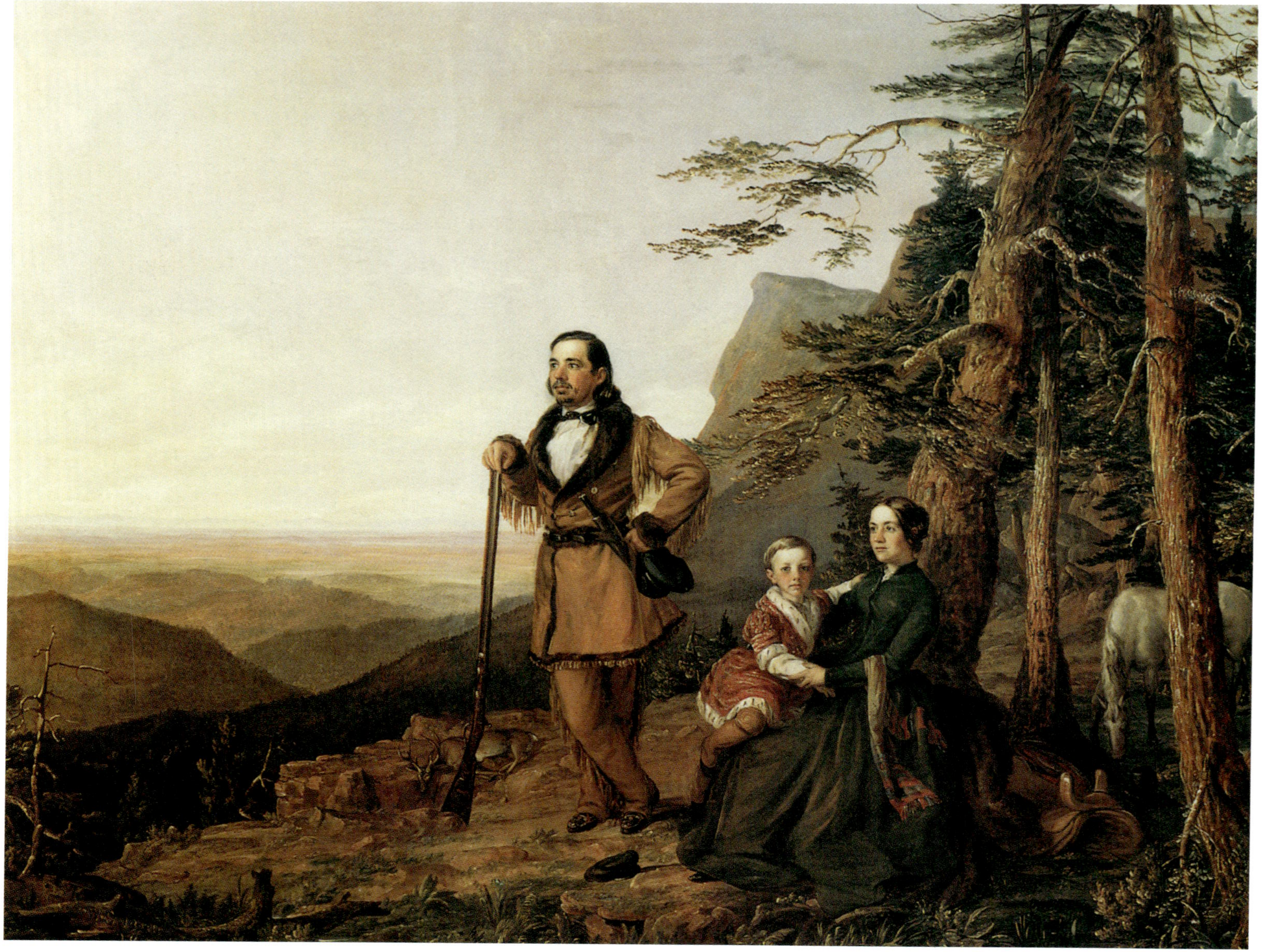

060. WILLIAM SMITH JEWETT (1812–1873)
The Promised Land—The Grayson Family, 1850
Oil on canvas. $50\frac{3}{4}$ x 64 in. (129 x 162.6 cm)

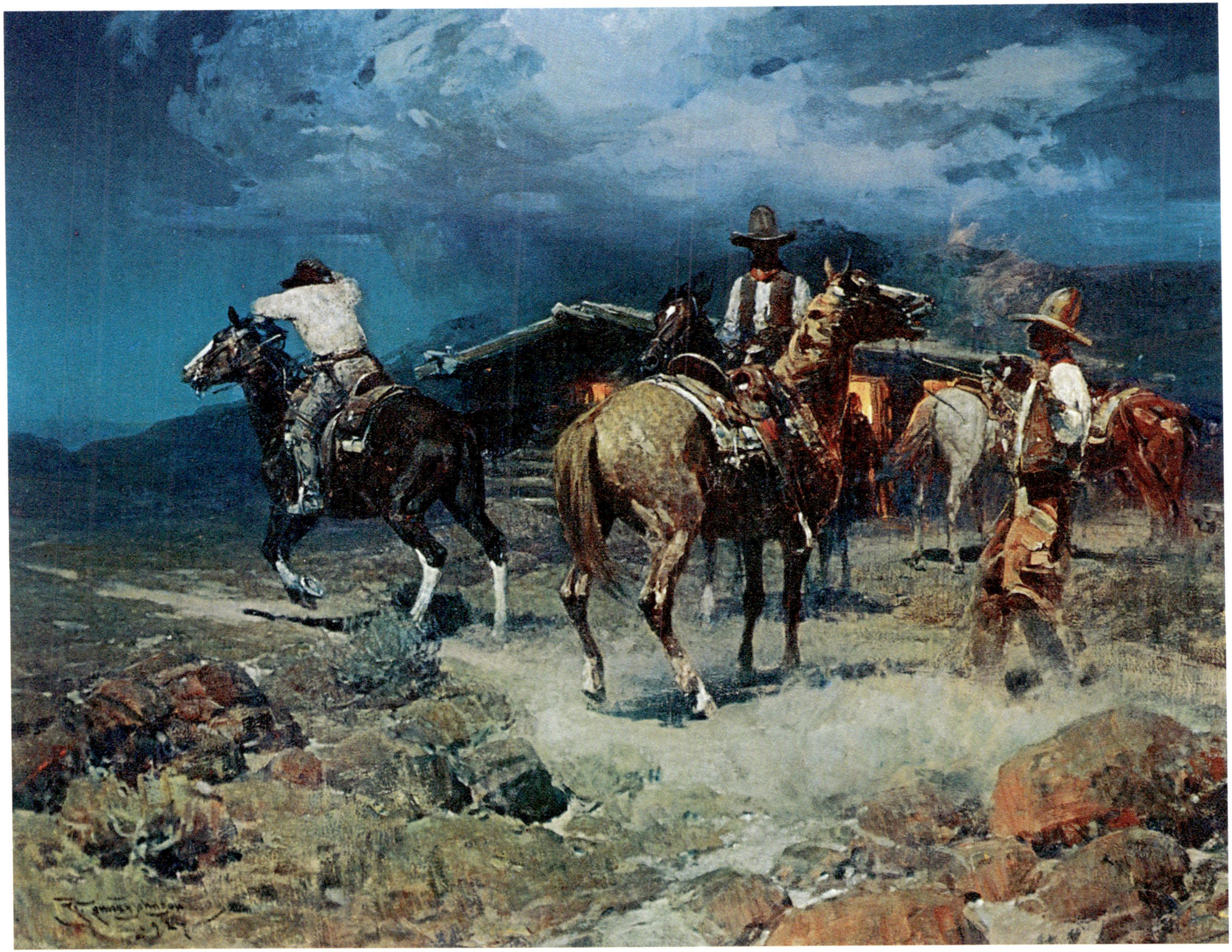

061. FRANK TENNEY JOHNSON (1874–1939)
The Pony Express, 1924
Watercolor on paper.

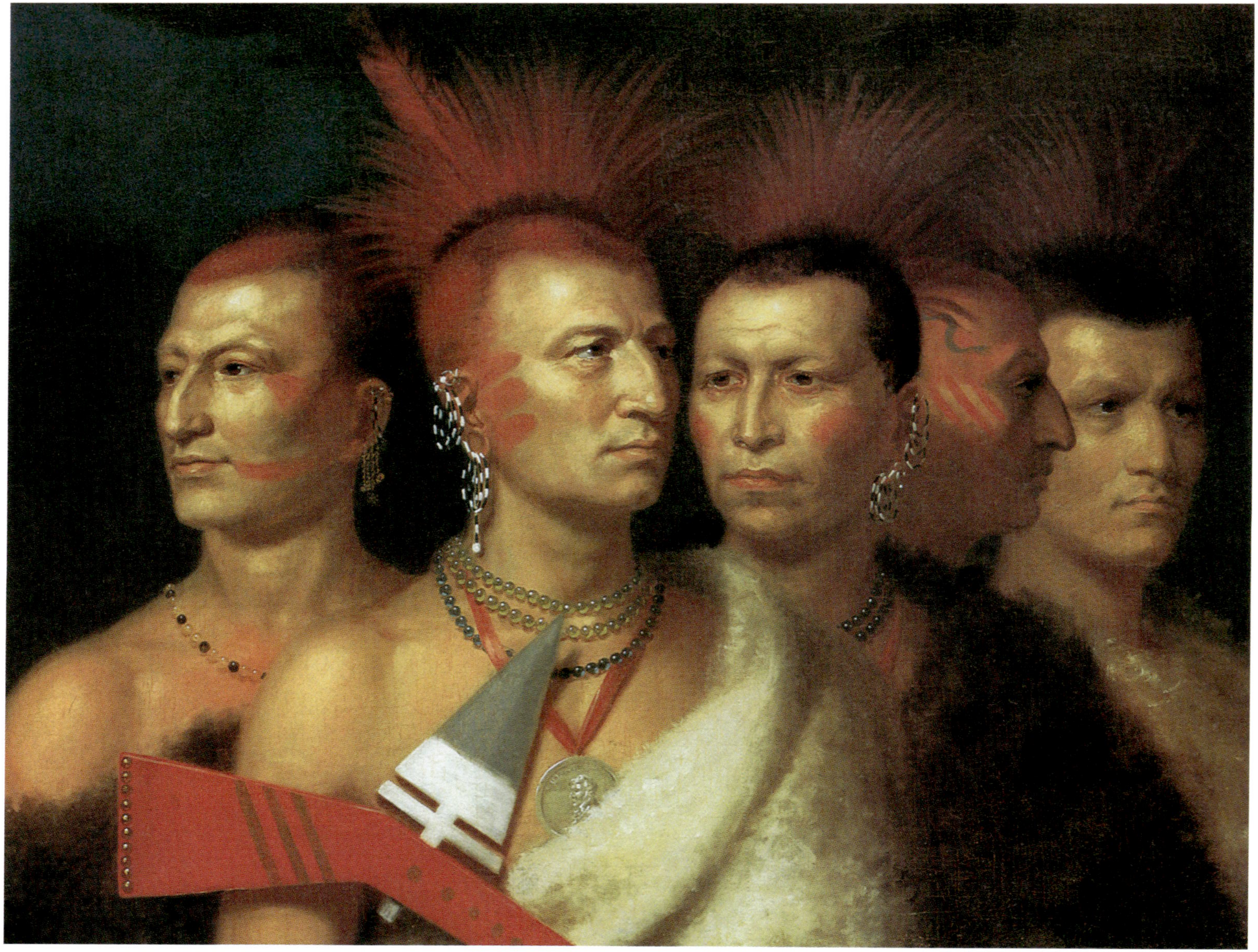

062. CHARLES BIRD KING (1785–1862)
Young Omaha, War Eagle, Little Missouri, and Pawnees, 1821
Oil on canvas. 36⅛ x 28 in. (91.8 x 71.1 cm)

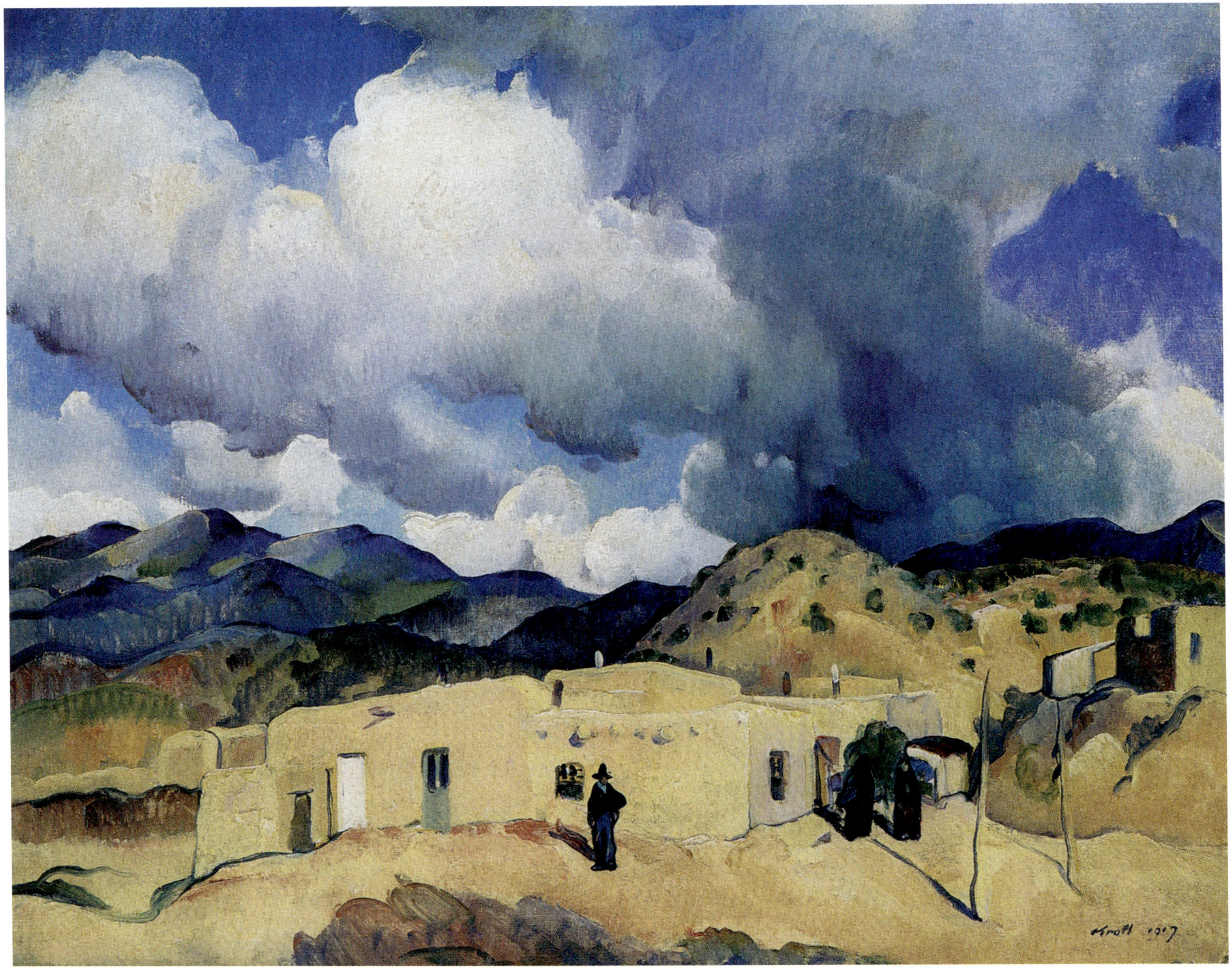

063. LEON KROLL (1884–1974)
Santa Fe Hills, 1917
Oil on canvas. 26 x 32 in. (66 x 81.3 cm)

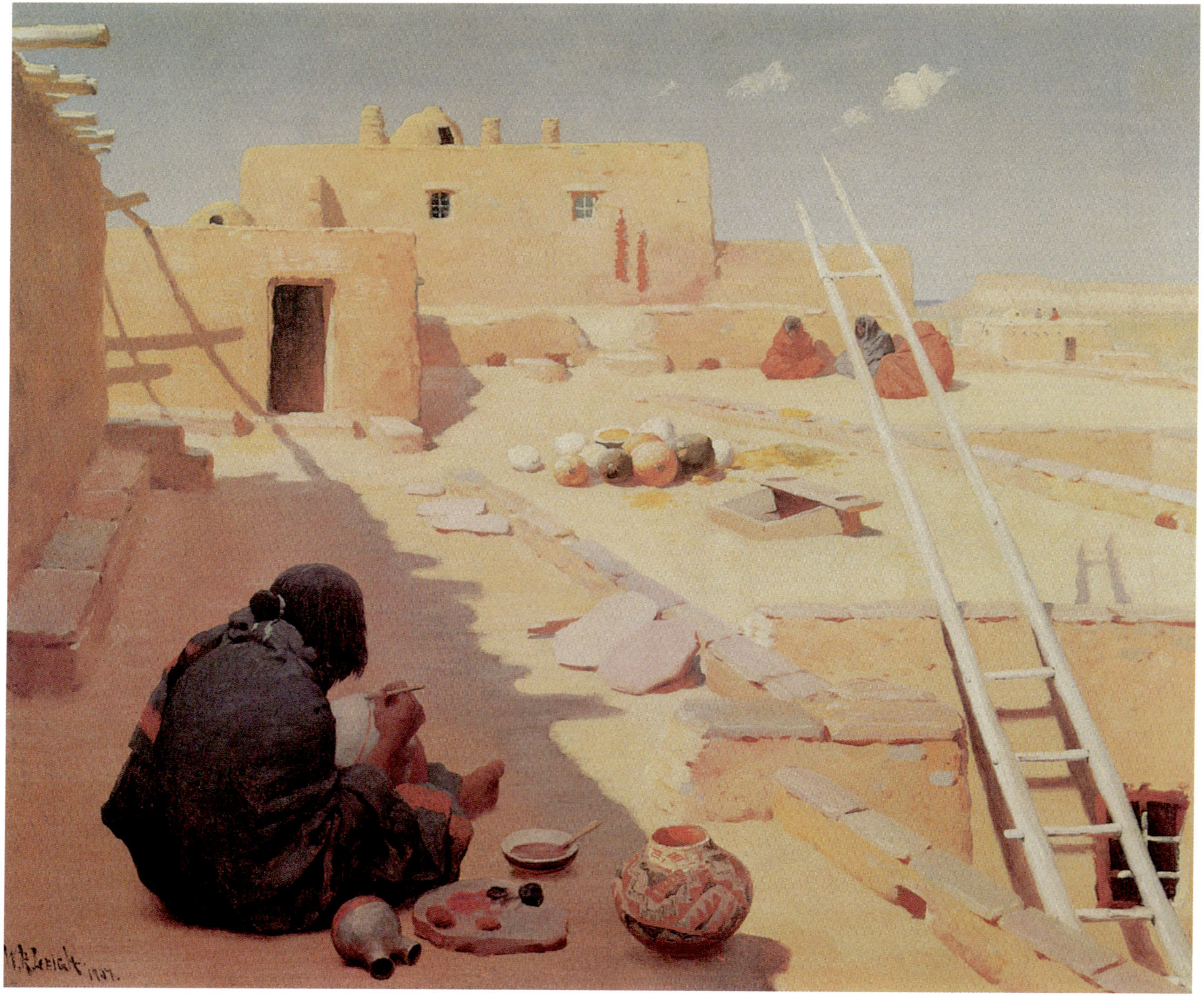

064. WILLIAM ROBINSON LEIGH (1866–1955)
Zuni Pottery Maker, 1907
Oil on canvas. 25 x 30 in. (63.5 x 76.2 cm)

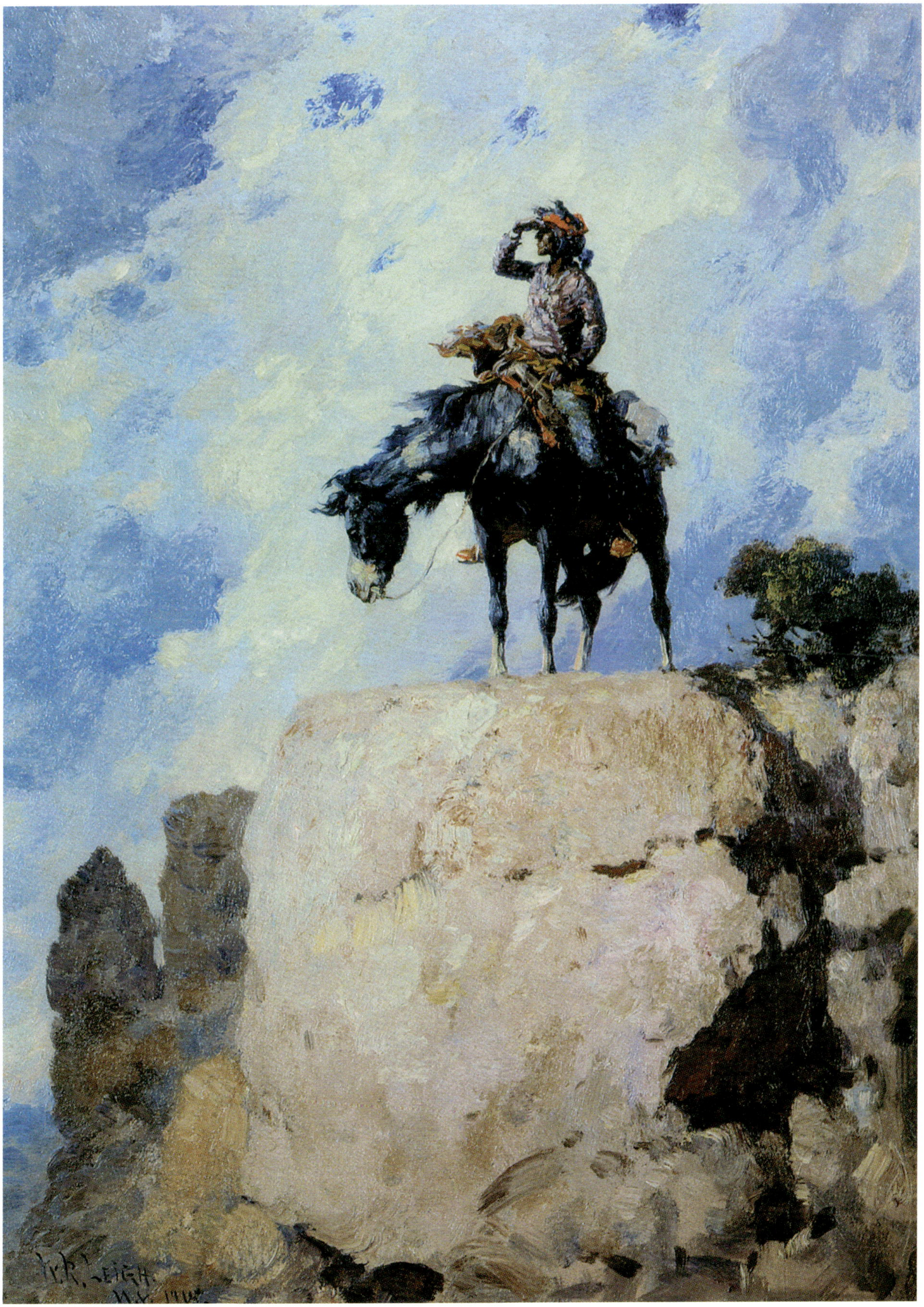

065. WILLIAM ROBINSON LEIGH (1866–1955)
Navajo Scout, 1915
Oil on canvas. 24 x 18 in. (61 x 45.7 cm)

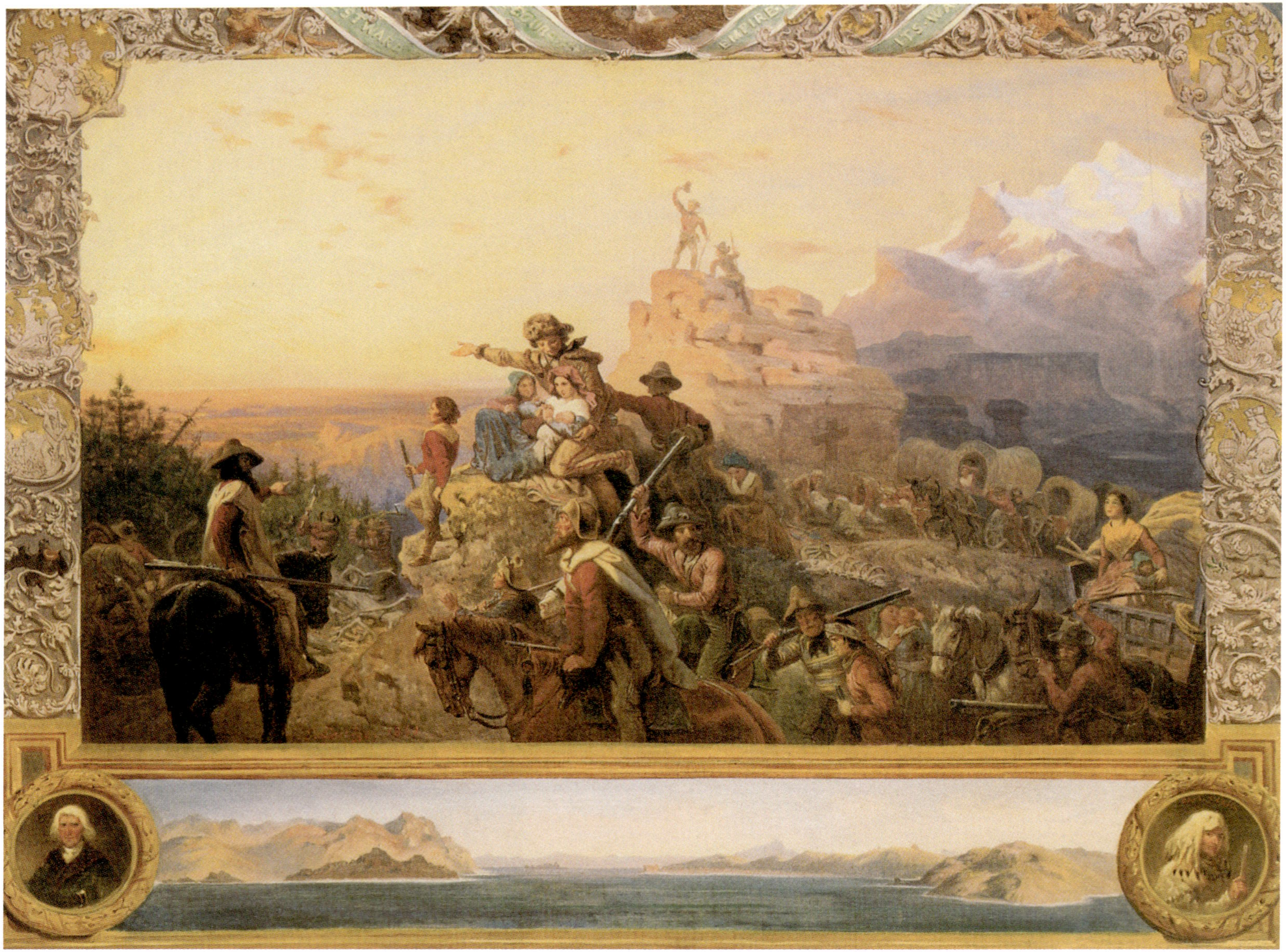

066. EMANUEL GOTTLIEB LEUTZE (1816–1868)
Westward the Course of Empire Takes Its Way, 1861
Oil. 33¼ x 43¼ in. (84.5 x 110 cm)

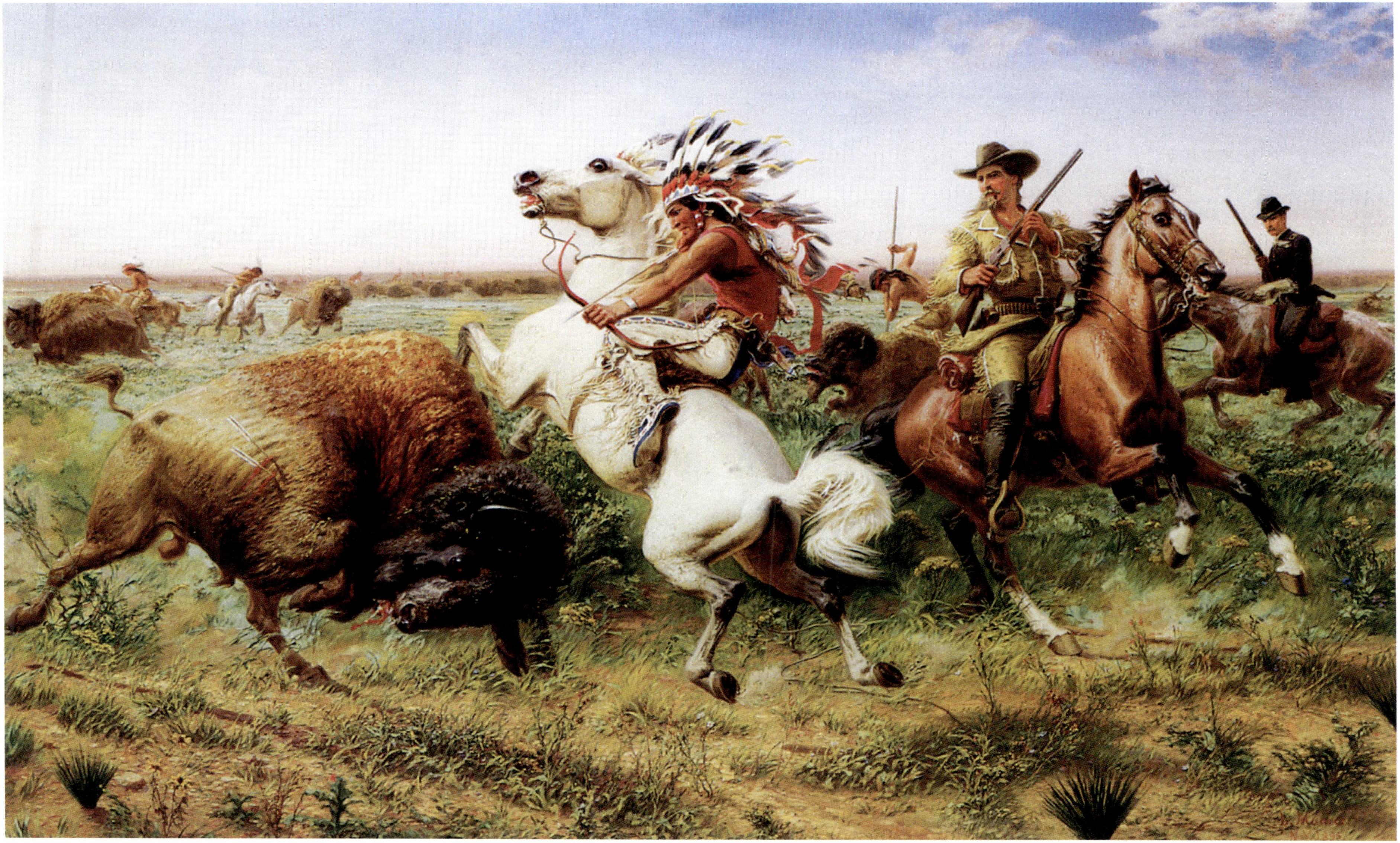

067. LOUIS MAURER (1832–1932)
The Great Royal Buffalo Hunt, 1895
Oil on canvas. 34 x 54 in. (86.4 x 137.2 cm)

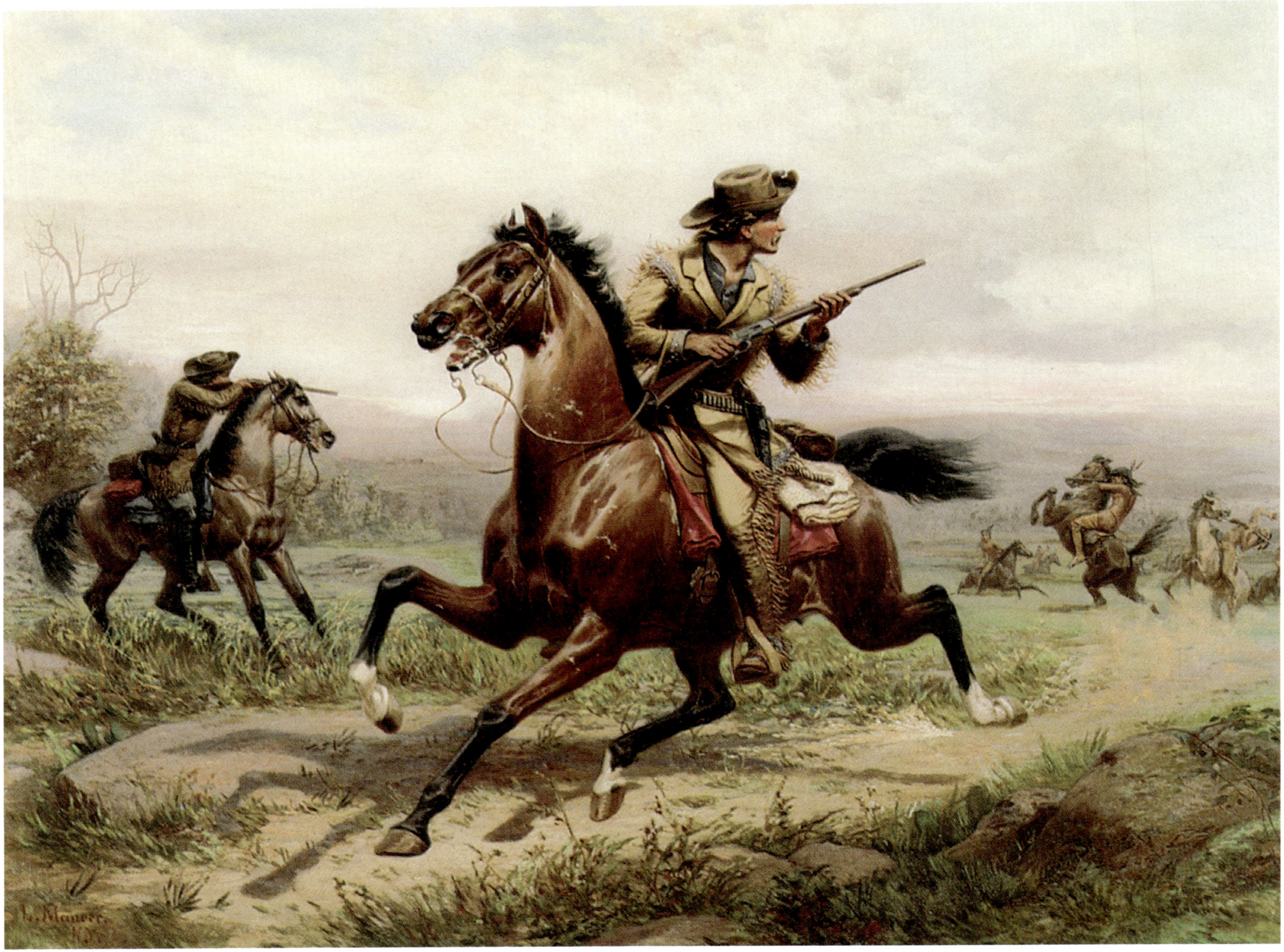

068. LOUIS MAURER (1832–1932)
Buffalo Bill Fighting Indians, c. 1885
Oil on canvas. 27 x 36 in. (69.7 x 91.4 cm)

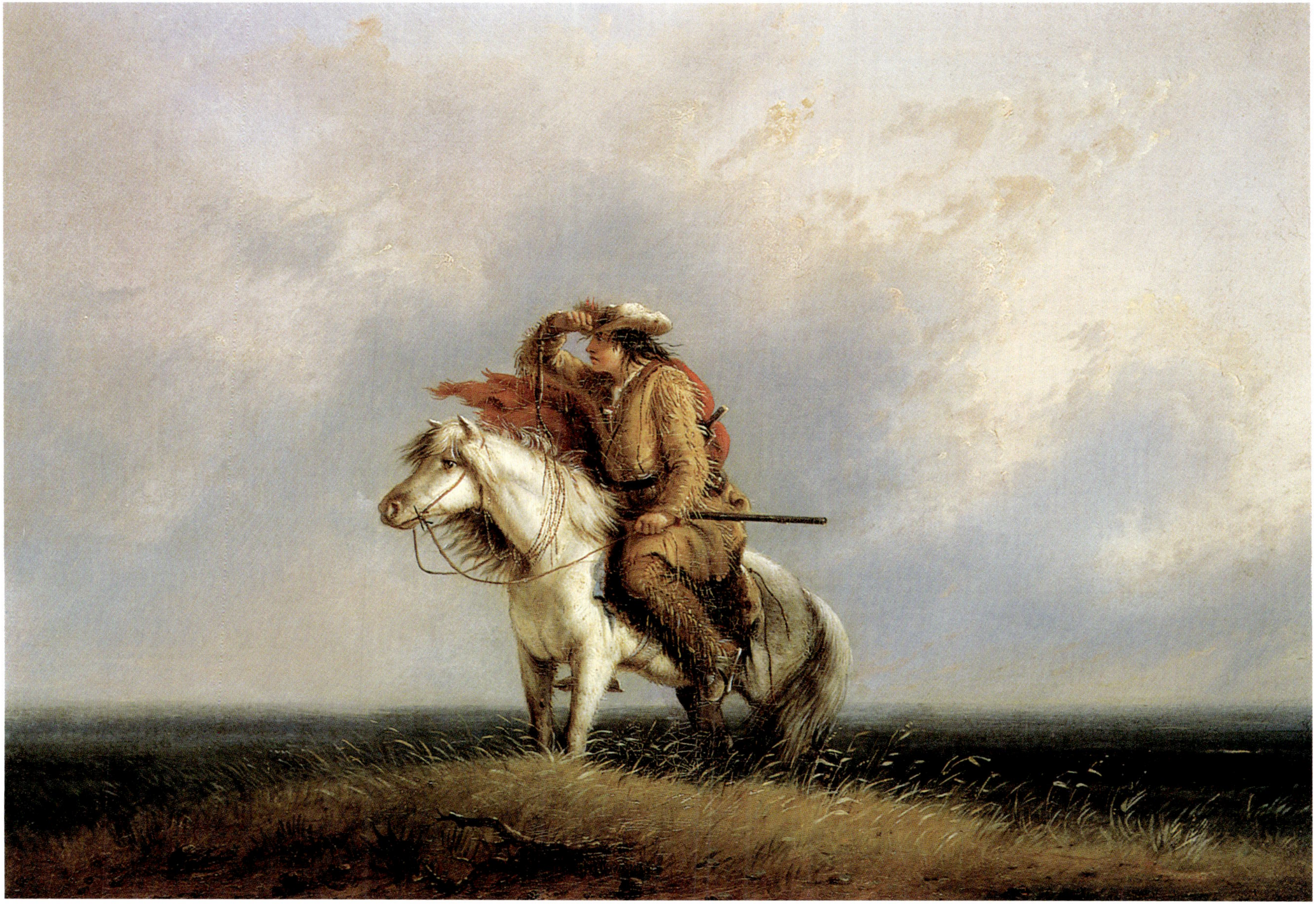

069. ALFRED JACOB MILLER (1810–1874)
The Lost Greenhorn, n.d.
Oil on canvas. 17⅞ x 23⅞ in. (45.4 x 60.6 cm)

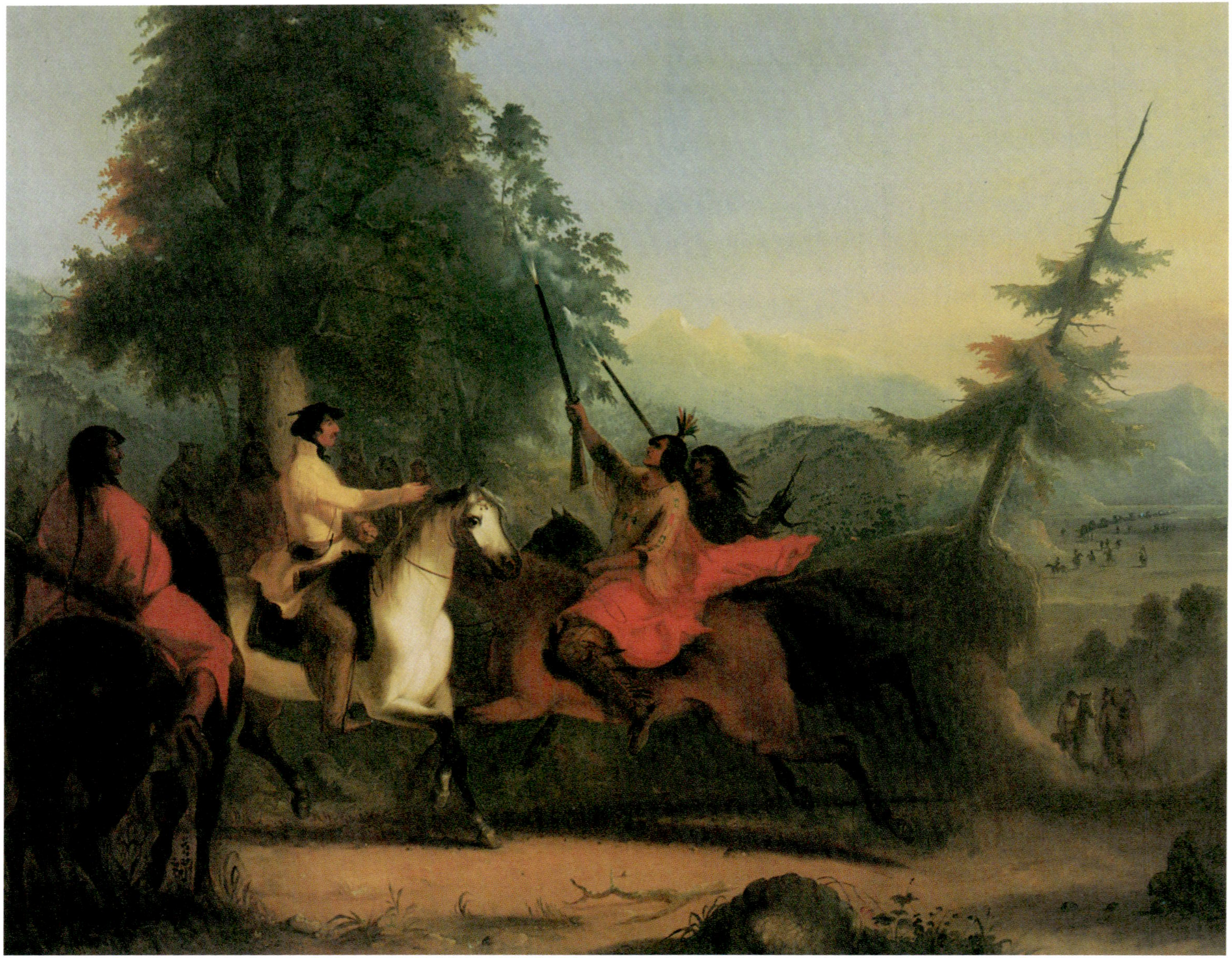

070. ALFRED JACOB MILLER (1810–1874)
Sir William Drummond Stewart Meeting Indian Chief, n.d.
Oil. 33 x 42 in. (83.8 x 106.7 cm)

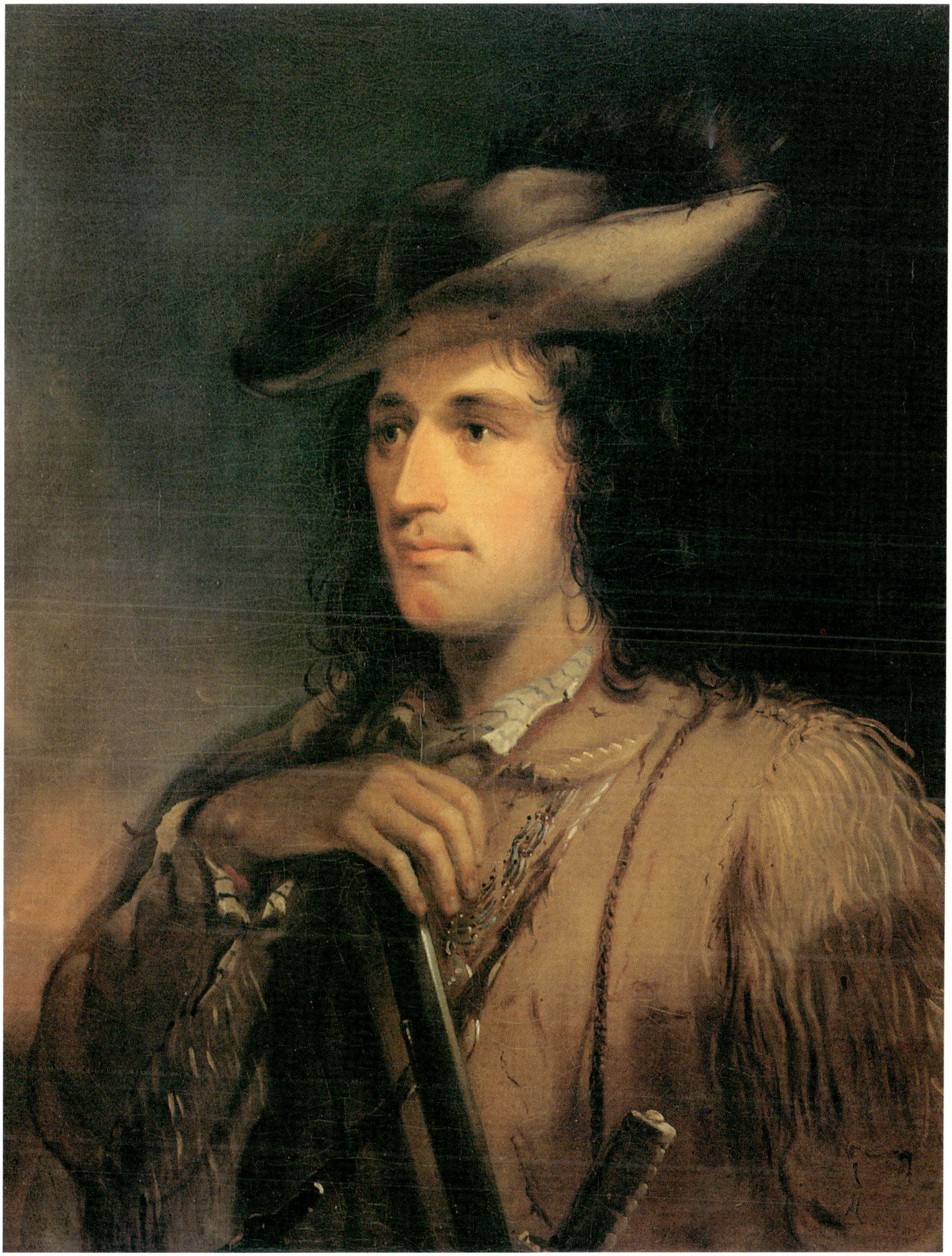

071. ALFRED JACOB MILLER (1810–1874)
Antoine Clement, the Great Hunter, 1837
Oil on canvas.

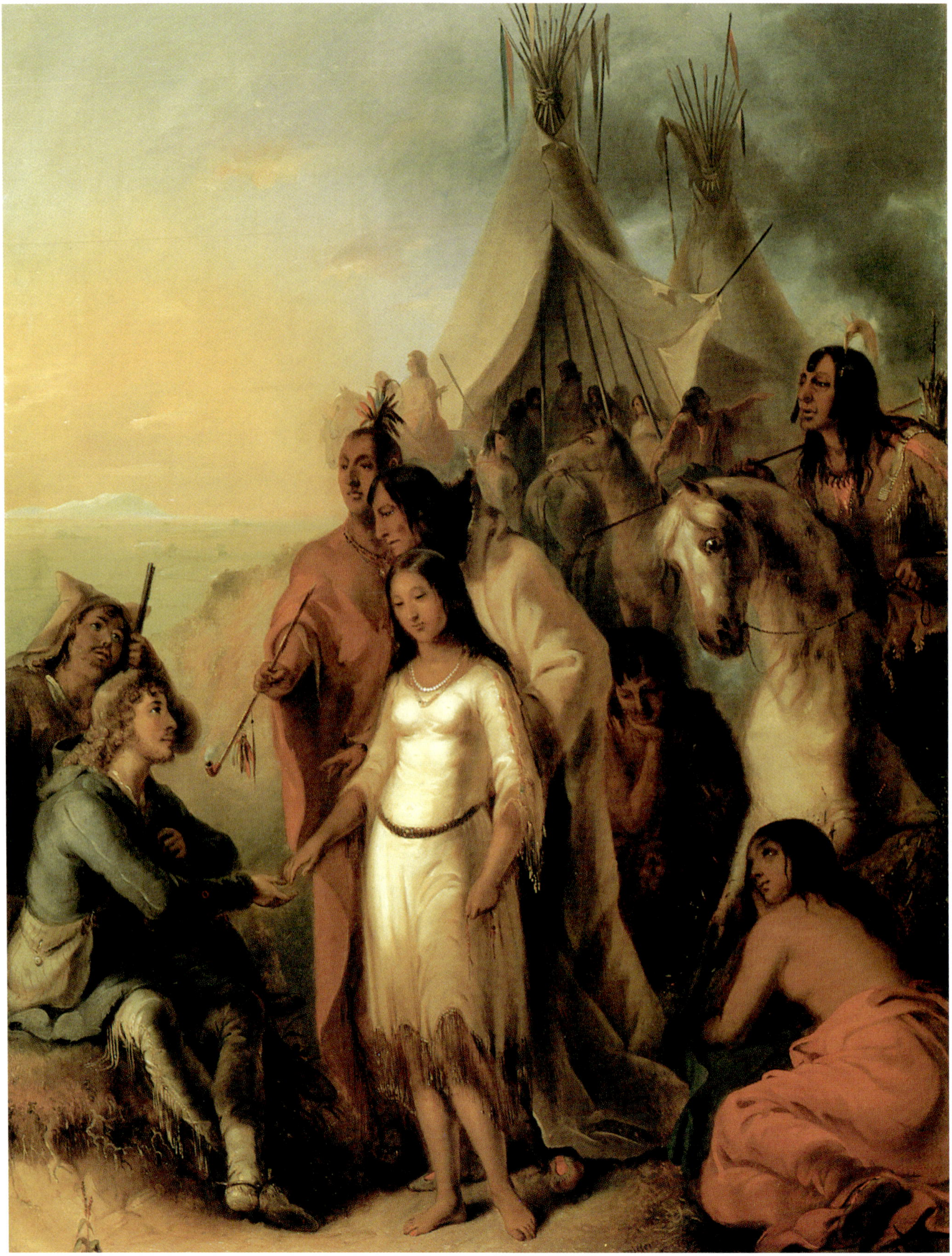

072. ALFRED JACOB MILLER (1810–1874)
The Trapper's Bride, 1845
Oil on canvas. 36 x 28 in. (91.4 x 71.1 cm)

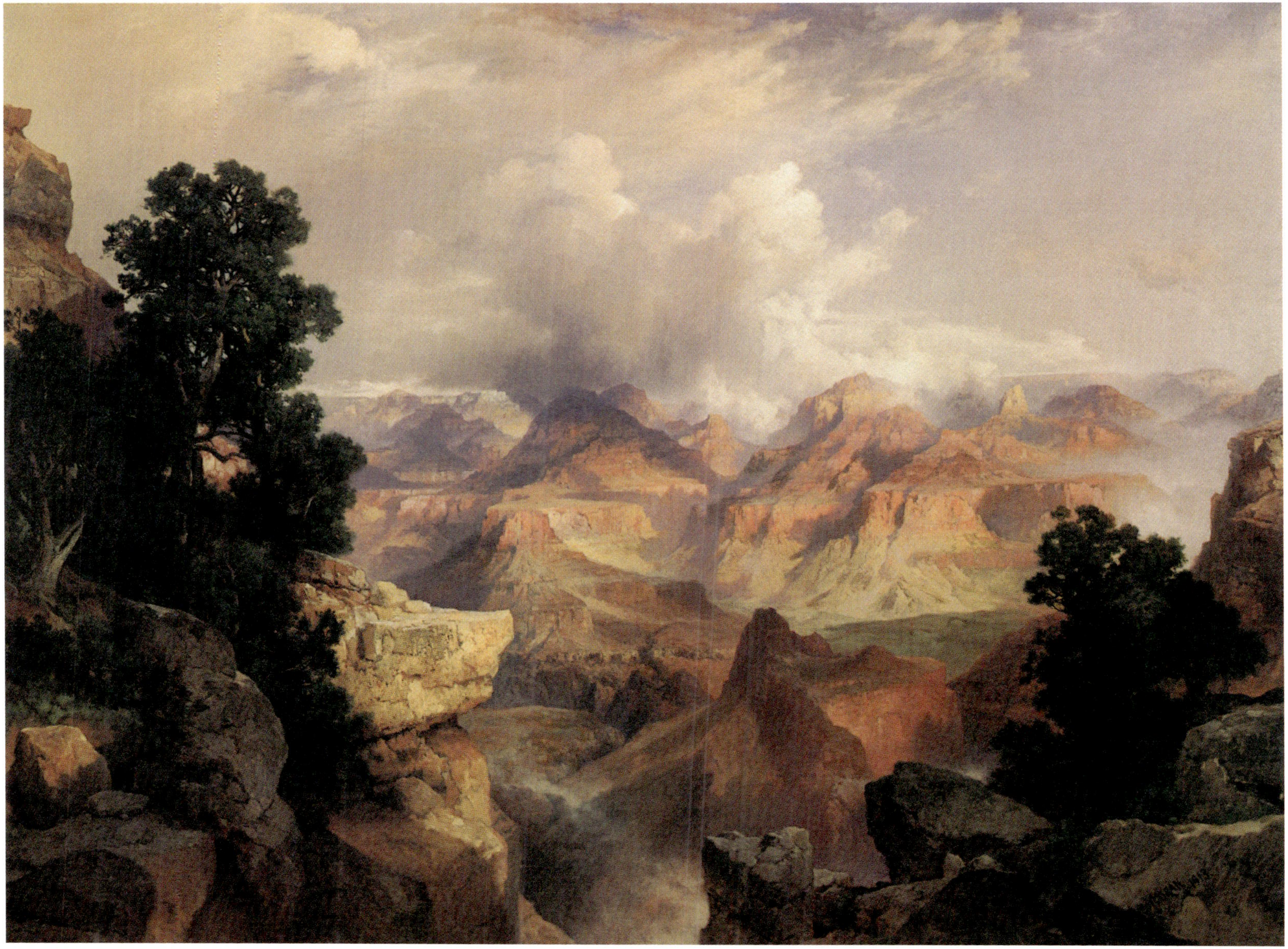

073. THOMAS MORAN (1837–1926)
The Grand Canyon, 1913
Oil. 30 x 40 in. (76.2 x 101.6 cm)

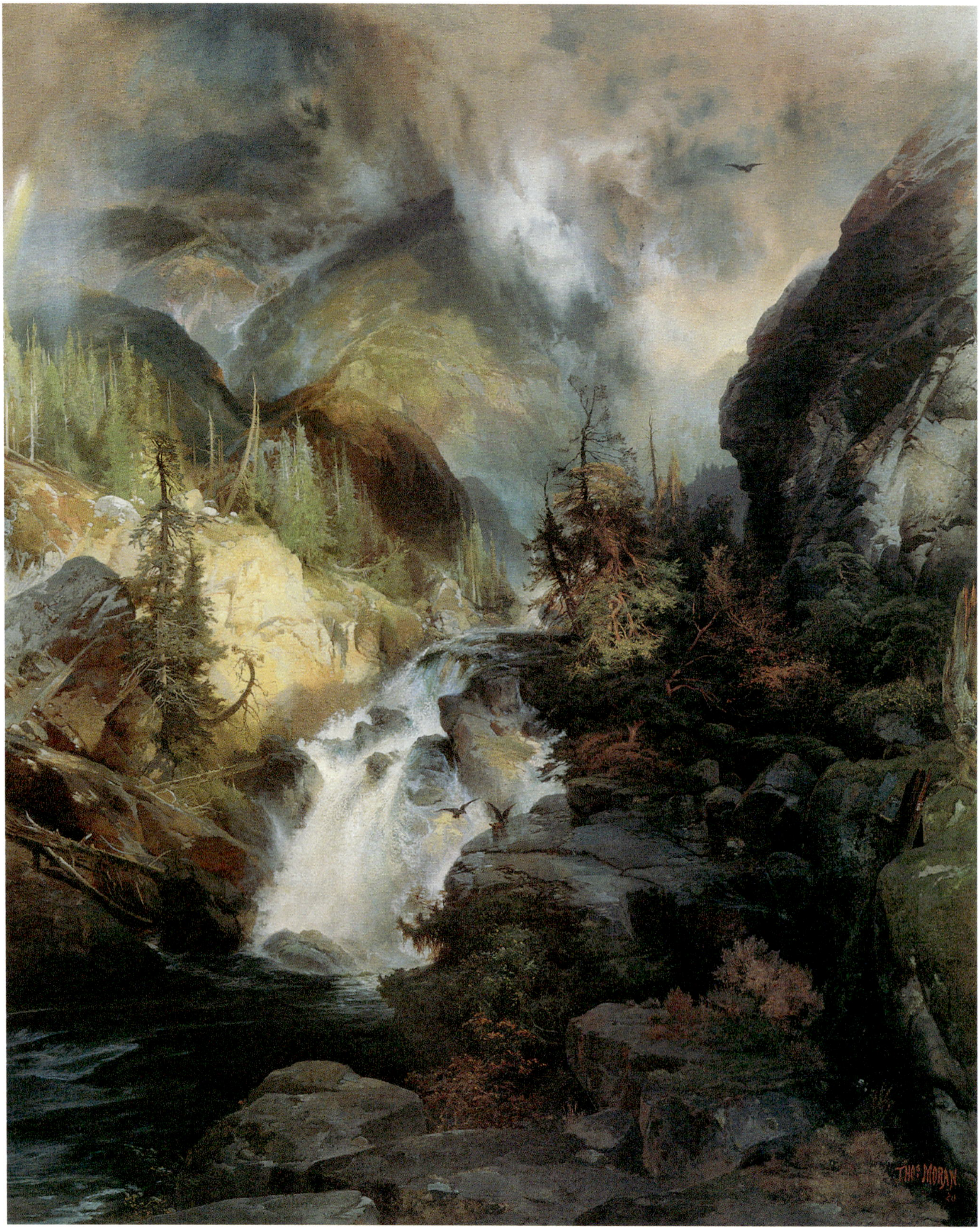

074. THOMAS MORAN (1837–1926)
Children of the Mountain, 1866
Oil on canvas. 62 x 55 in. (158 x 132.5 cm)

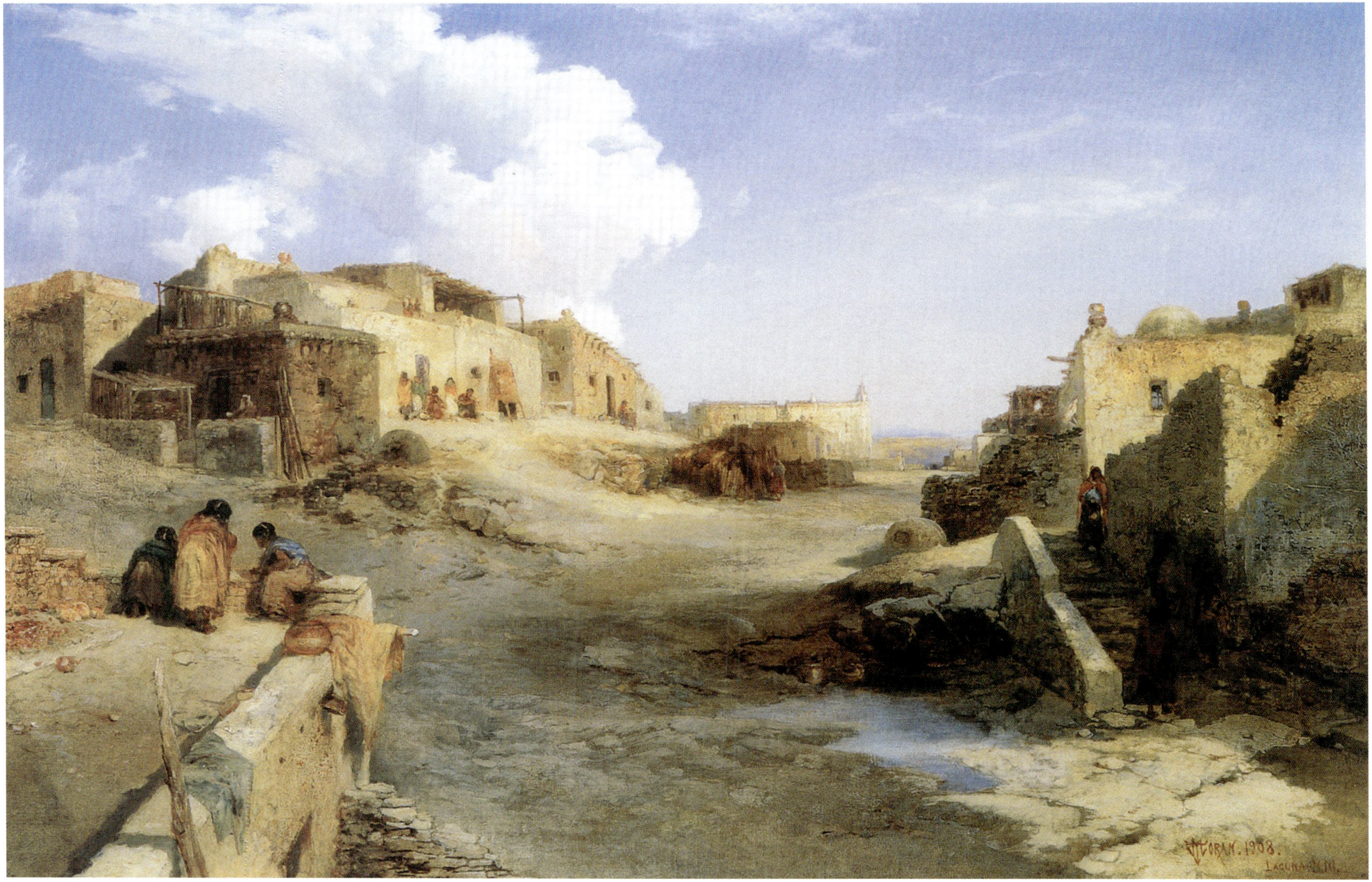

075. THOMAS MORAN (1837–1926)
An Indian Pueblo, Laguna, New Mexico, 1908
Oil on canvas. 25¼ x 30¼ in. (64.1 x 76.8 cm)

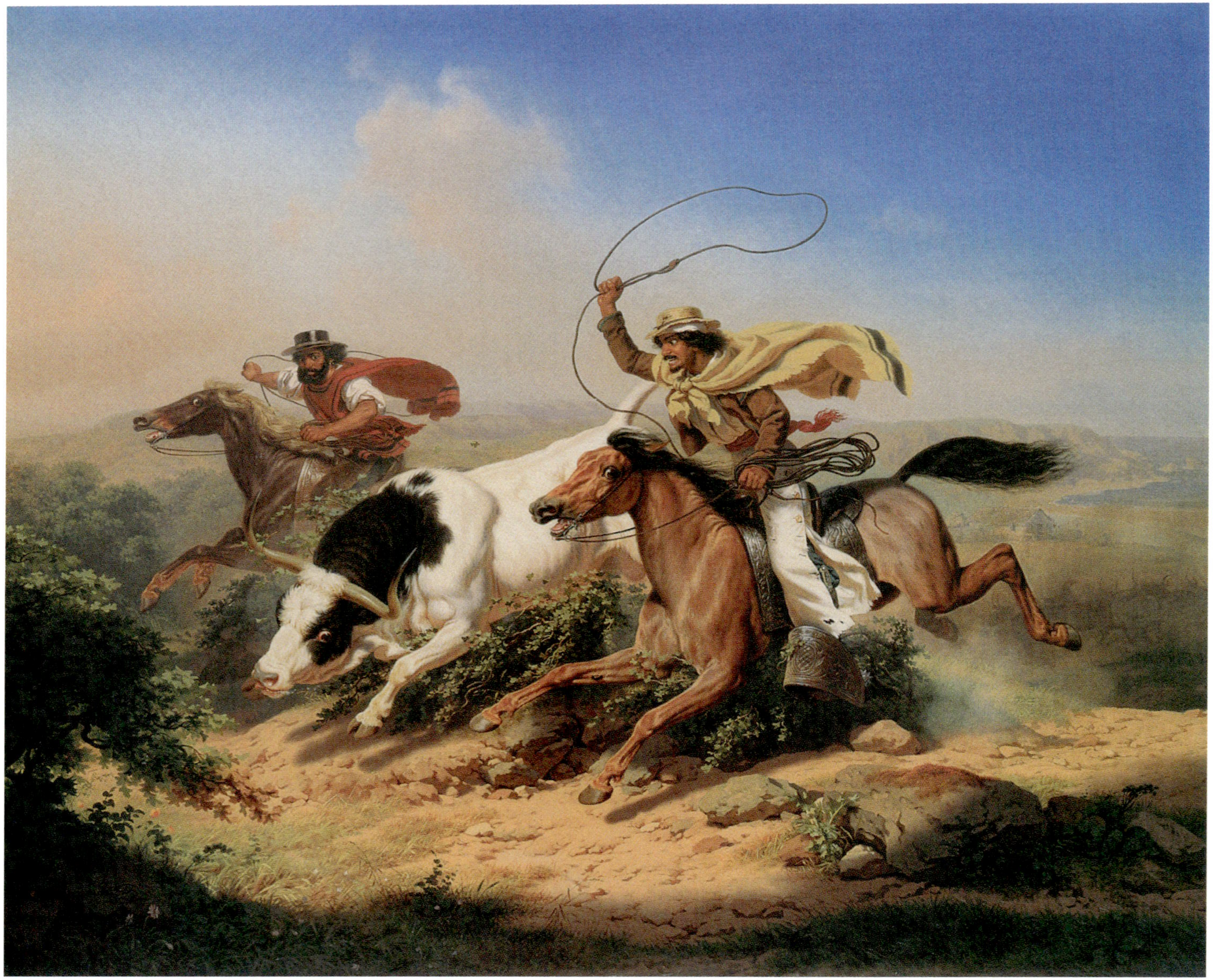

076. CHARLES CHRISTIAN NAHL (1818–1878)
Vaqueros Roping a Steer, 1866
Oil on canvas. 42 x 51⅝ in. (106.7 x 131.1 cm)

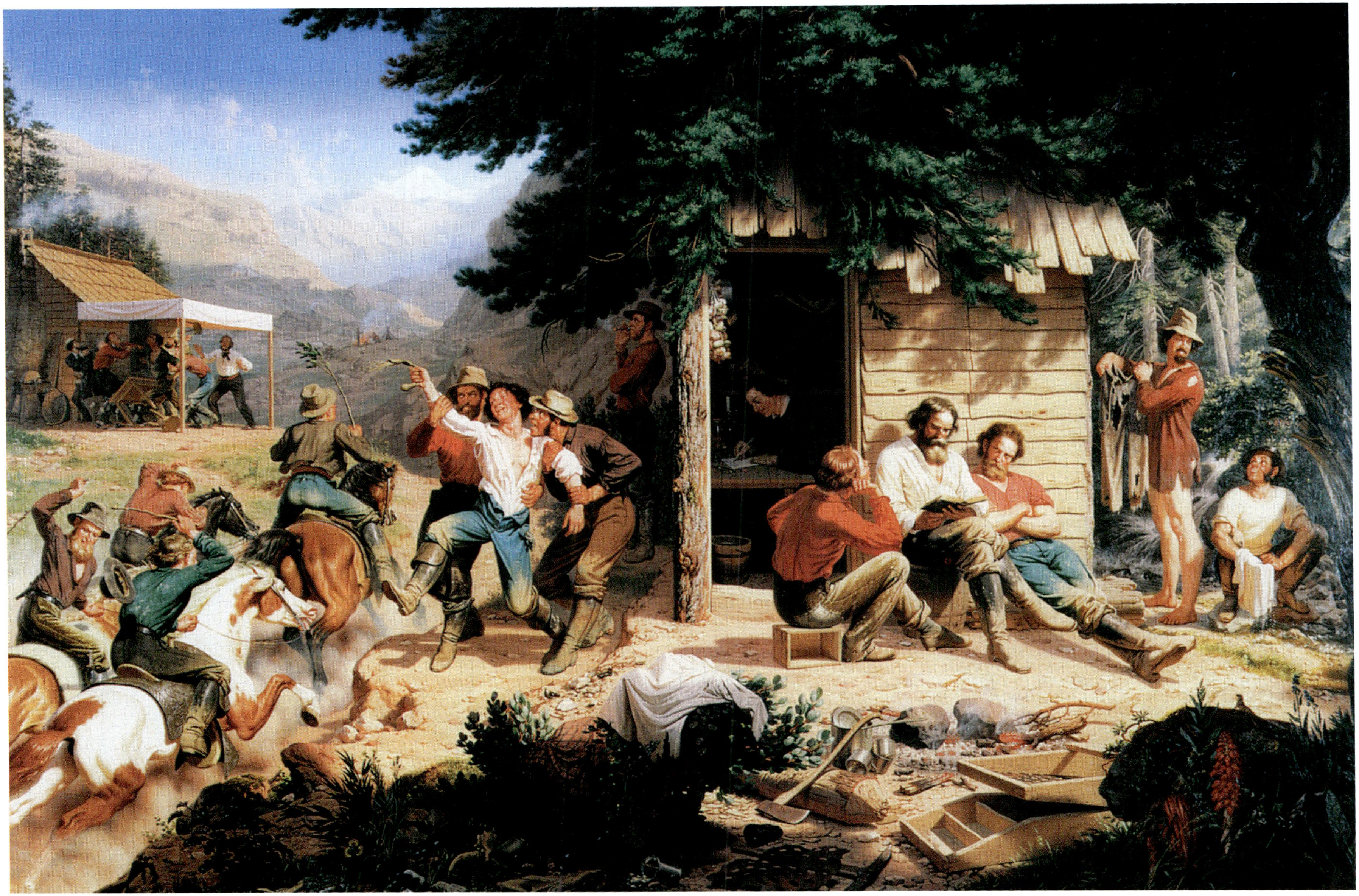

077. CHARLES CHRISTIAN NAHL (1818–1878)
Sunday Morning in the Mines, 1872
Oil on canvas. 72 x 108 in. (183 x 274.5 cm)

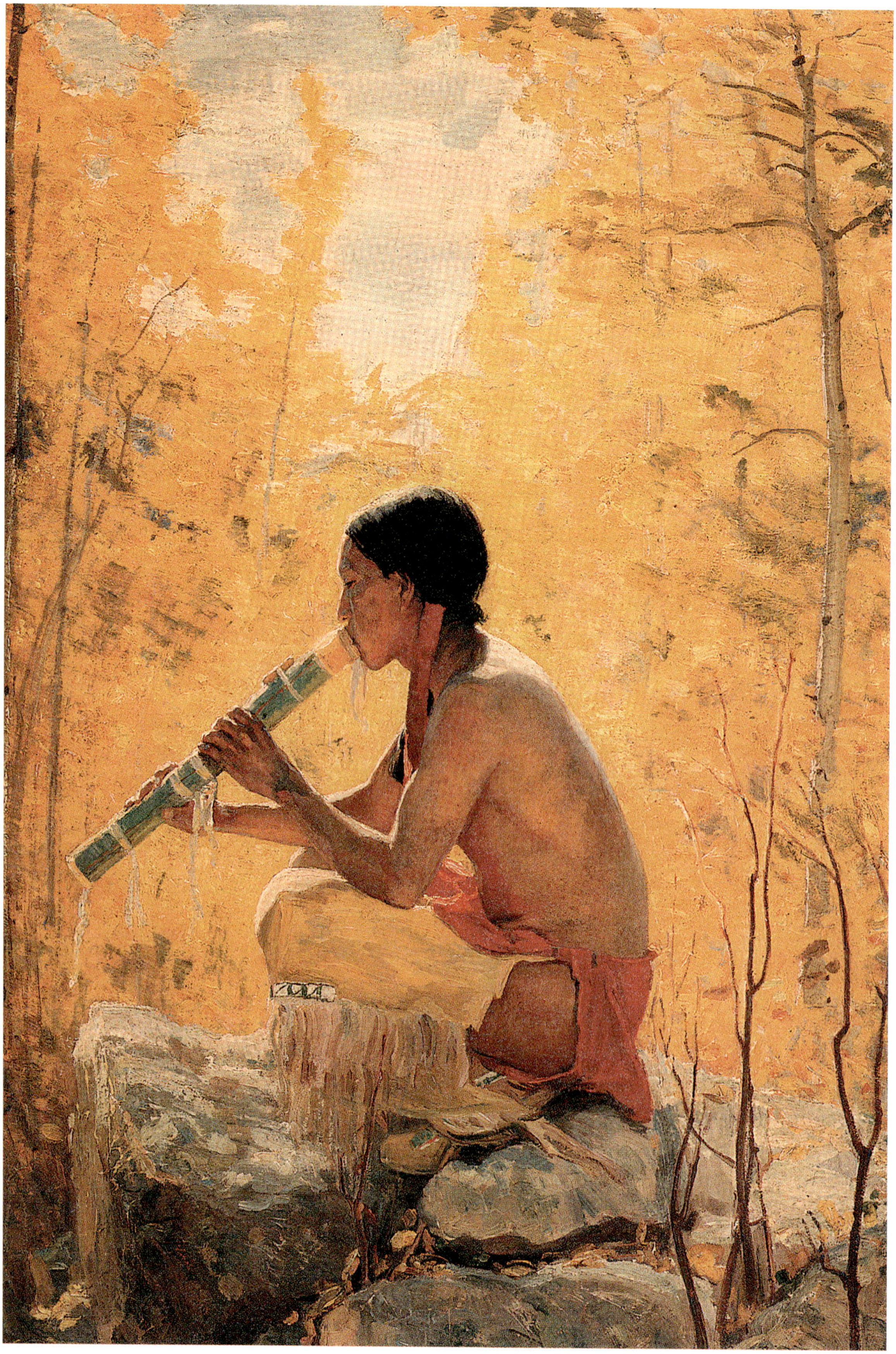

078. BERT GEER PHILLIPS (1868–1956)
Song of the Aspen, c. 1926–28
Oil on canvas. 40 x 27 in. (101.6 x 68.6 cm)

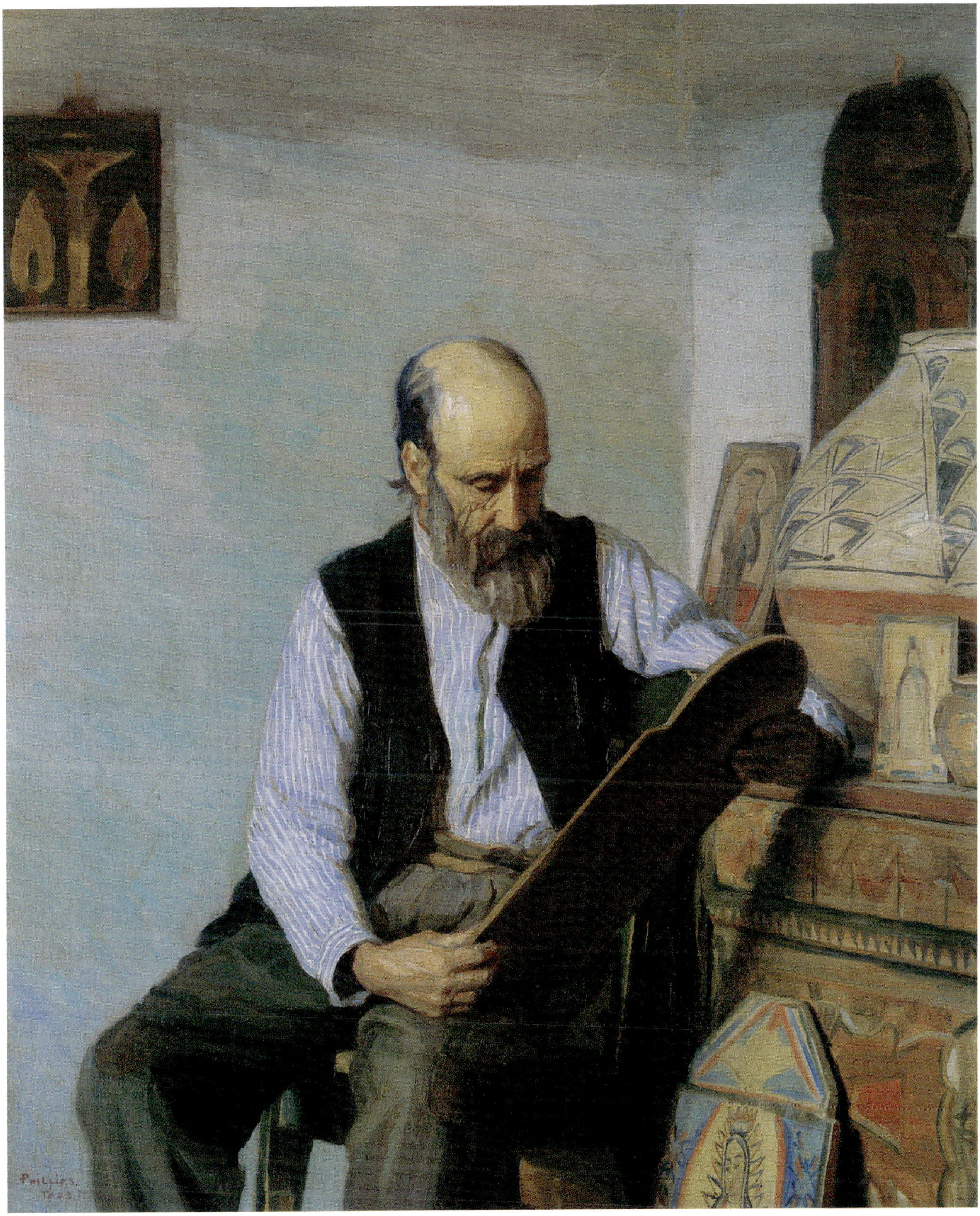

079. BERT GEER PHILLIPS (1868–1956)
The Santero, c. 1918
Oil on canvas. 30¼ x 25 in. (76.8 x 63.5 cm)

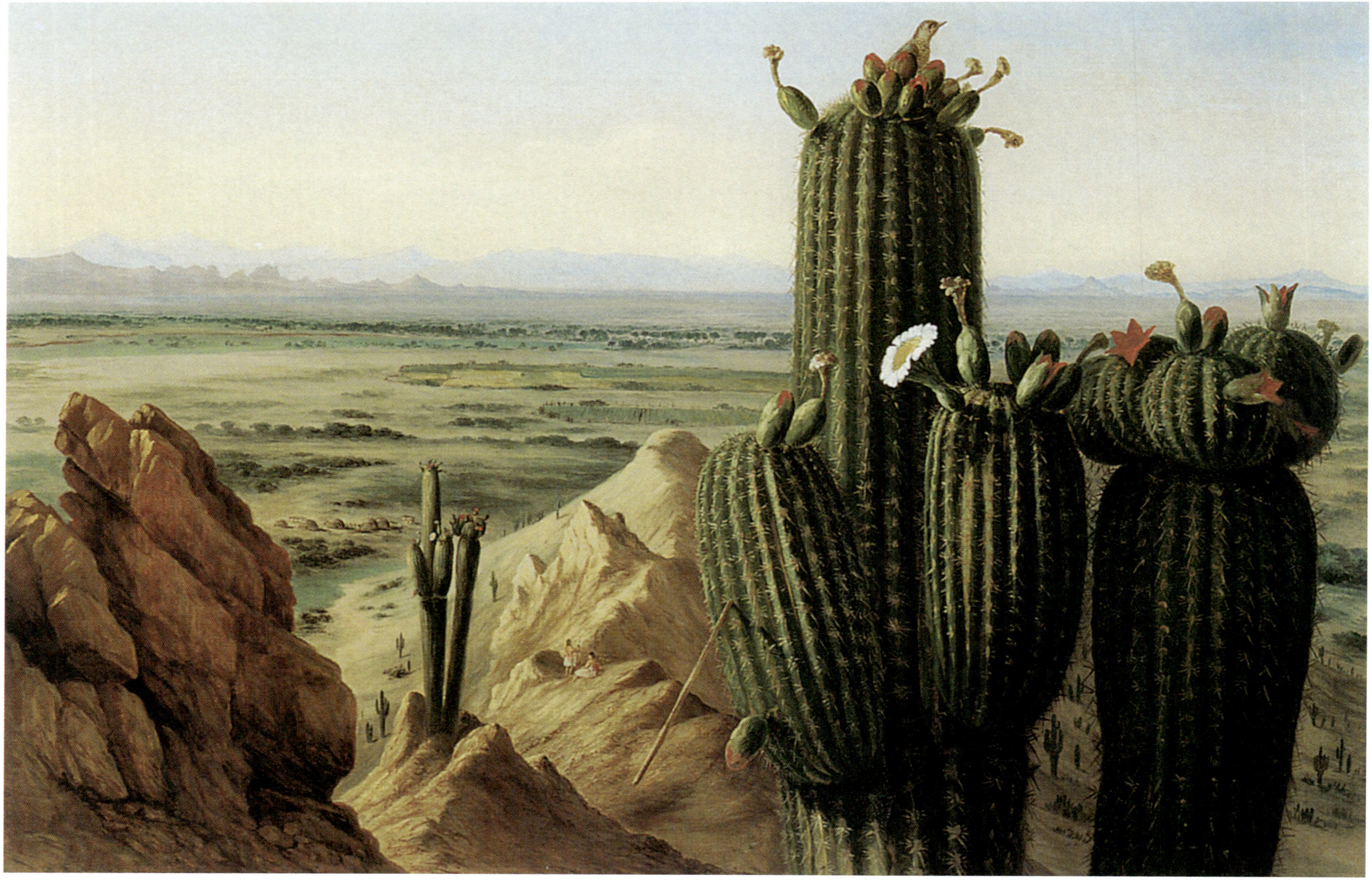

080. HENRY CHEEVER PRATT (1803–1880)
View from Maricopa Mountain near the Rio Gila, 1855
Oil on canvas. 33 x 48 in. (83.8 x 121.9 cm)

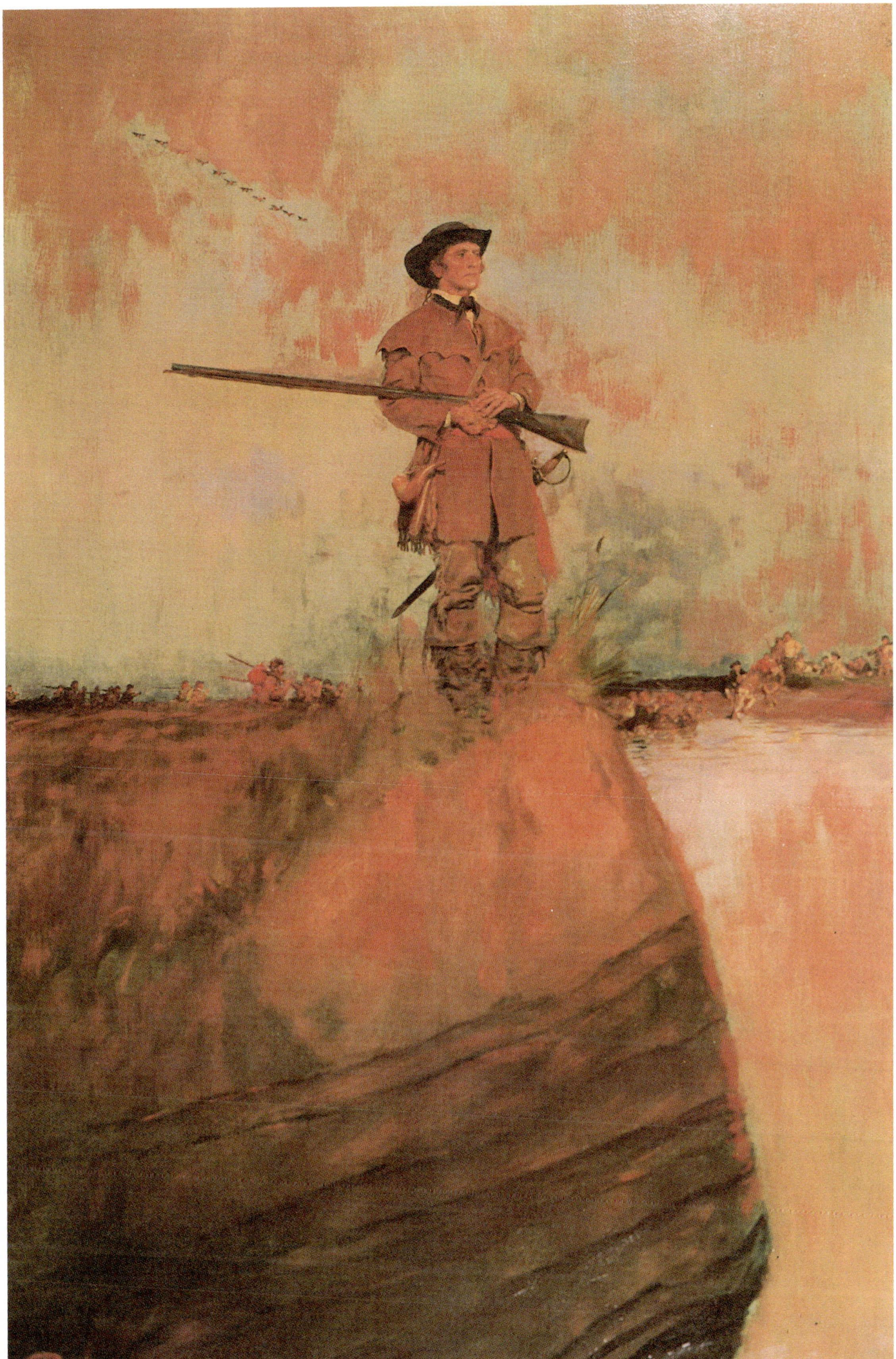

081. HOWARD PYLE (1853–1911)
George Rogers Clark on His Way to Kaskaskia, n.d.
Oil. 30 x 42 in. (76.2 x 106.7 cm)

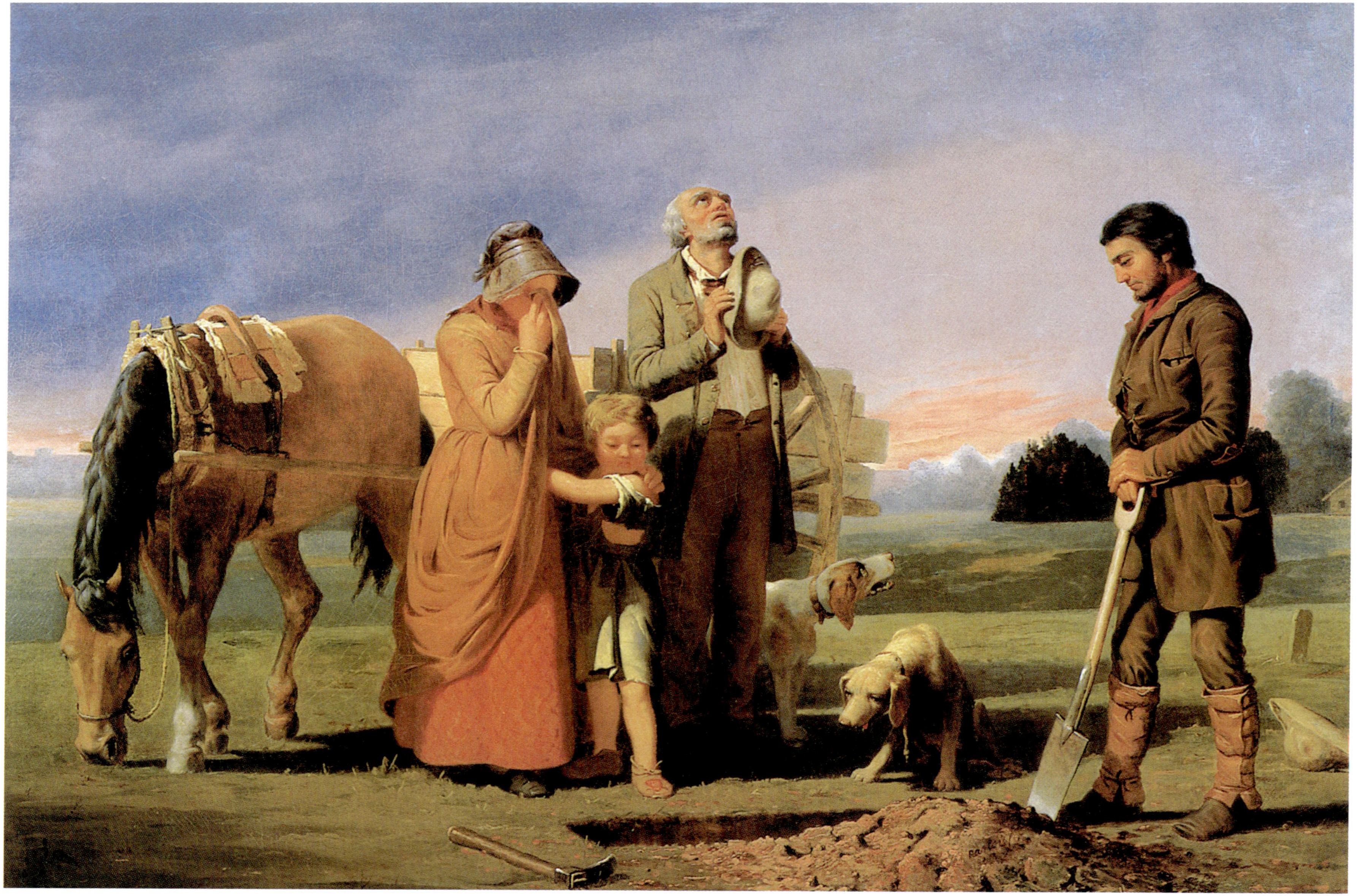

082. WILLIAM TYLEE RANNEY (1813–1857)
Prairie Burial, 1848
Oil on canvas. 28½ x 41 in. (72.4 x 104.1 cm)

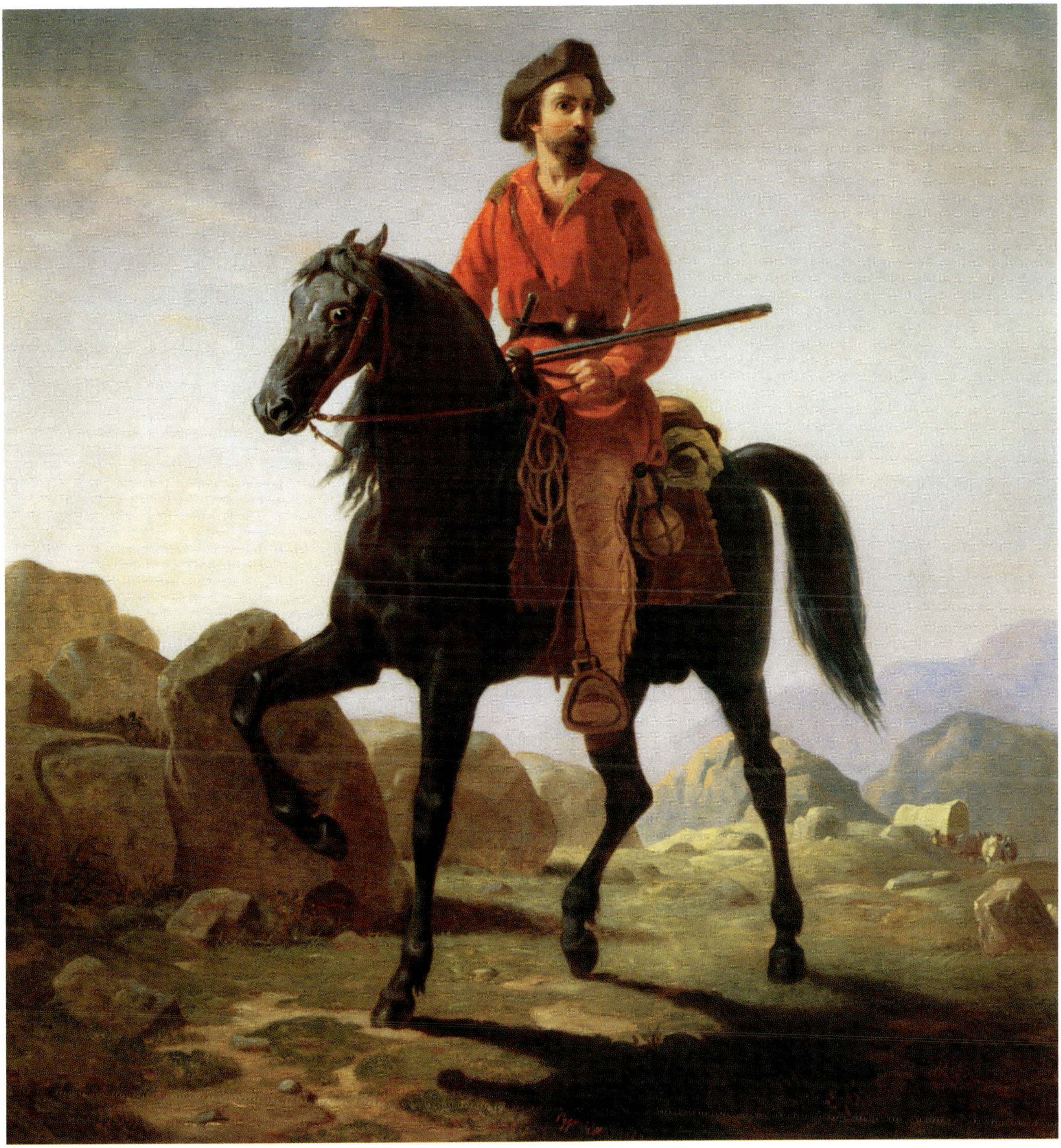

083. WILLIAM TYLEE RANNEY (1813–1857)
Kit Carson, 1854
Oil on canvas. 29 x 24½ in. (73.7 x 62.2 cm)

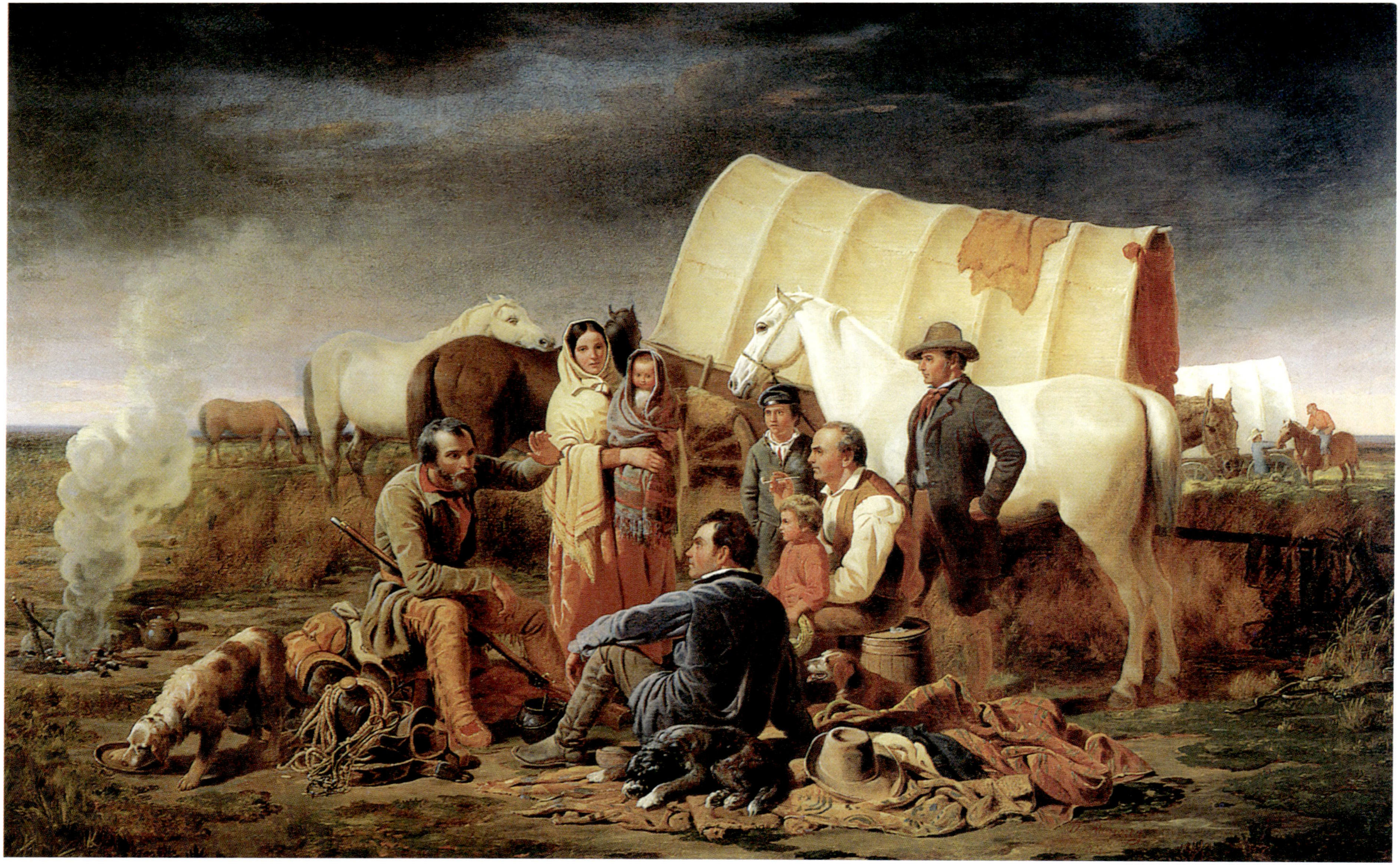

084. WILLIAM TYLEE RANNEY (1813–1857)
Advice on the Prairie, 1853
Oil on canvas. 40 x 54 in. (101.6 x 137.2 cm)

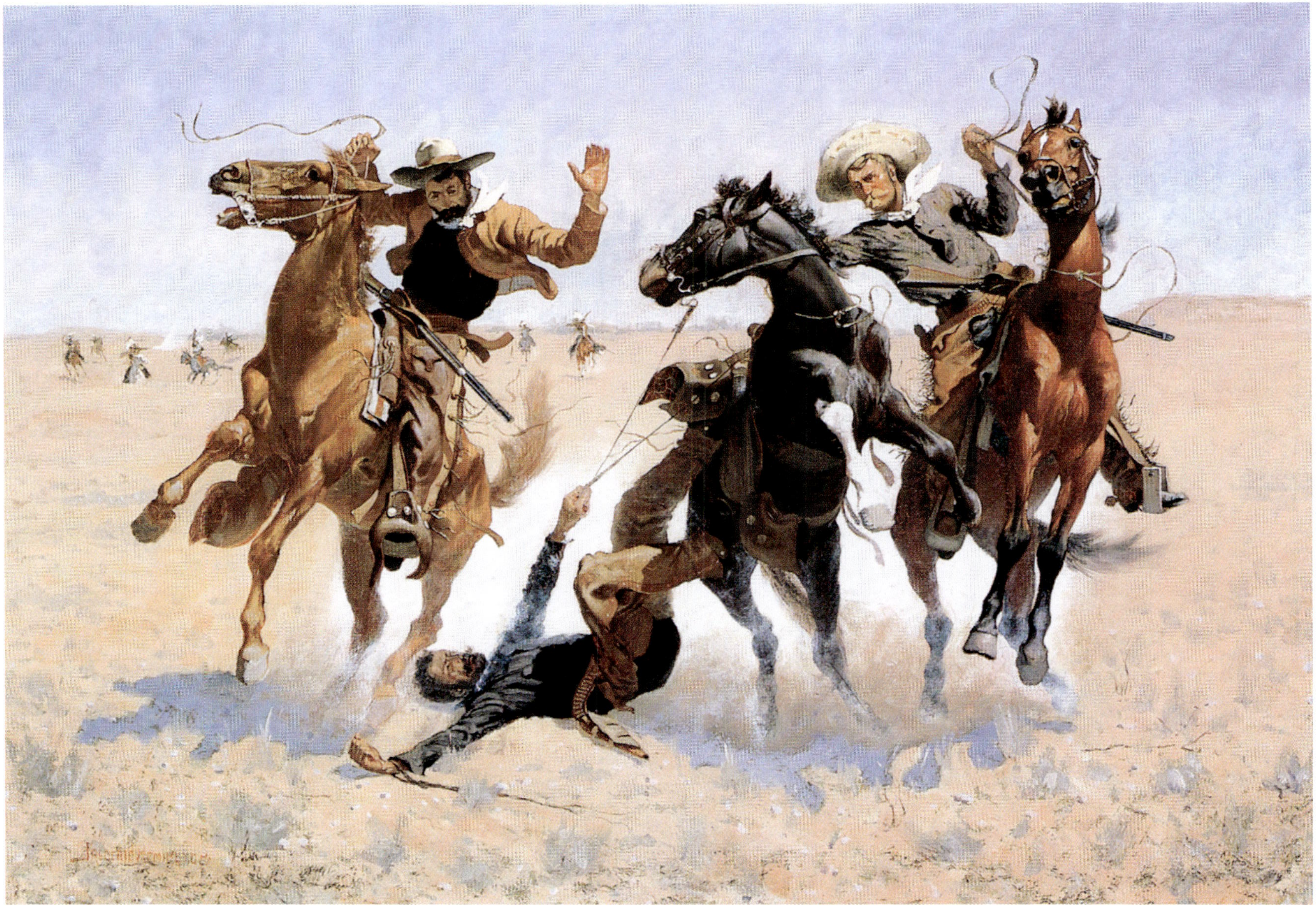

085. FREDERIC REMINGTON (1861–1909)
Aiding a Comrade, c. 1890
Oil on canvas. 34¼ x 48⅛ in. (87.2 x 122.2 cm)

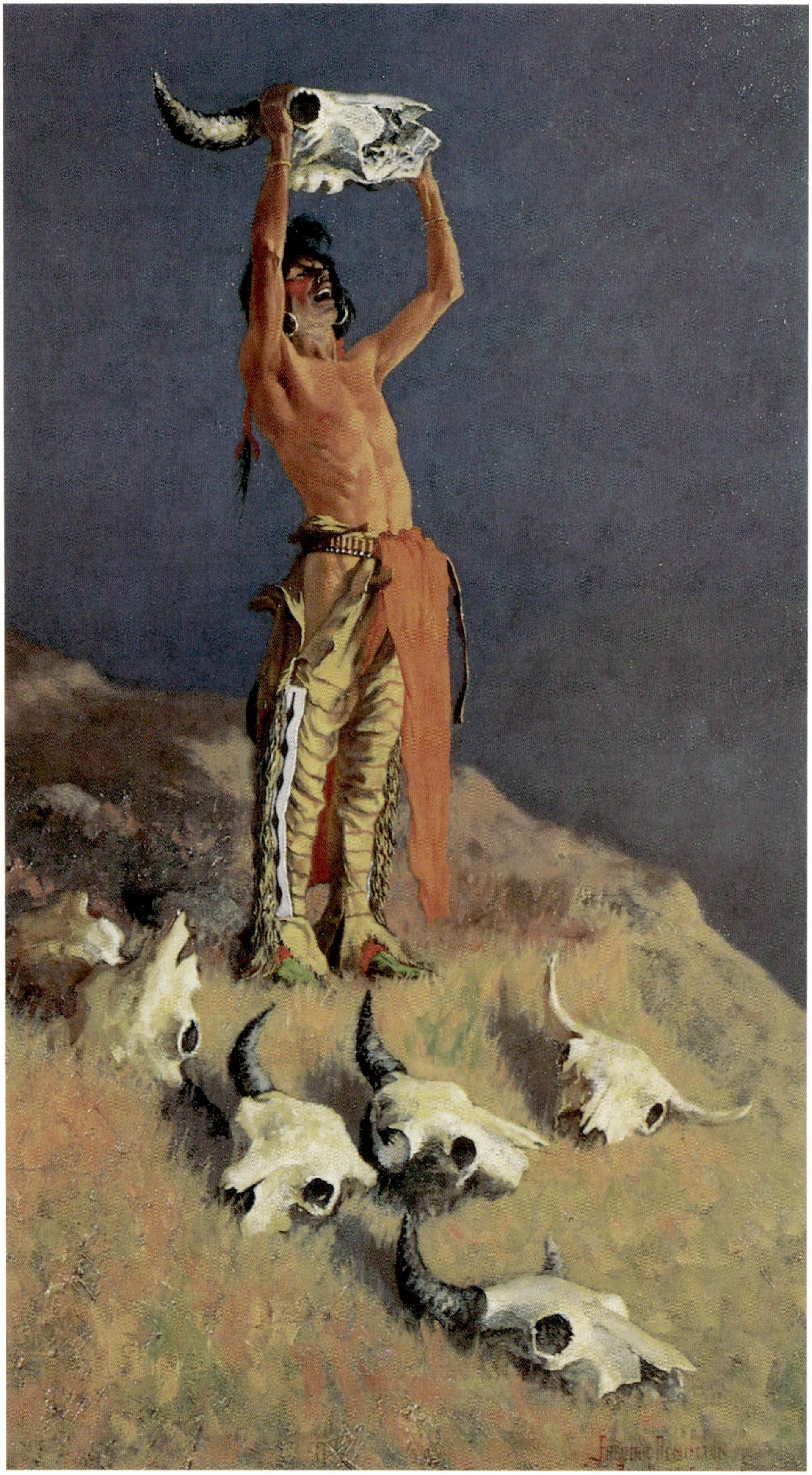

086. FREDERIC REMINGTON (1861–1909)
Conjuring Back the Buffalo, 1892
Oil on canvas. 35 x 20 in. (88.9 x 50.8 cm)

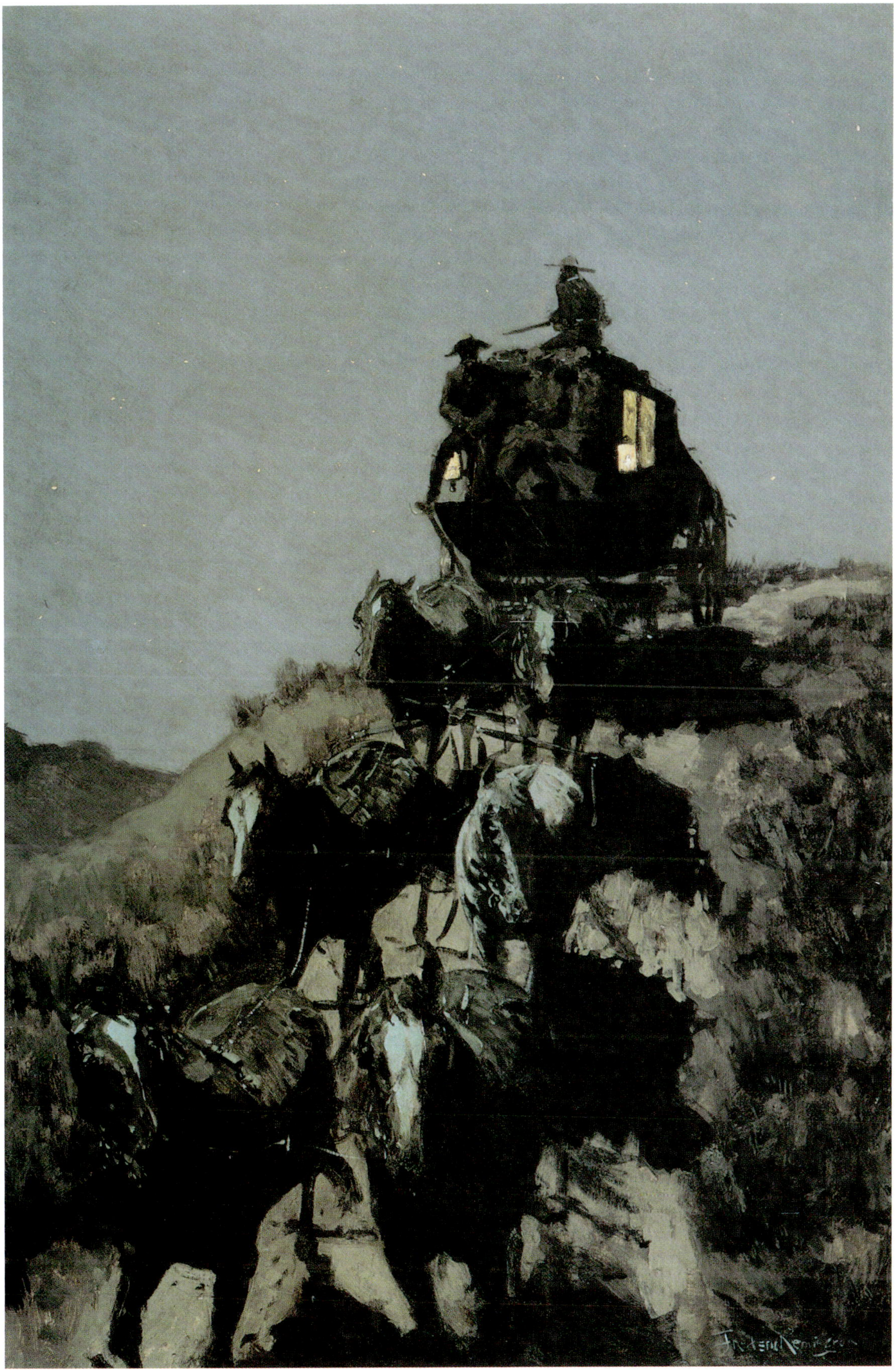

087. FREDERIC REMINGTON (1861–1909)
Old Stage Coach of the Plains, 1901
Oil on canvas. 40¼ x 27¼ in. (102.2 x 69.2 cm)

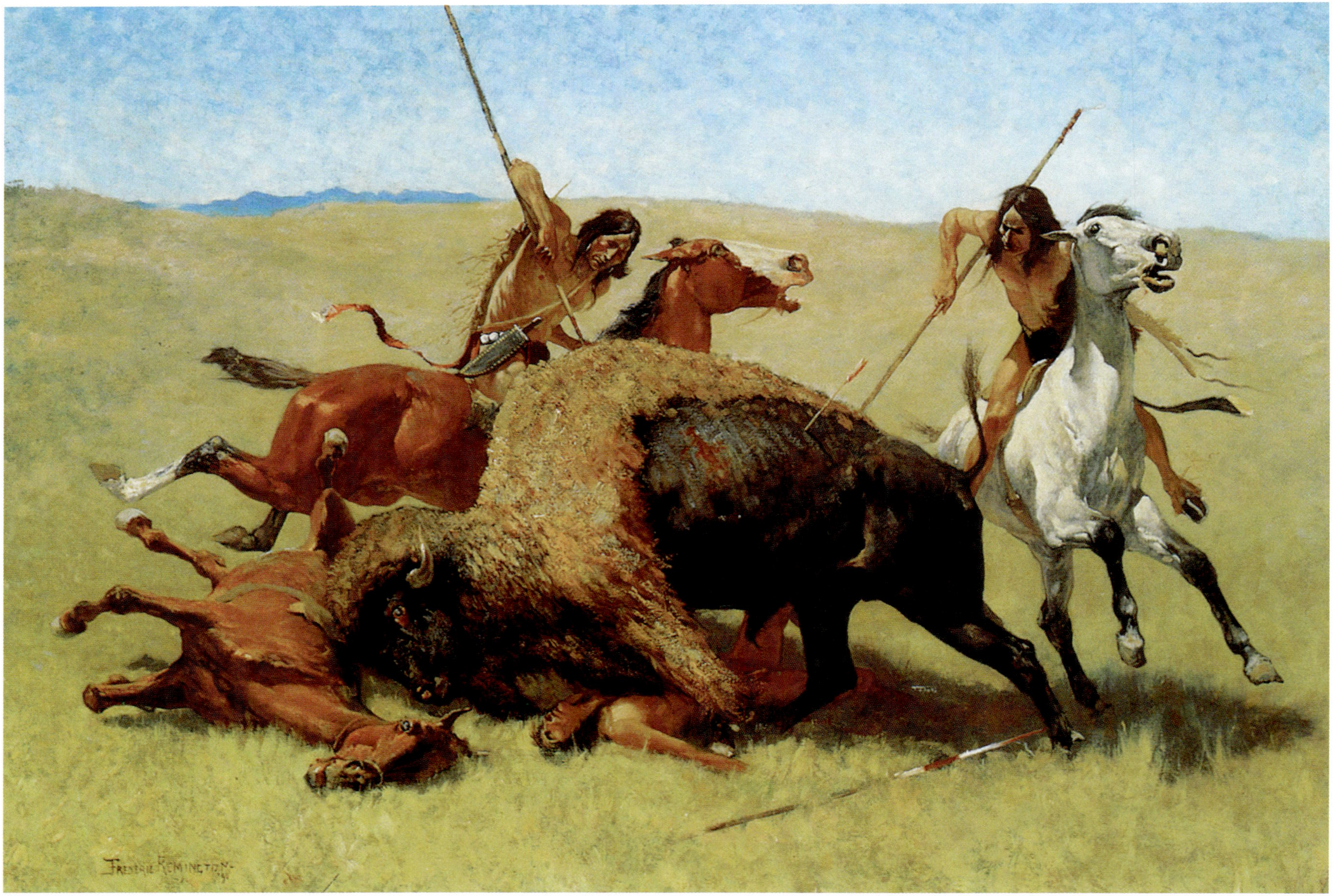

088. FREDERIC REMINGTON (1861–1909)
The Buffalo Hunt, 1890
Oil on canvas. 34 x 49 in. (86.4 x 124.5 cm)

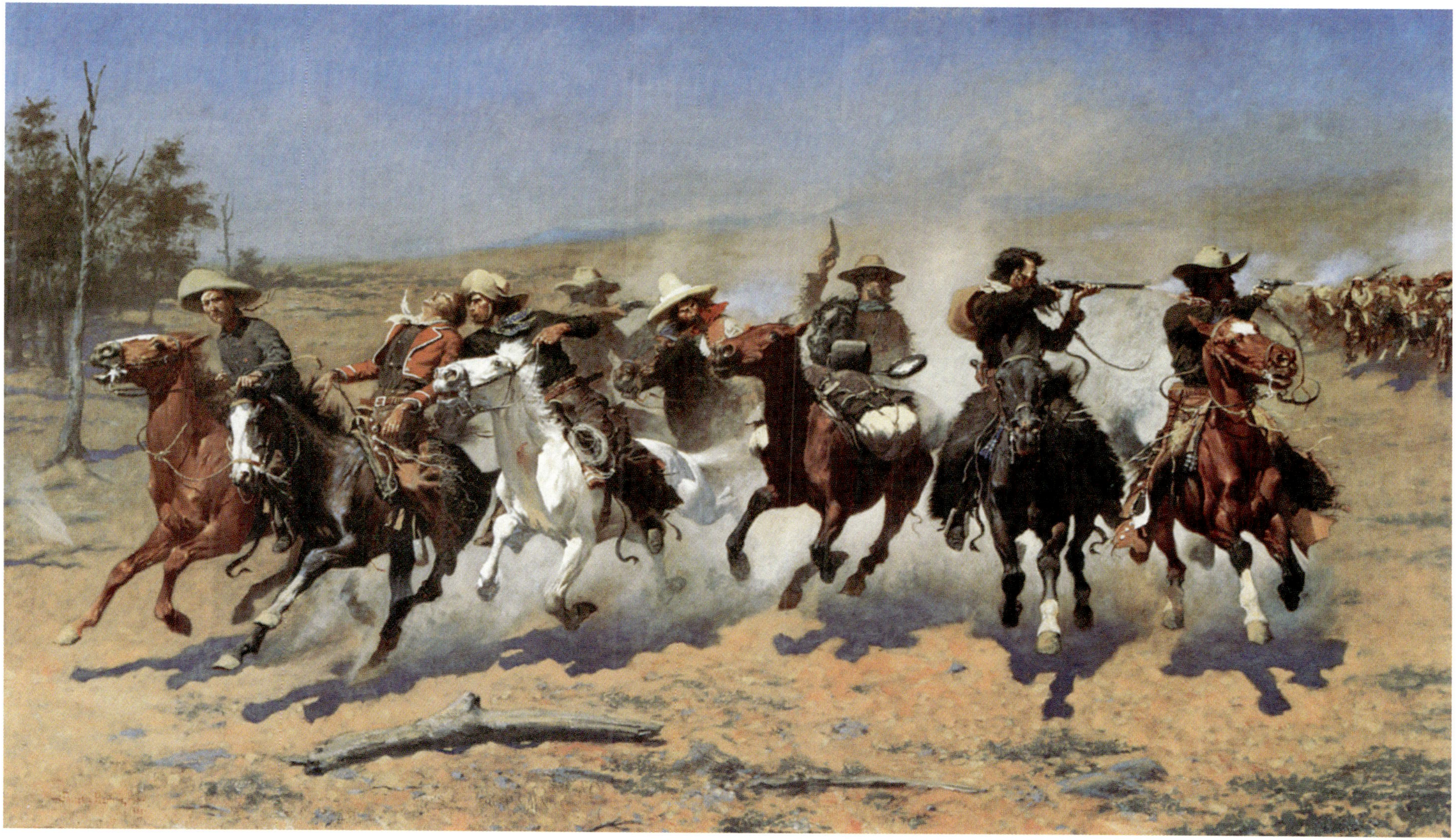

089. FREDERIC REMINGTON (1861–1909)
A Dash for the Timber, 1889
Oil on canvas. 48¼ x 84⅛ in. (122.6 x 213.7 cm)

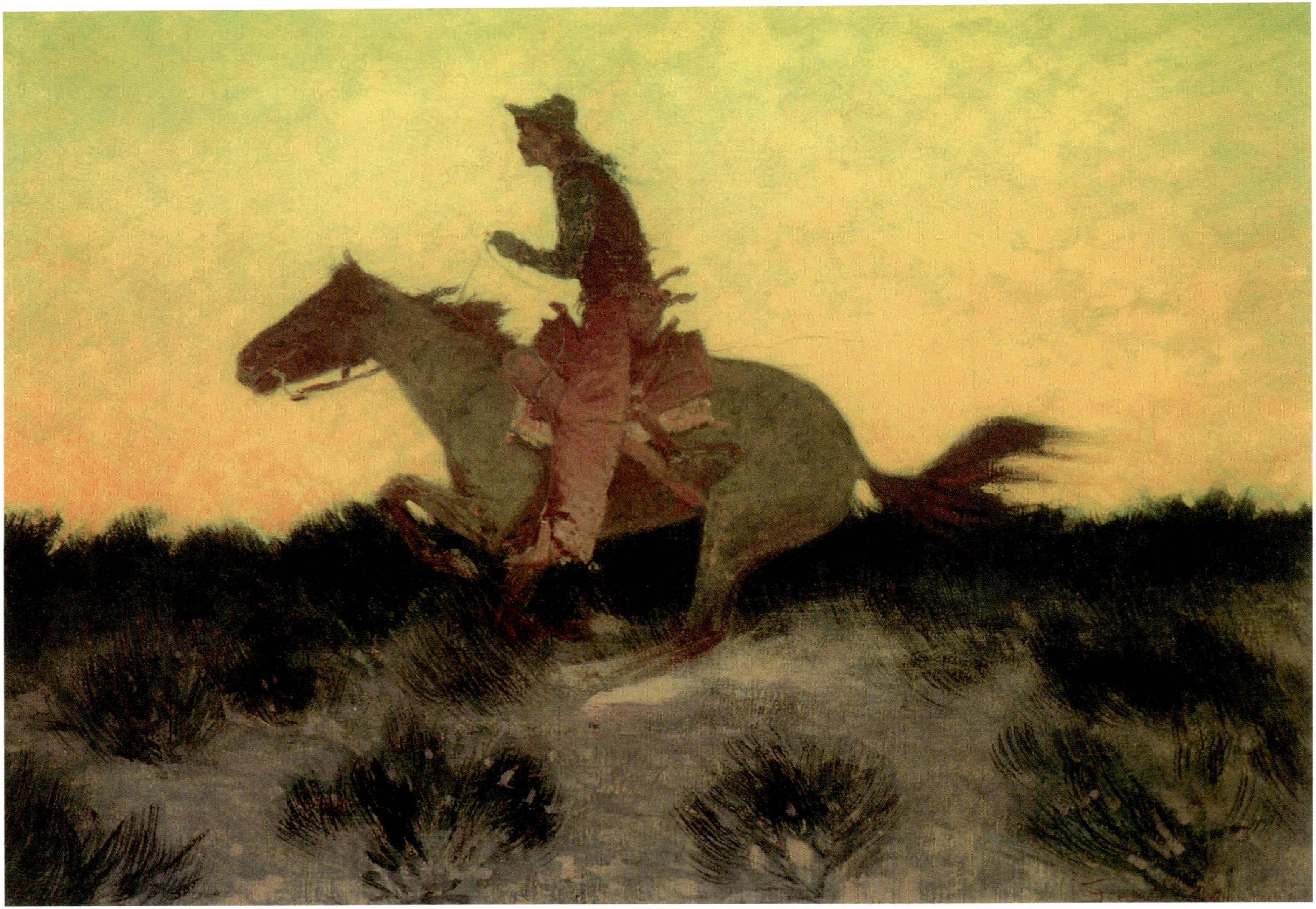

090. FREDERIC REMINGTON (1861–1909)
Against the Sunset, 1906
Oil on canvas. 22 x 30 in. (55.9 x 76.2 cm)

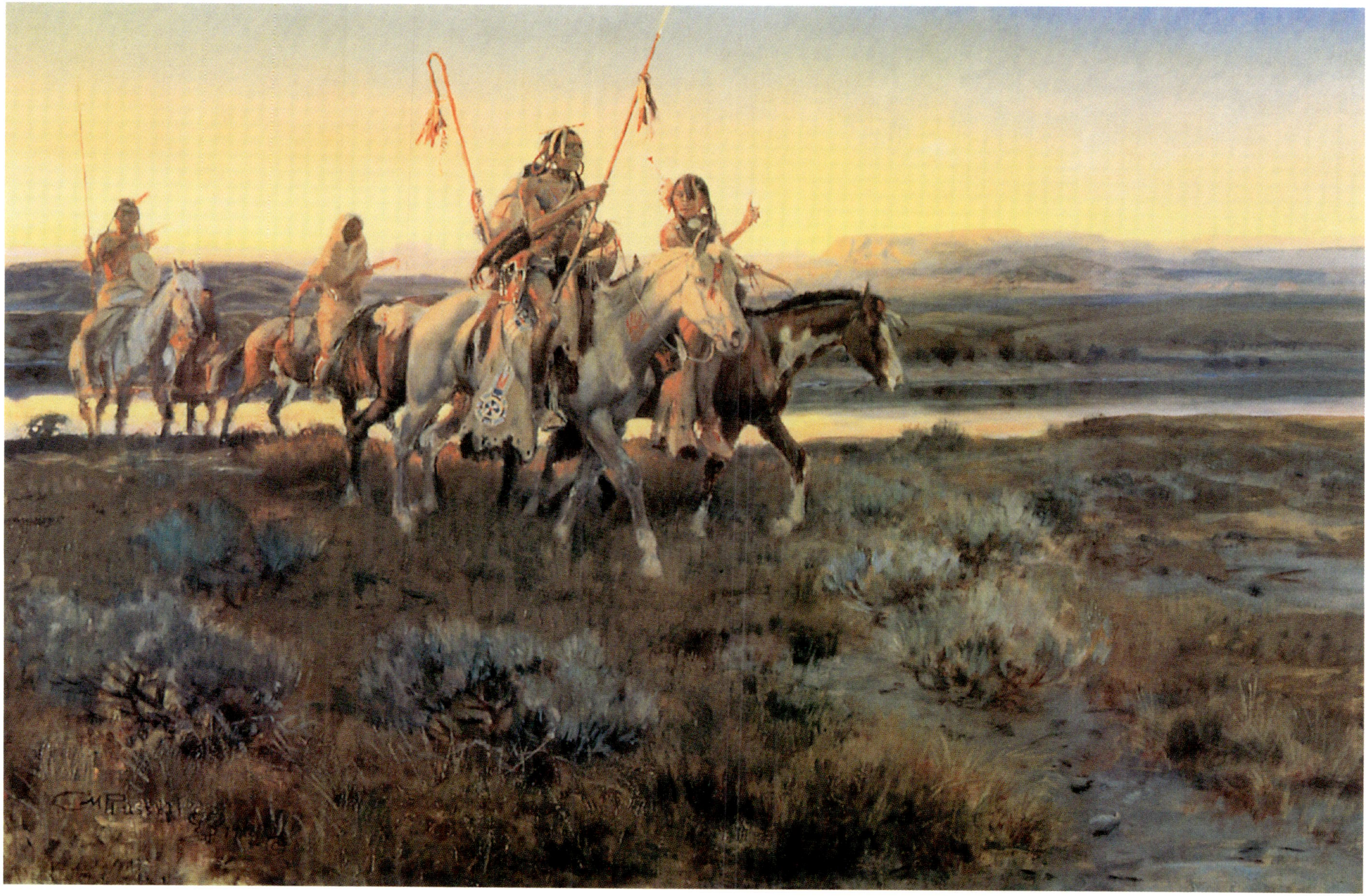

091. CHARLES M. RUSSELL (1864–1926)
Piegans, 1918
Oil on canvas. 24 x 36 in. (61 x 91.4 cm)

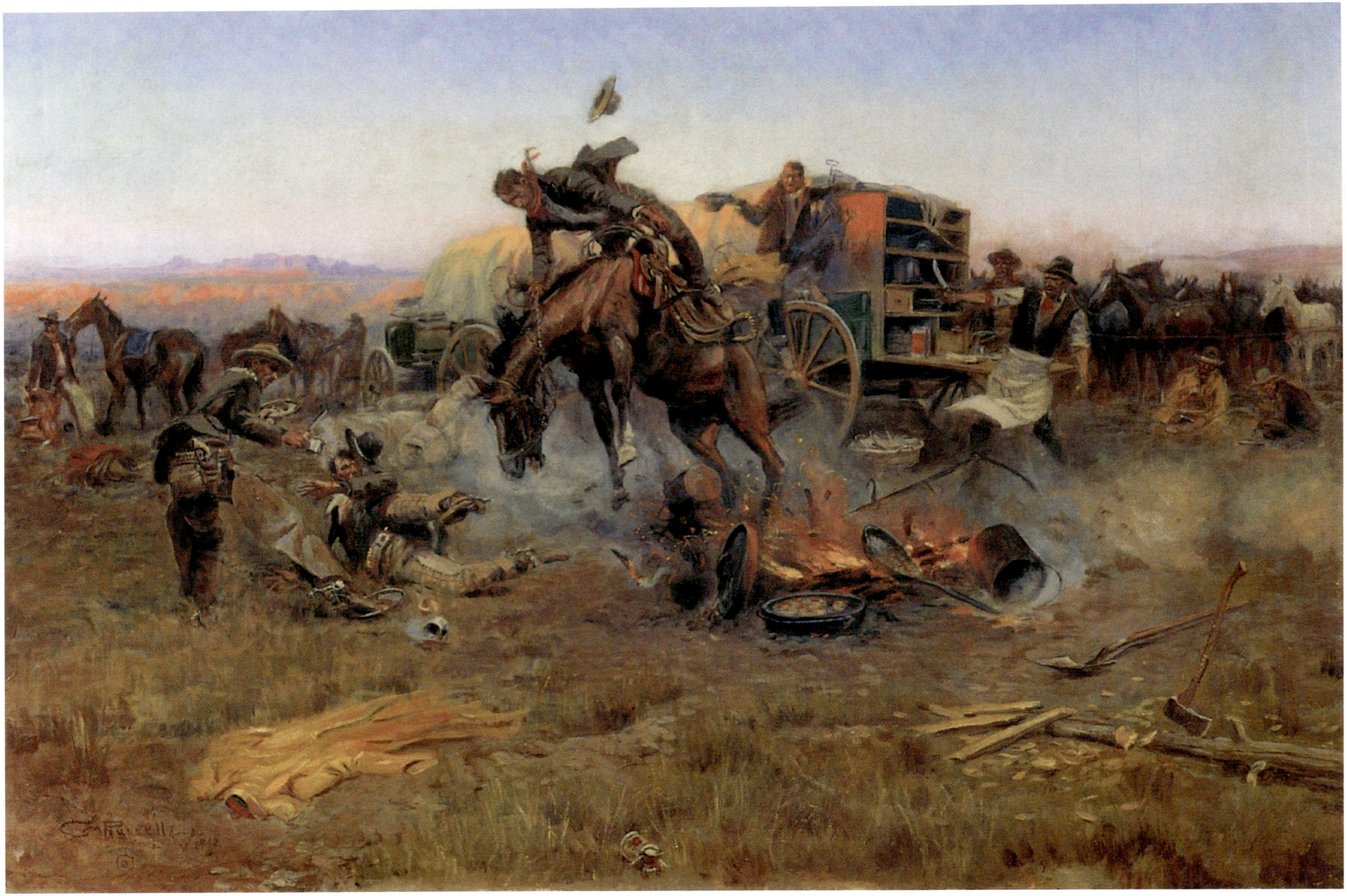

092. CHARLES M. RUSSELL (1864–1926)
Camp Cook's Troubles, 1912
Oil on canvas. 29 x 43 in. (73.7 x 109.2 cm)

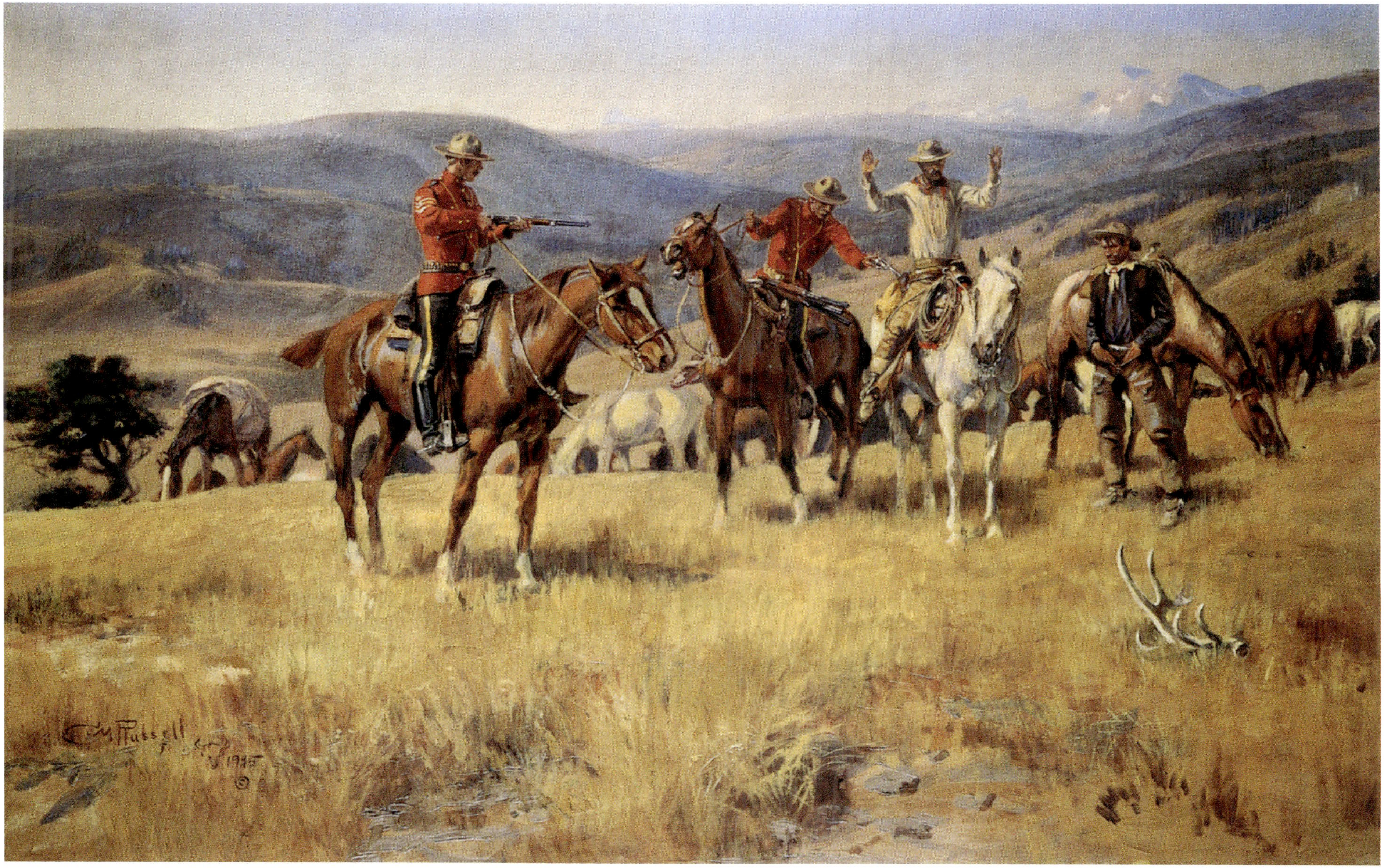

093. CHARLES M. RUSSELL (1864–1926)
When Law Dulls the Edge of Chance, 1915
Oil on canvas. 29½ x 47½ in. (74.9 x 120.6 cm)

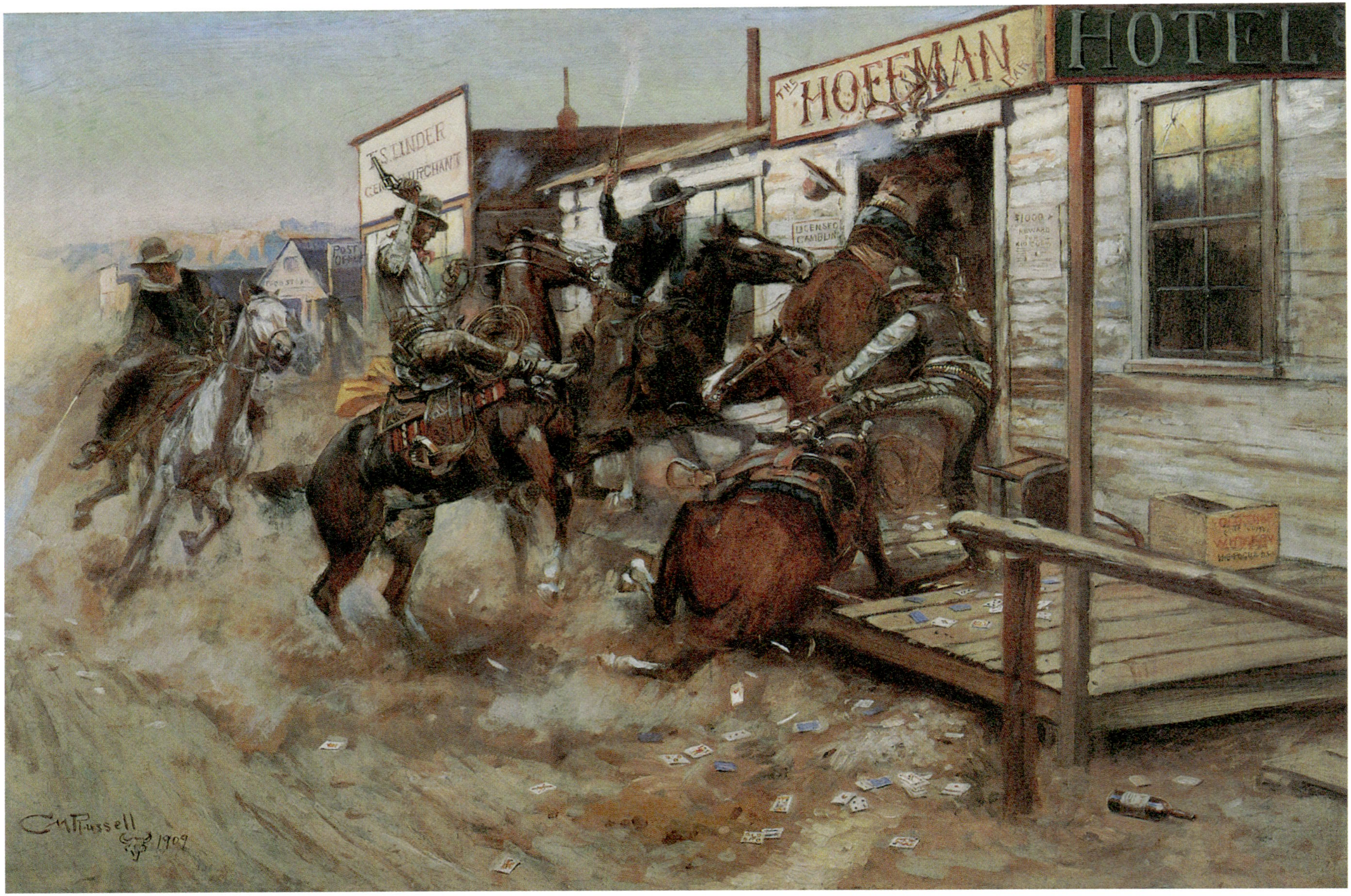

094. CHARLES M. RUSSELL (1864–1926)
In Without Knocking, 1909
Oil on canvas. 20⅛ x 29⅞ in. (51.1 x 75.9 cm)

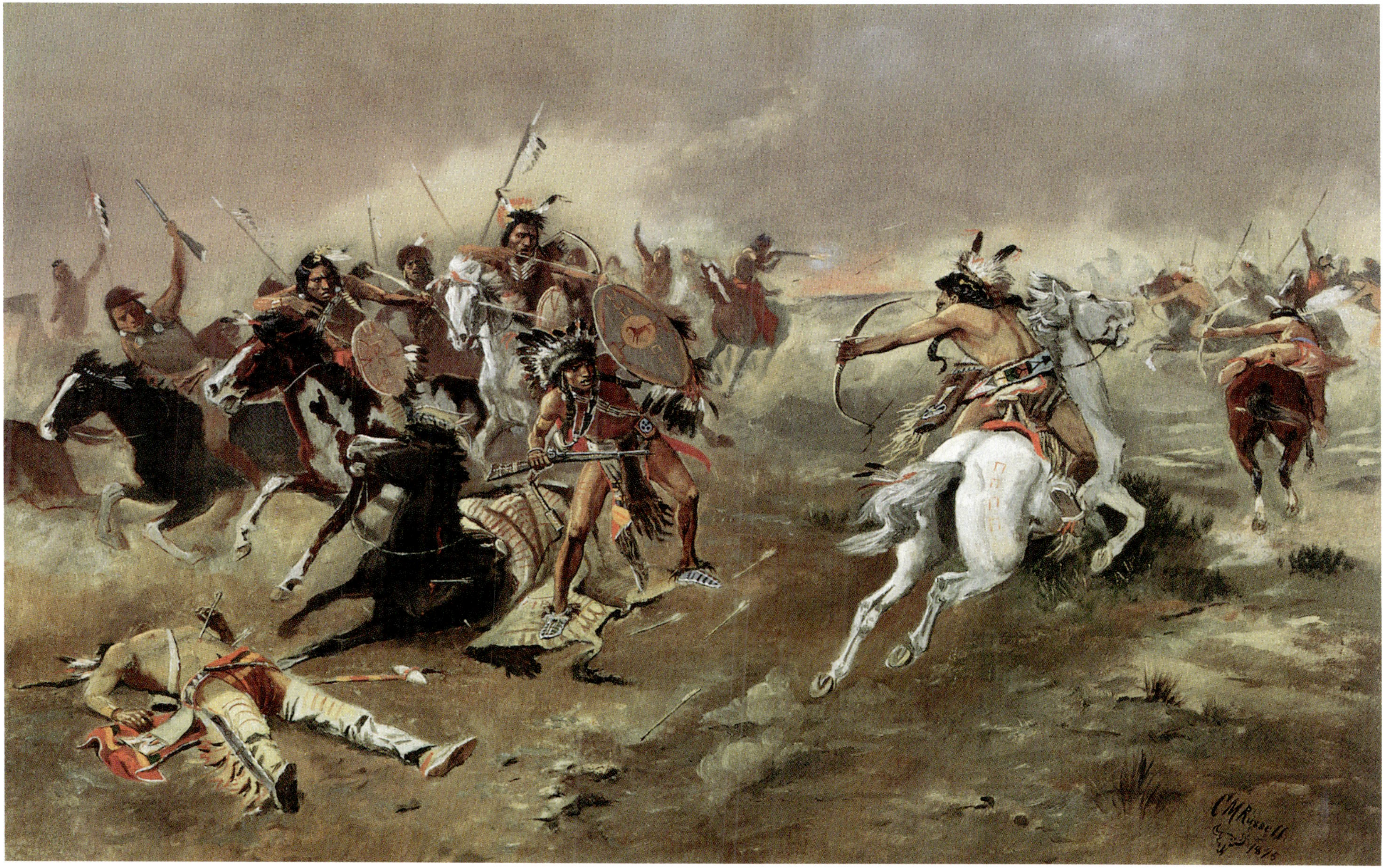

095. CHARLES M. RUSSELL (1864–1926)
For Supremacy, 1895
Oil on canvas. 23⅛ x 35 in. (58.7 x 88.9 cm)

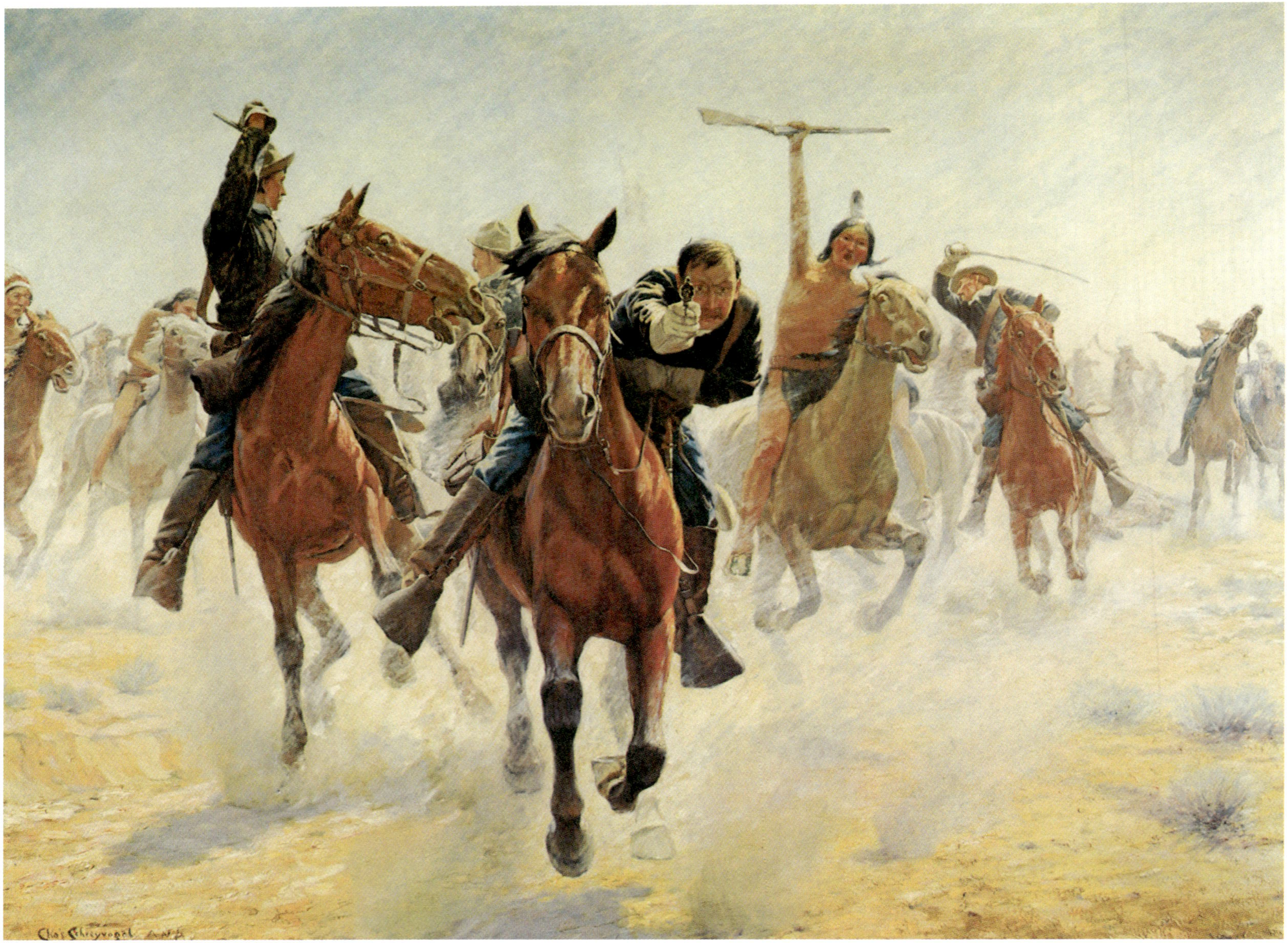

096. CHARLES SCHREYVOGEL (1861–1912)
Breaking Through the Line, n.d.
Oil. 39 x 52 in. (99.1 x 132.1 cm)

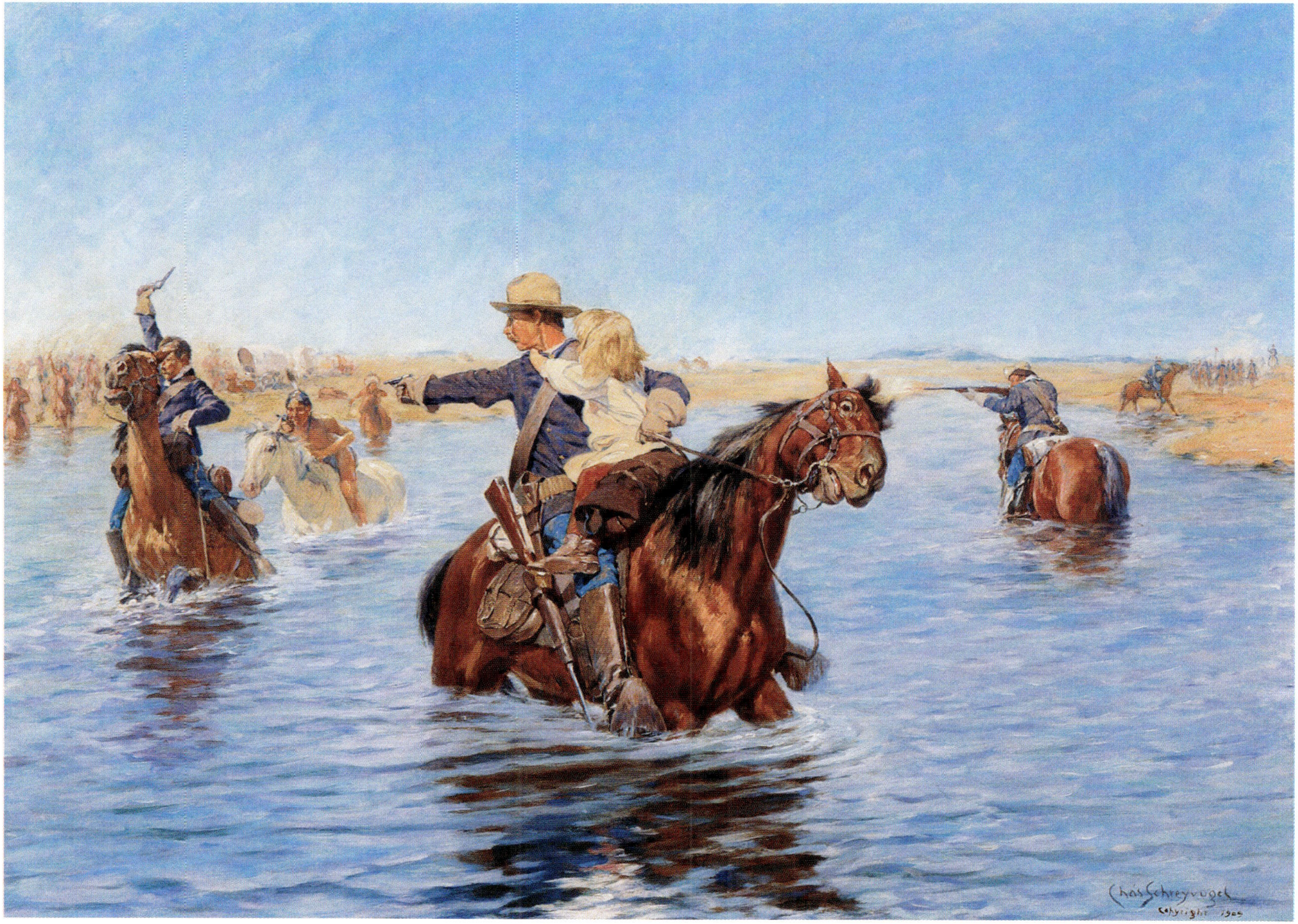

097. CHARLES SCHREYVOGEL (1861–1912)
In Safe Hands, 1909
Oil on canvas. 25¼ x 34 in. (64.1 x 86.4 cm)

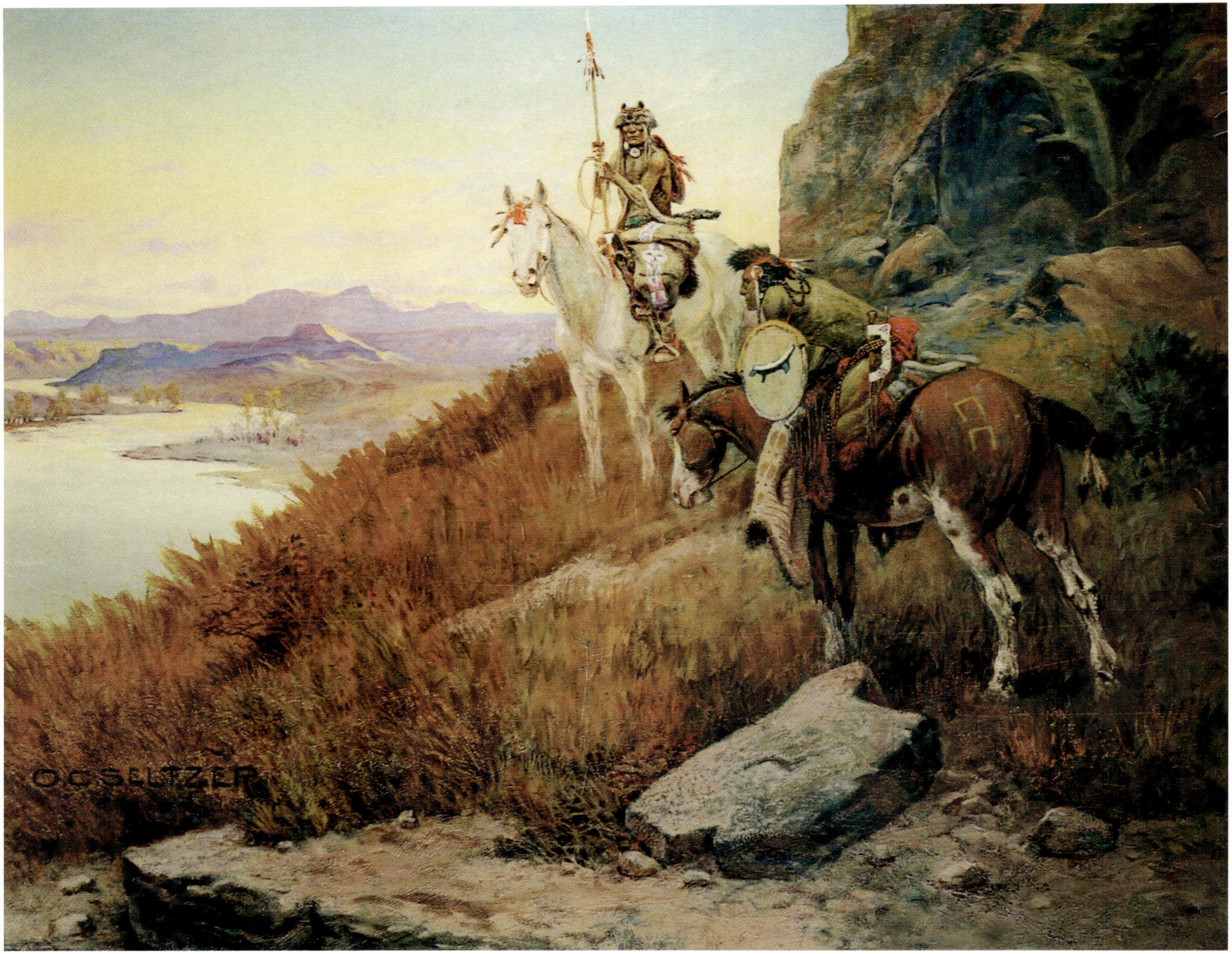

098. OLAF C. SELTZER (1877–1957)
Watching for the White Man's Boats, n.d.
Oil on canvas. 42¼ x 53¾ in. (107.3 x 136.5 cm)

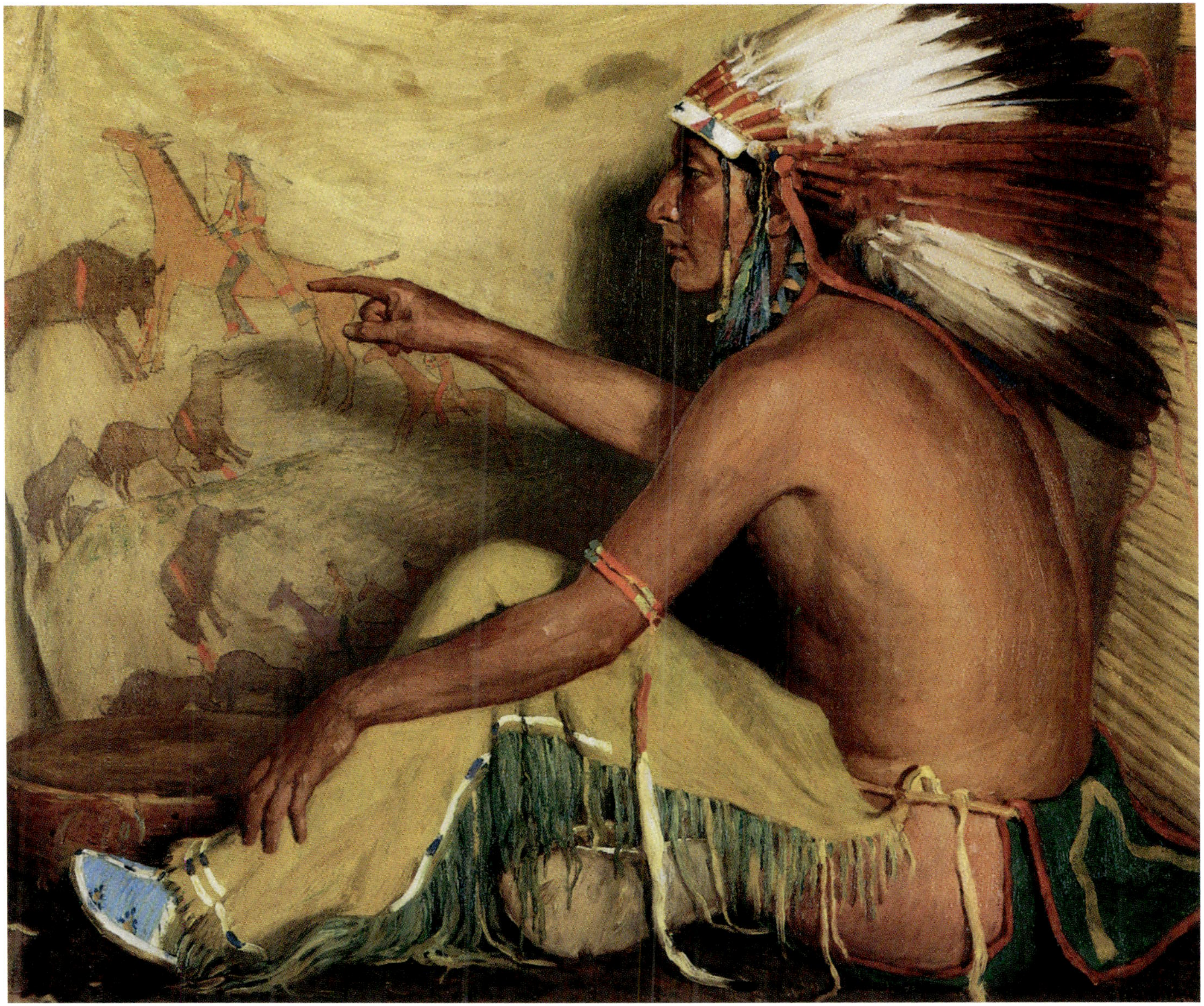

099. JOSEPH HENRY SHARP (1859–1953)
Pointing with Pride to His Record, c. 1920–24
Oil on canvas. 25 x 30 in. (63.5 x 76.2 cm)

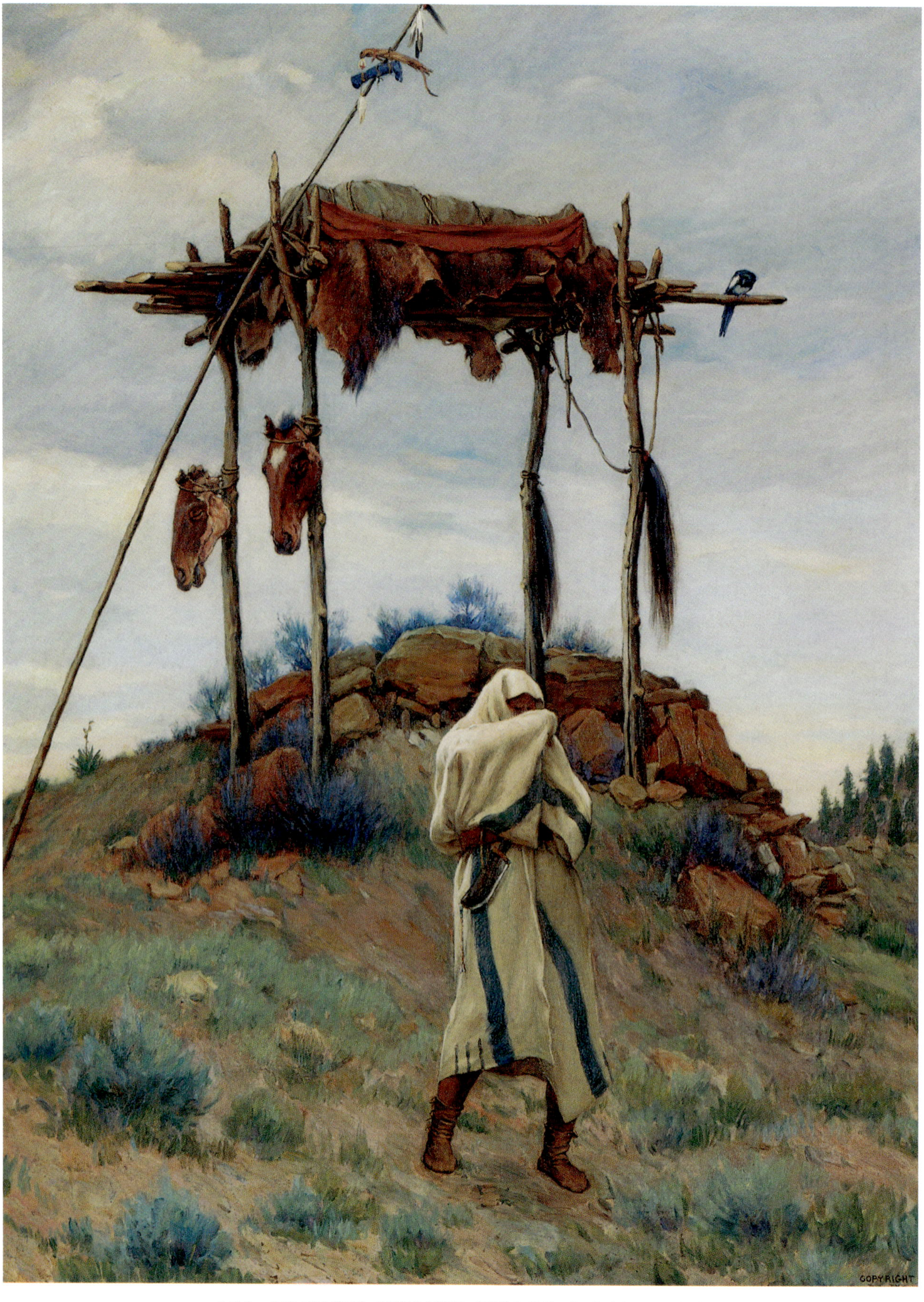

100. JOSEPH HENRY SHARP (1859–1953)
The Voice of the Great Spirit, 1906
Oil on canvas. 40 x 30 in. (101.6 x 76.2 cm)

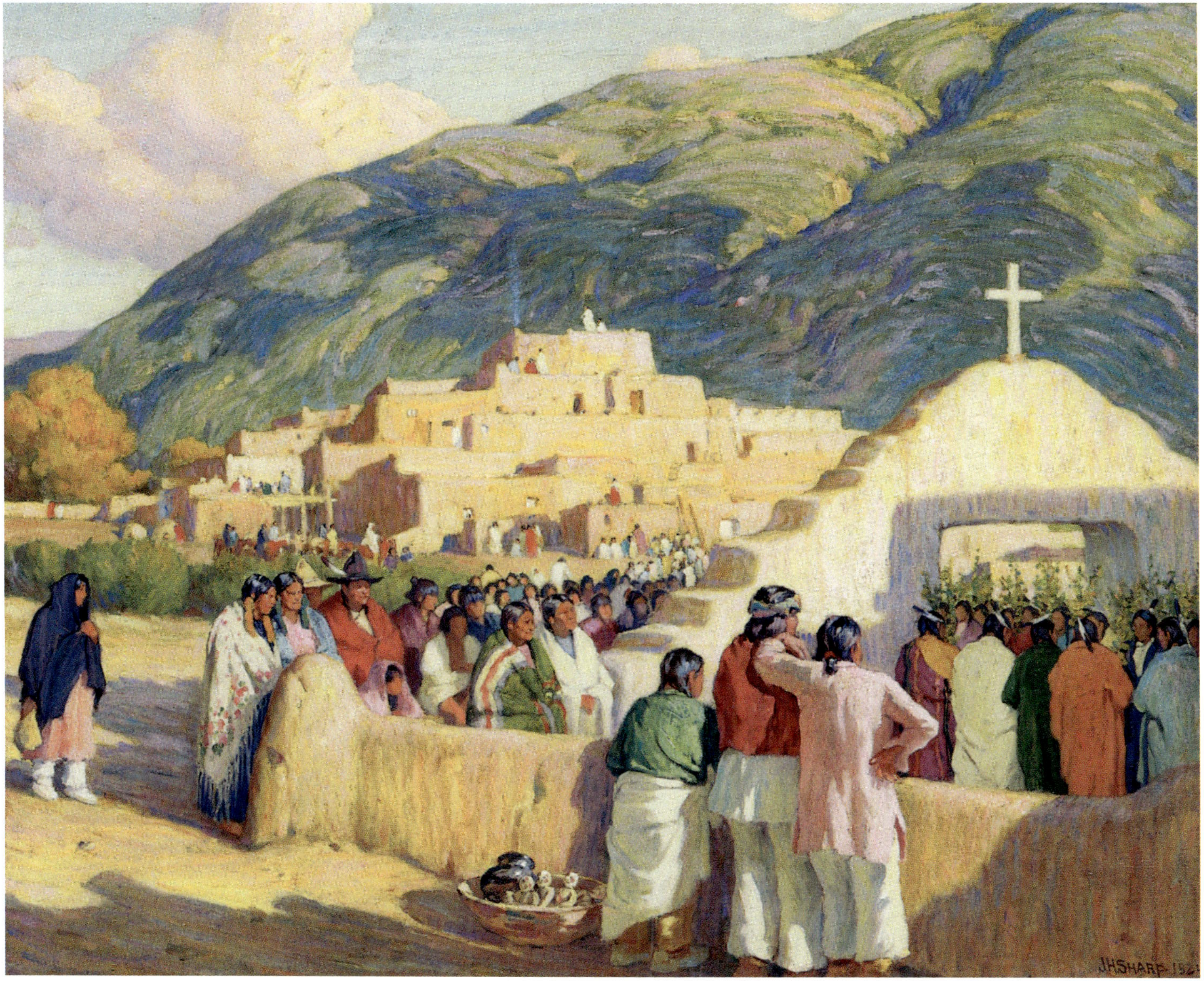

101. JOSEPH HENRY SHARP (1859–1953)
Sunset Dance—Ceremony to the Evening Sun, 1924
Oil on canvas. 25⅛ x 30 in. (63.8 x 76.2 cm)

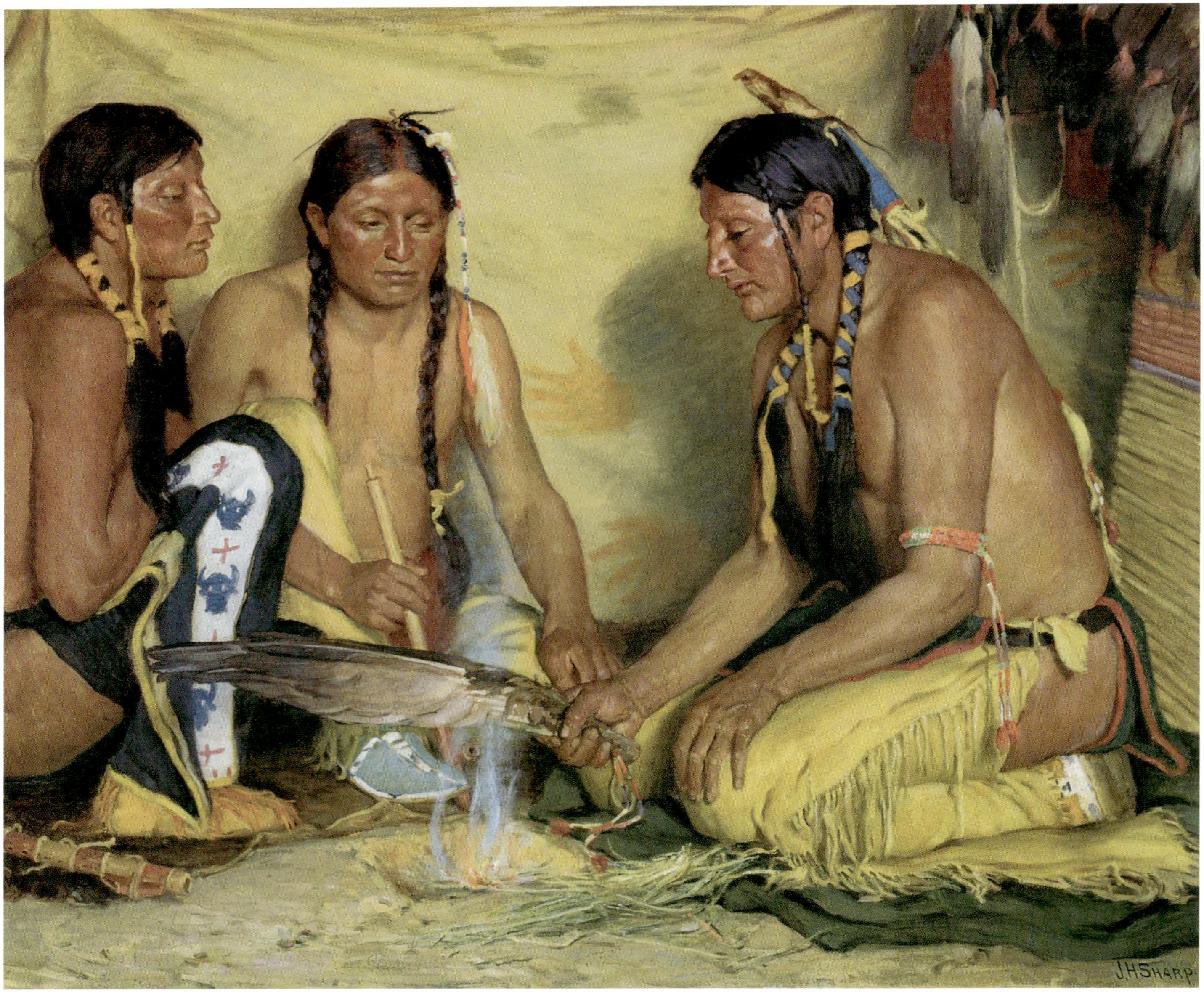

102. JOSEPH HENRY SHARP (1859–1953)
Making Sweet Grass Medicine, Blackfoot Ceremony, c. 1920
Oil. 30 x 36 in. (76.2 x 91.4 cm)

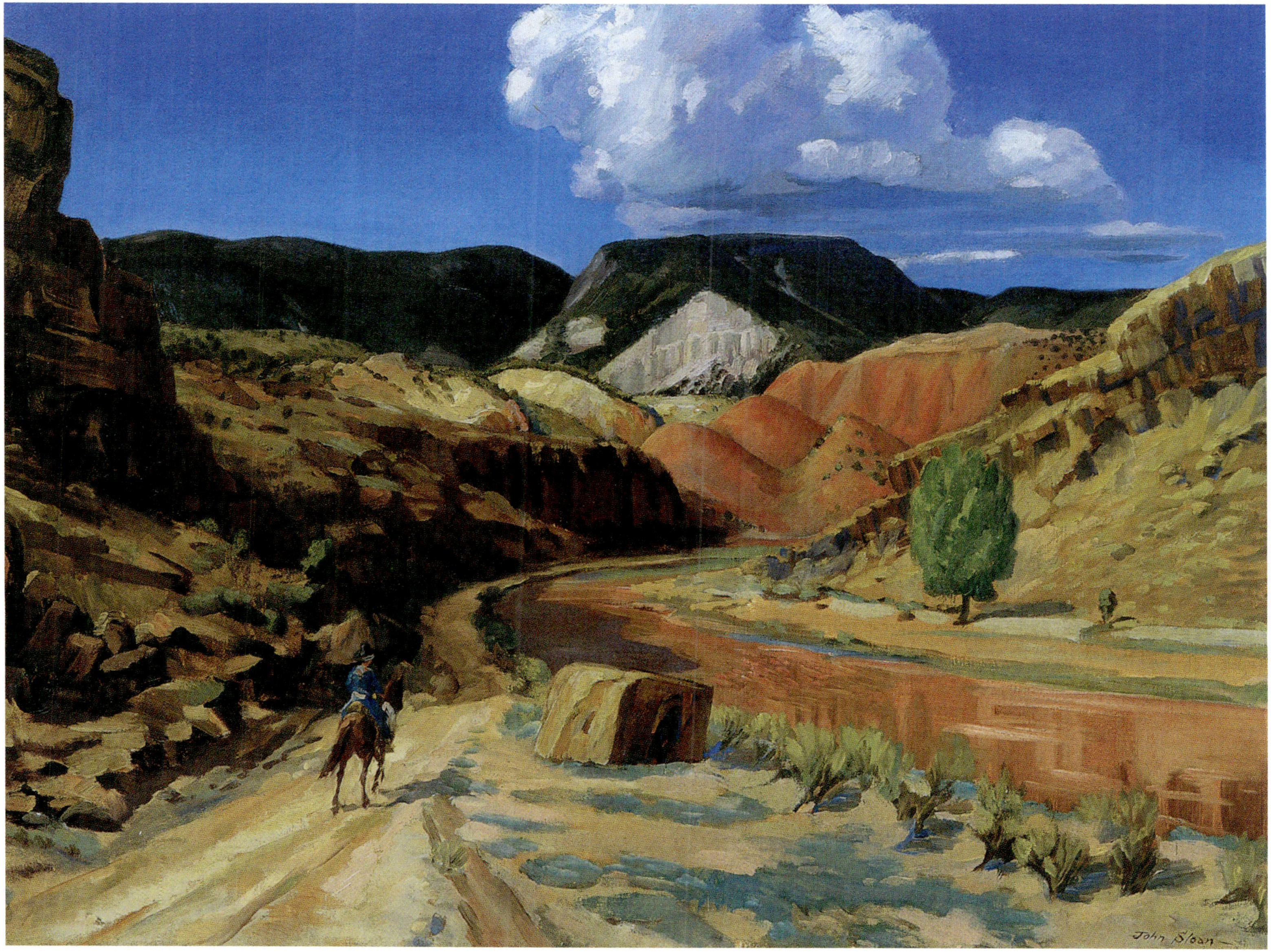

103. JOHN SLOAN (1871–1951)
Chama Running Red, 1925
Oil on canvas. 30½ x 40¼ in. (77.5 x 102.2 cm)

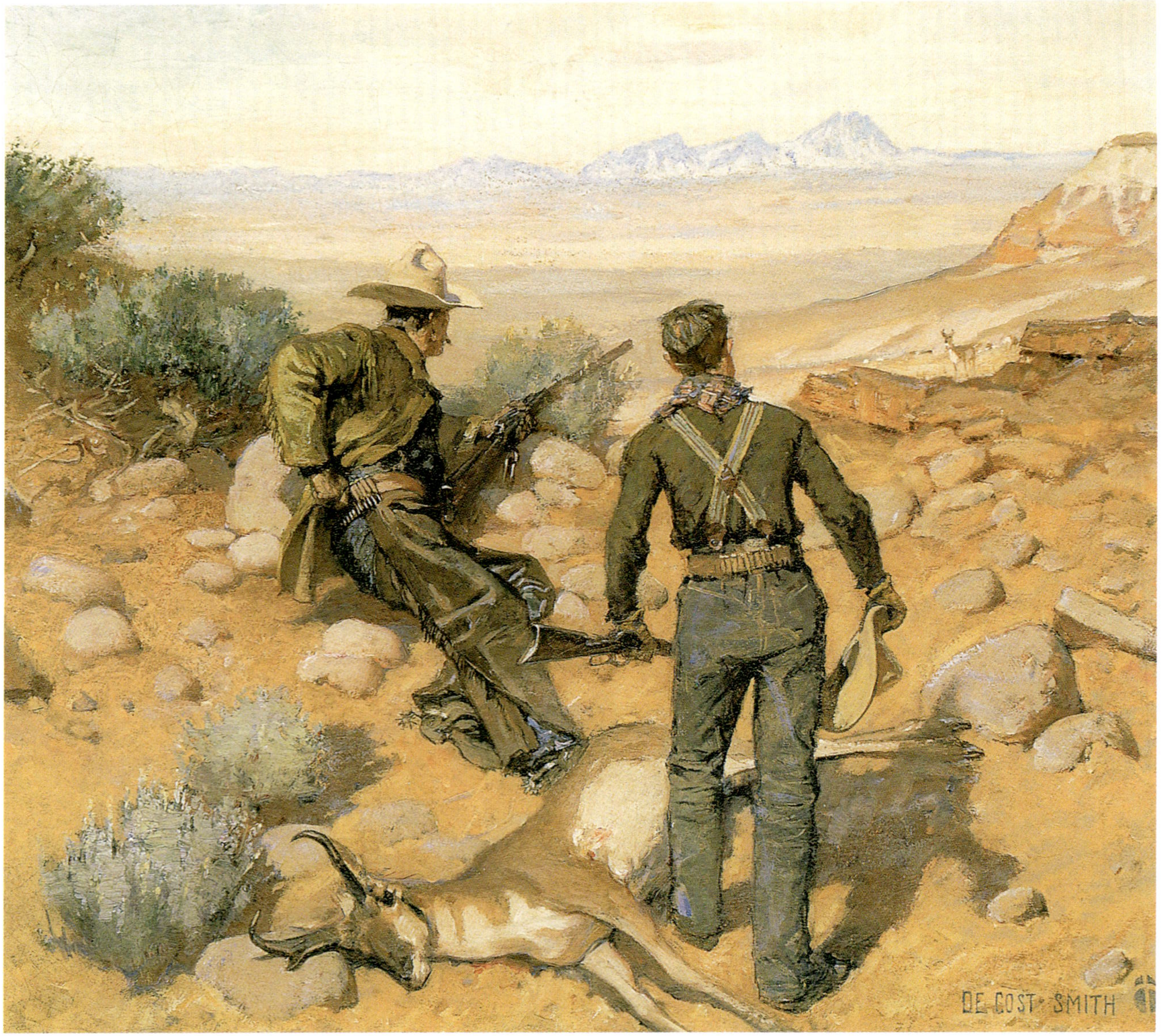

104. DE COST SMITH (1864–1939)
Antelope Hunting—South Dakota, c. 1880s
Oil on canvas. 22 x 24 in. (55.9 x 61 cm)

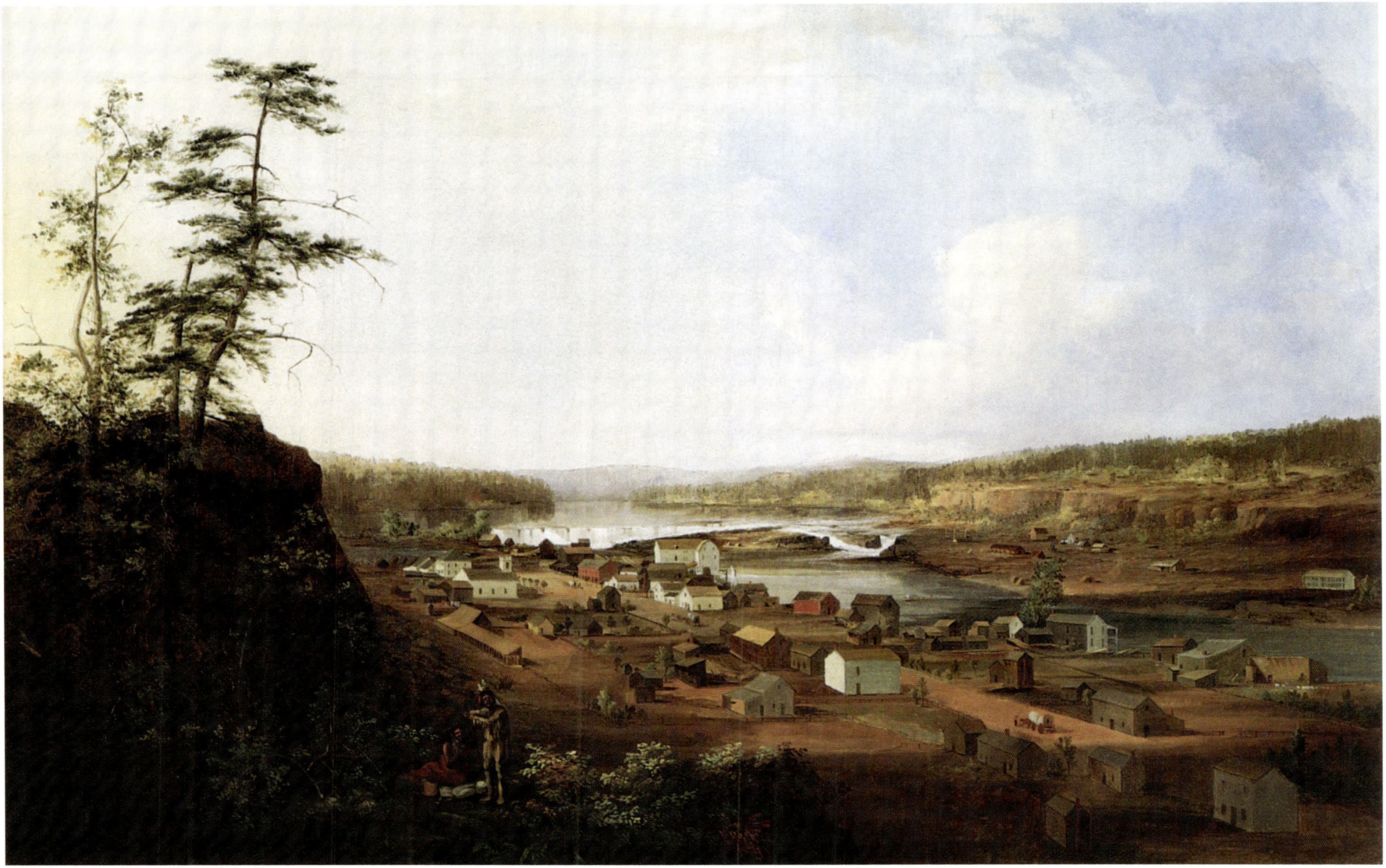

105. JOHN MIX STANLEY (1814–1872)
Oregon City on the Willamette River, c. 1850–58
Oil on canvas. 26½ x 40 in. (67.3 x 101.6 cm)

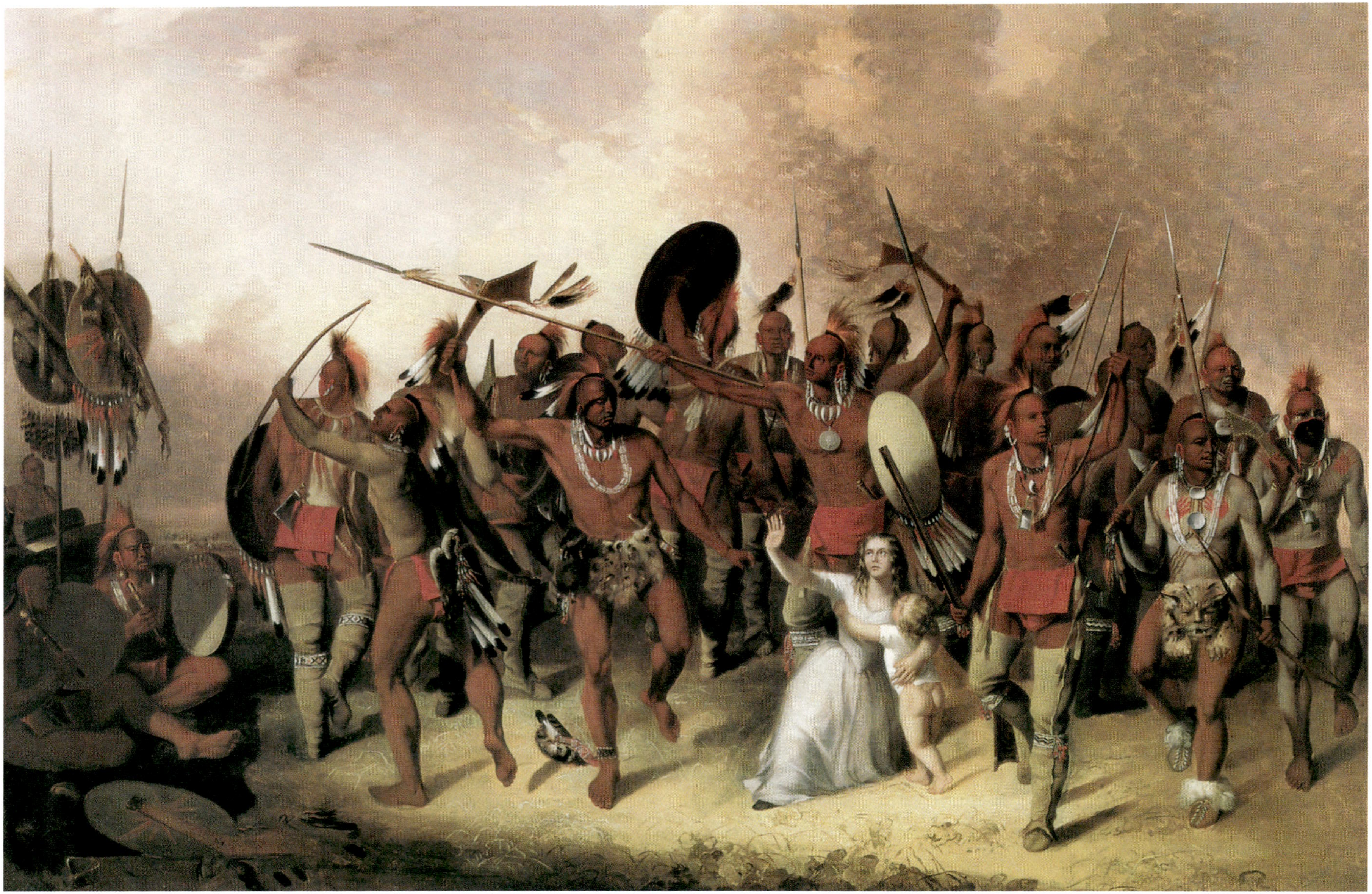

106. JOHN MIX STANLEY (1814–1872)
Osage Scalp Dance, 1845
Oil. 40¾ x 60½ in. (103.5 x 153.6 cm)

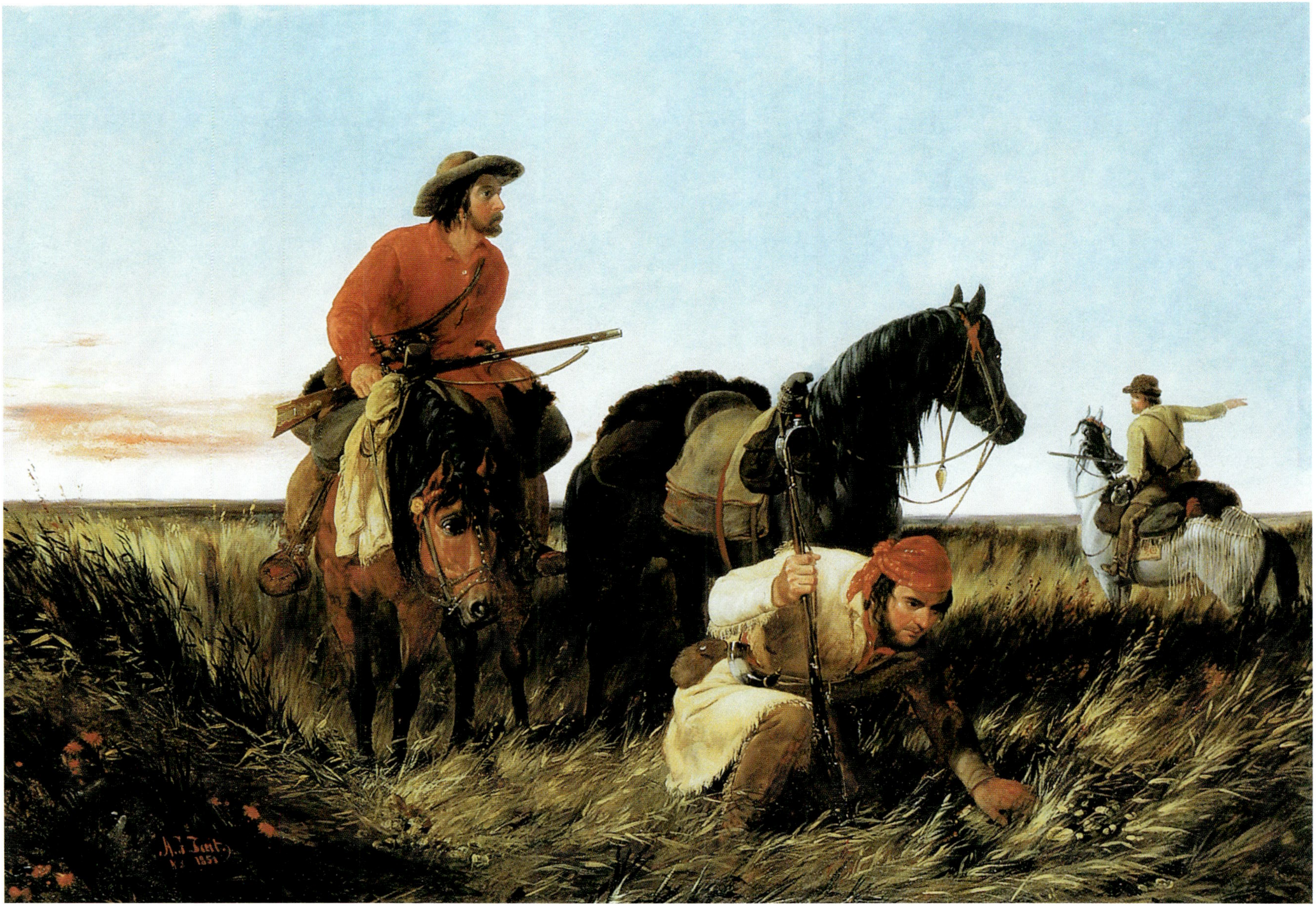

107. ARTHUR FITZWILLIAM TAIT (1819–1905)
Trappers Following the Trail: At Fault, 1851
Oil on canvas. 36 x 50 in. (91.4 x 127 cm)

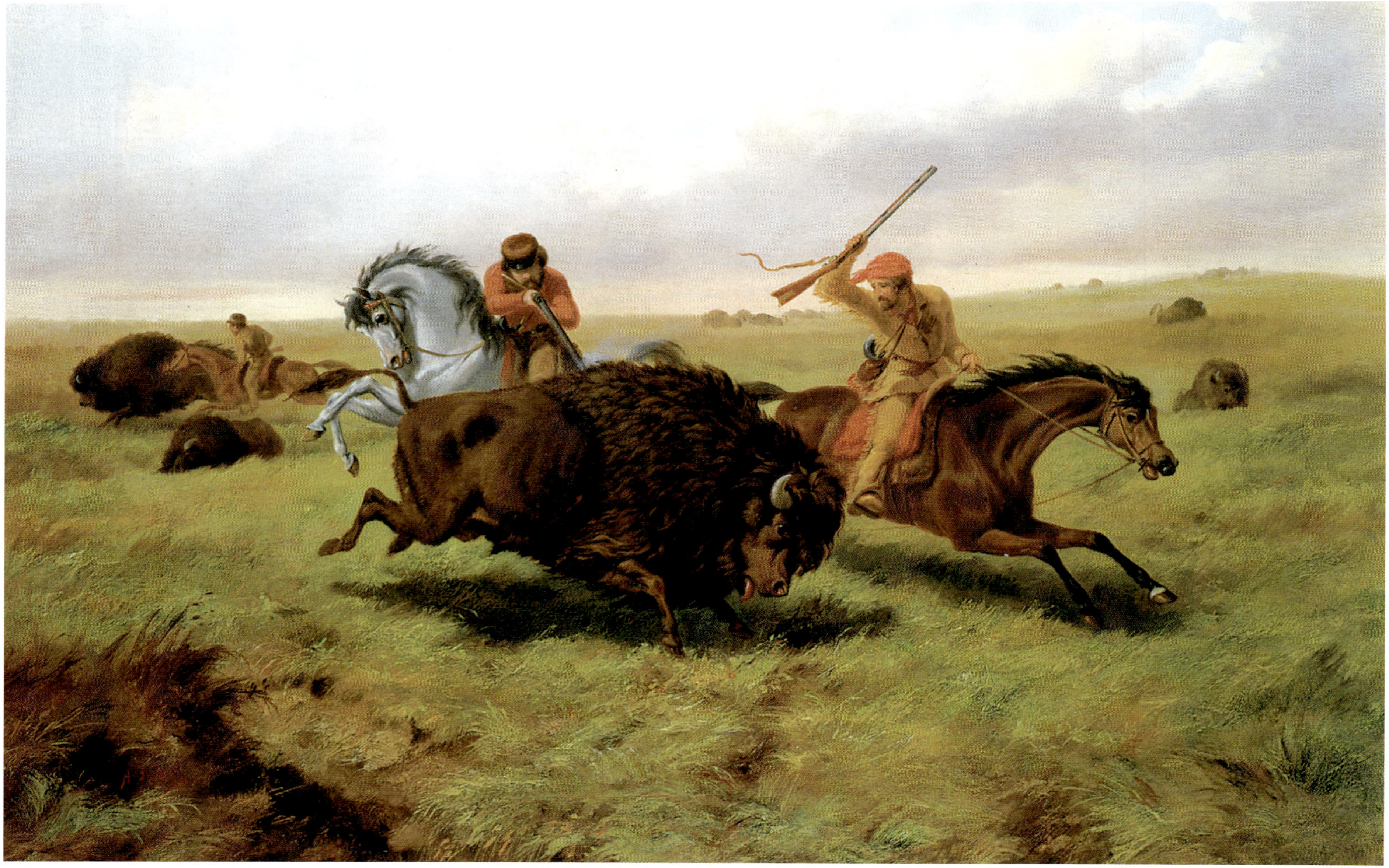

108. ARTHUR FITZWILLIAM TAIT (1819–1905)
Buffalo Hunt, 1861
Oil on canvas. 24½ x 36½ in. (62.2 x 92.7 cm)

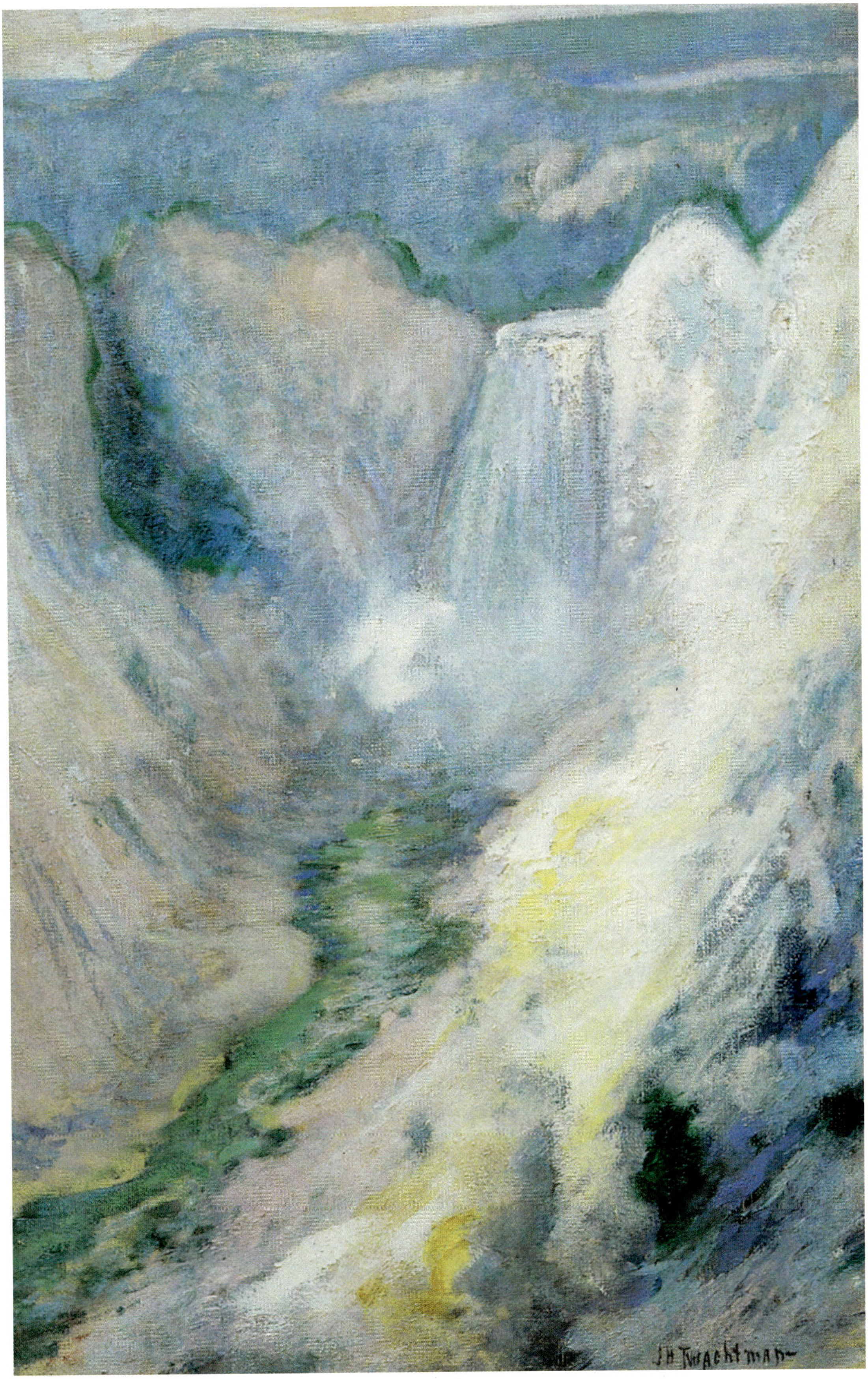

109. JOHN HENRY TWACHTMAN (1853–1902)
Waterfall in Yellowstone, c. 1895
Oil on canvas. 23⅜ x 16½ in. (59.4 x 41.9 cm)

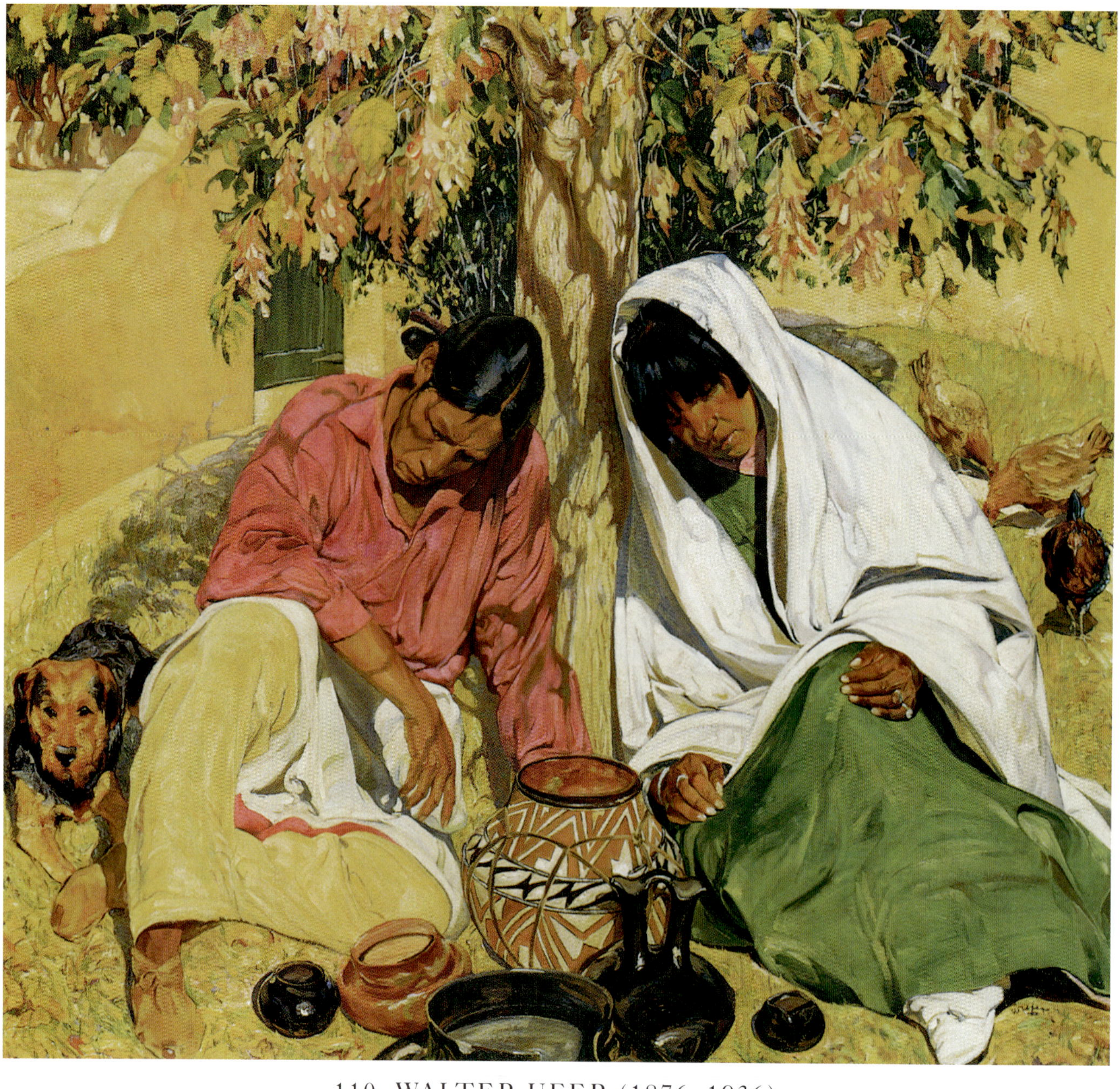

110. WALTER UFER (1876–1936)
Autumn, c. 1926
Oil on canvas. 45 x 48 in. (114.3 x 121.9 cm)

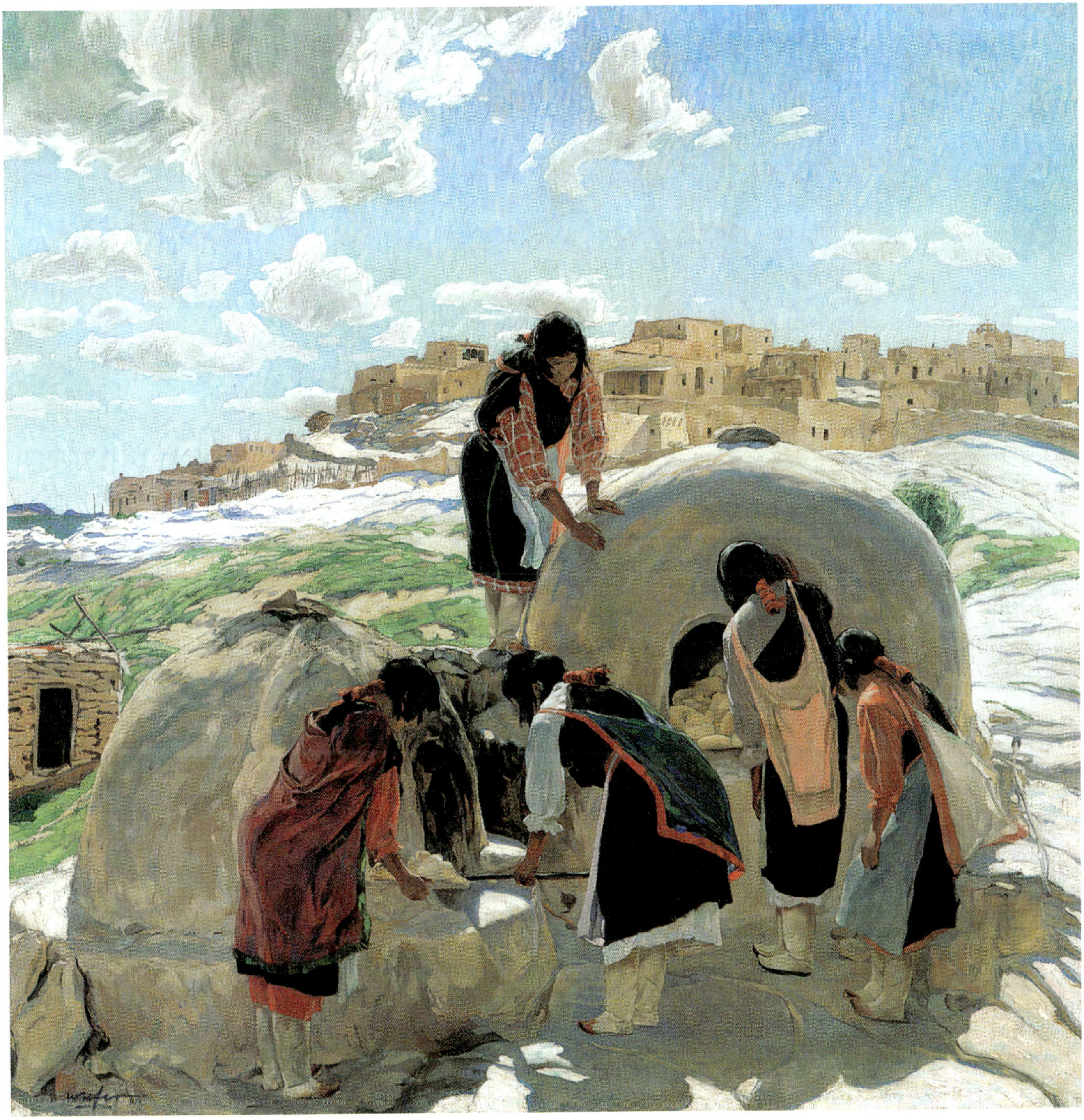

111. WALTER UFER (1876–1936)
The Bakers, 1917
Oil on canvas. 50¼ x 50¼ in. (127.6 x 127.6 cm)

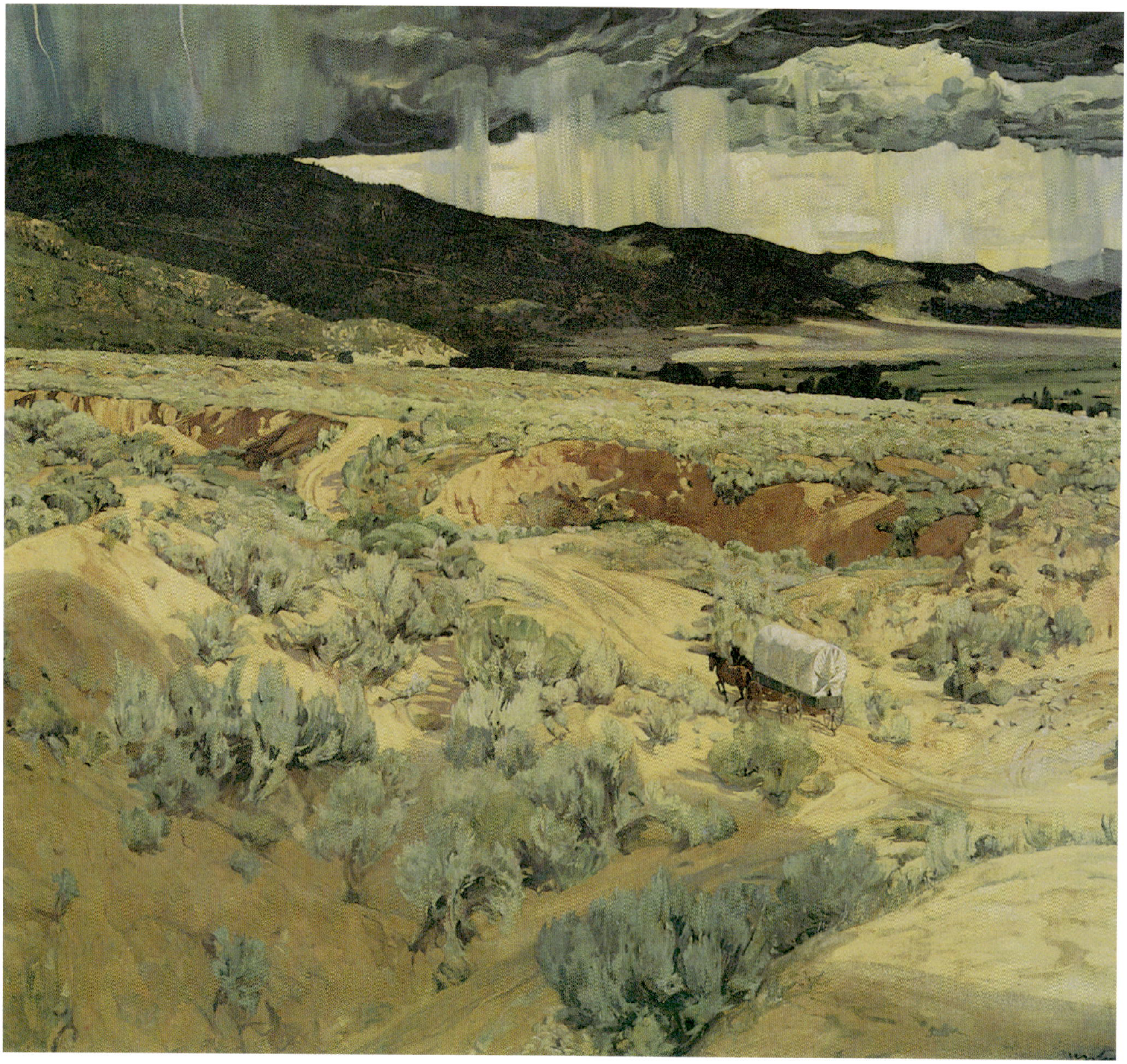

112. WALTER UFER (1876–1936)
Where the Desert Meets the Mountain, before 1922
Oil on canvas. 36½ x 40¼ in. (92.8 x 102.2 cm)

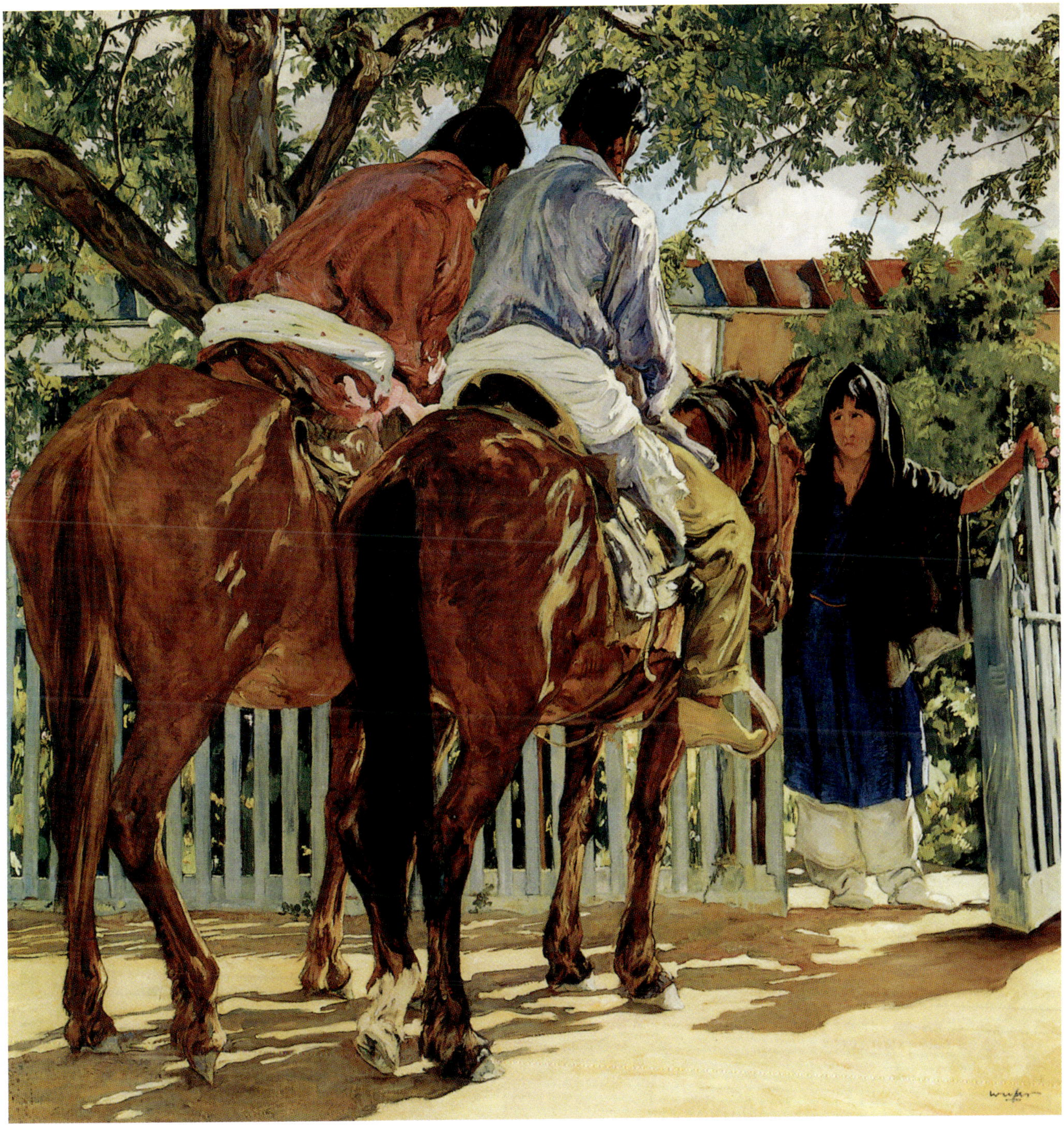

113. WALTER UFER (1876–1936)
Callers, c. 1926
Oil on canvas. 50½ x 50½ in. (128.3 x 128.3 cm)

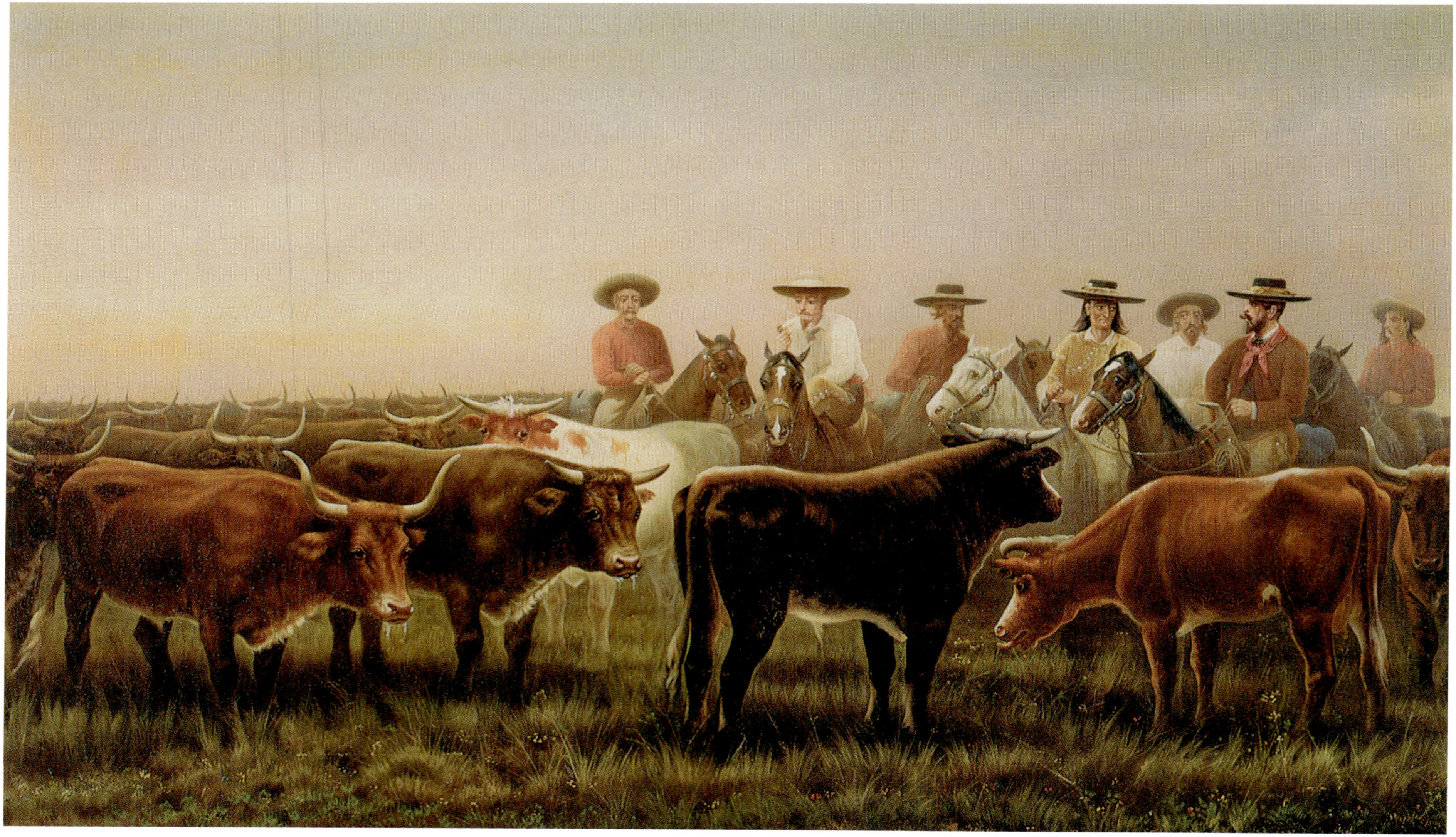

114. JAMES WALKER (1819–1889)
Judges of the Plains, 1877
Oil on canvas. 30 x 50 in. (76.2 x 127 cm)

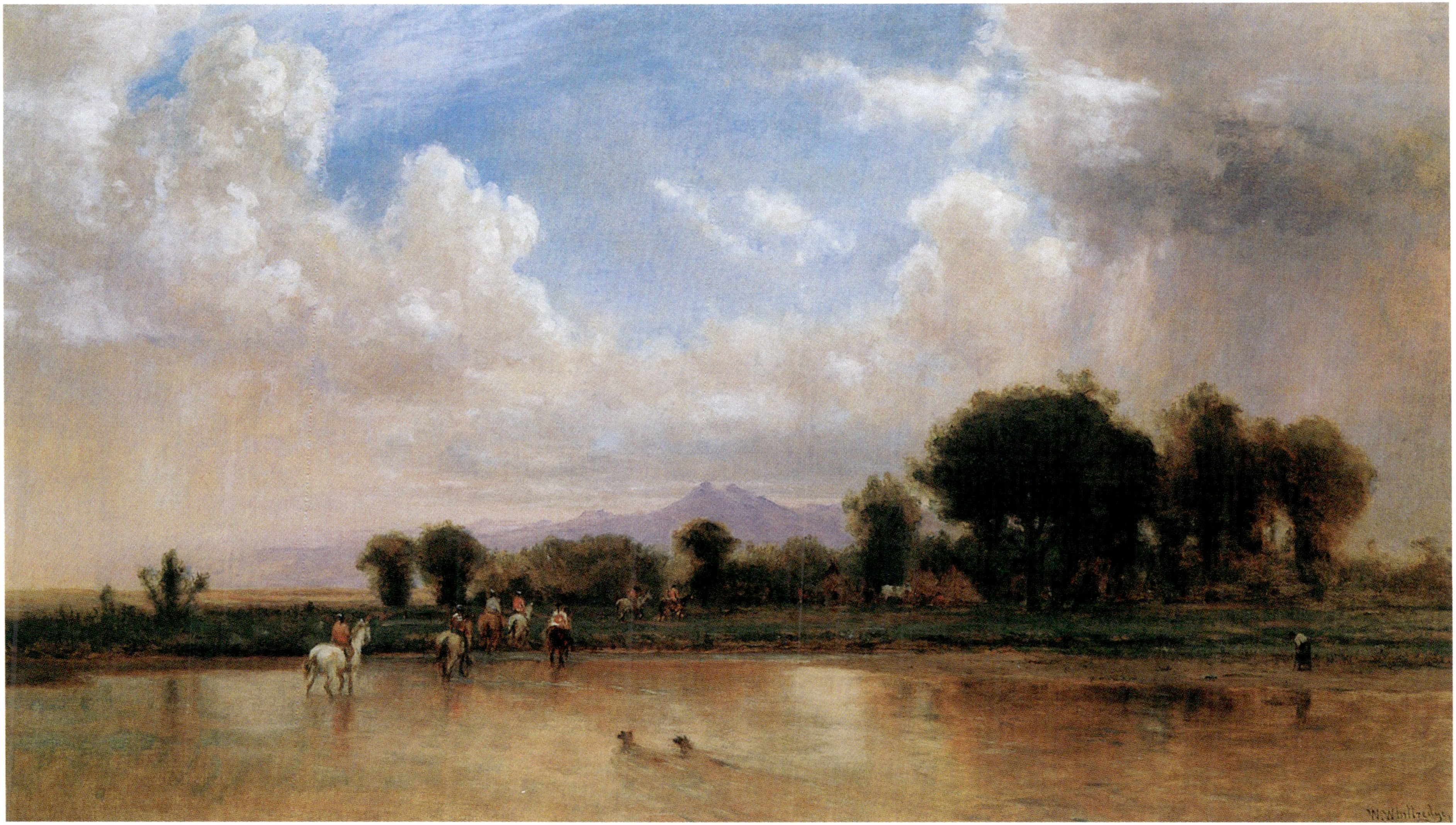

115. THOMAS WORTHINGTON WHITTREDGE (1820–1910)
On the Plains, Cache la Poudre River, 1865
Oil on canvas. 24 x 42 in. (61 x 106.7 cm)

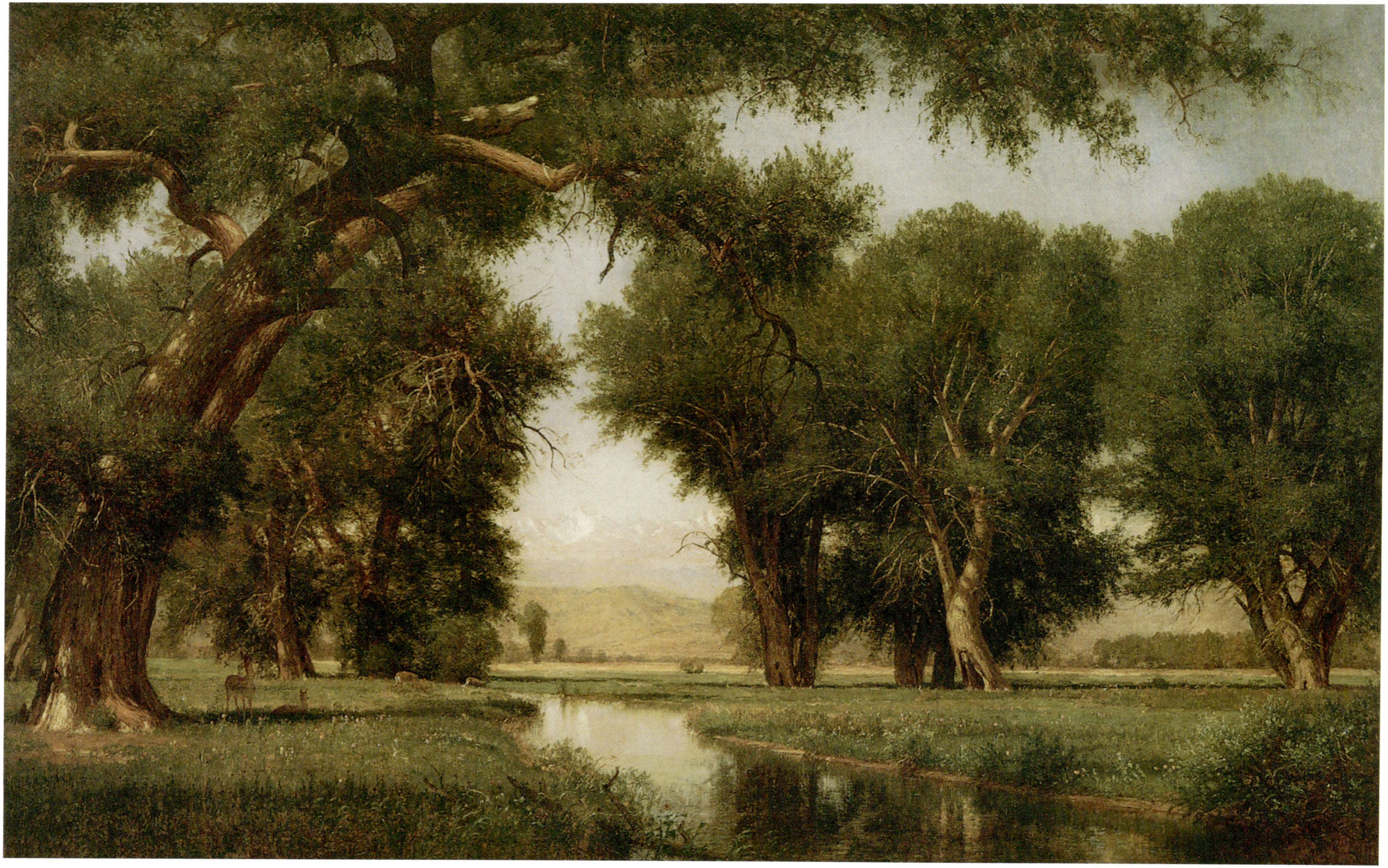

116. THOMAS WORTHINGTON WHITTREDGE (1820–1910)
On the Cache la Poudre River, Colorado, 1876
Oil on canvas. 40⅜ x 60⅜ in. (102.6 x 153.4 cm)

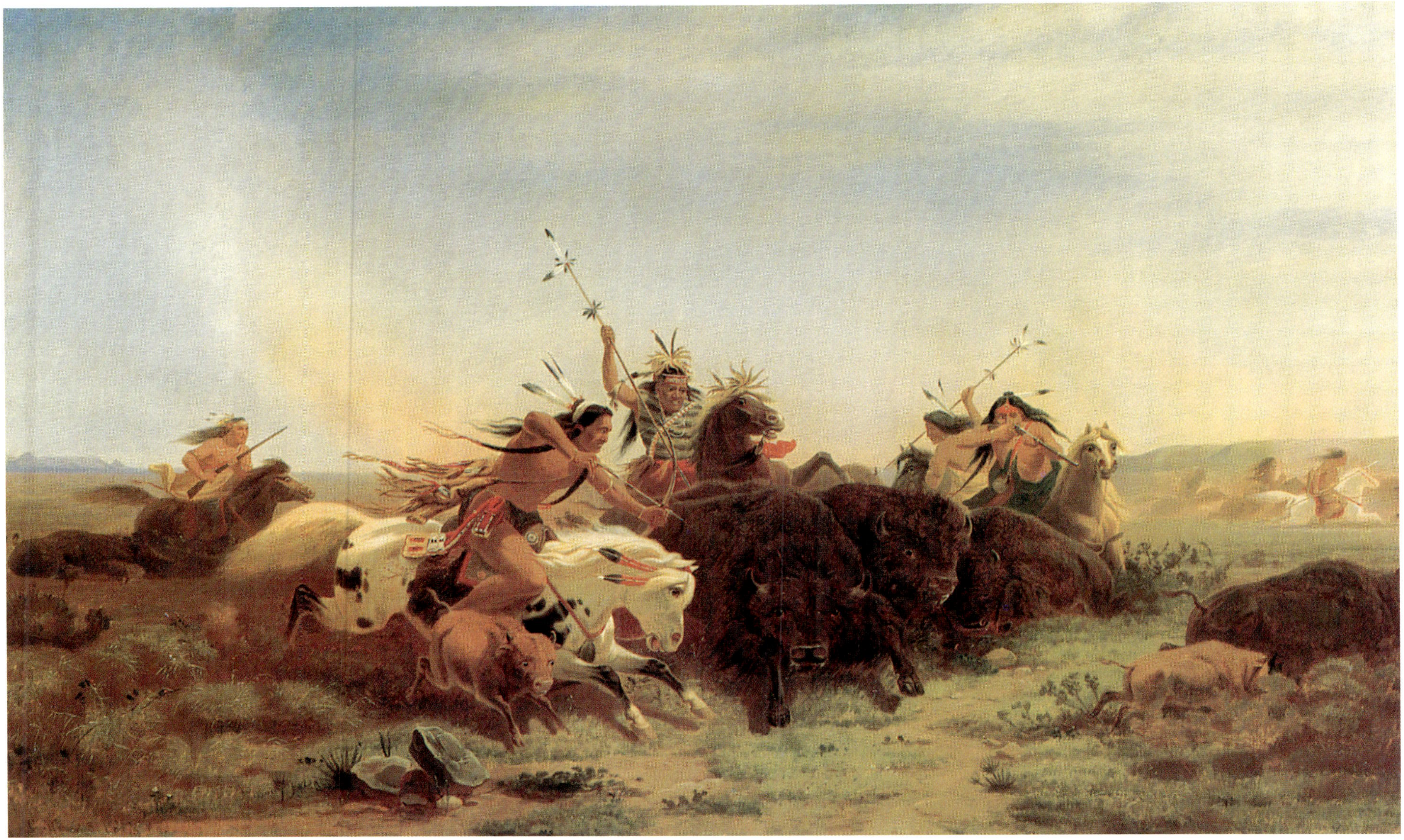

117. CHARLES WIMAR (1828–1862)
Buffalo Hunt, 1861
Oil on canvas. 36 x 61 in. (91.4 x 154.9 cm)

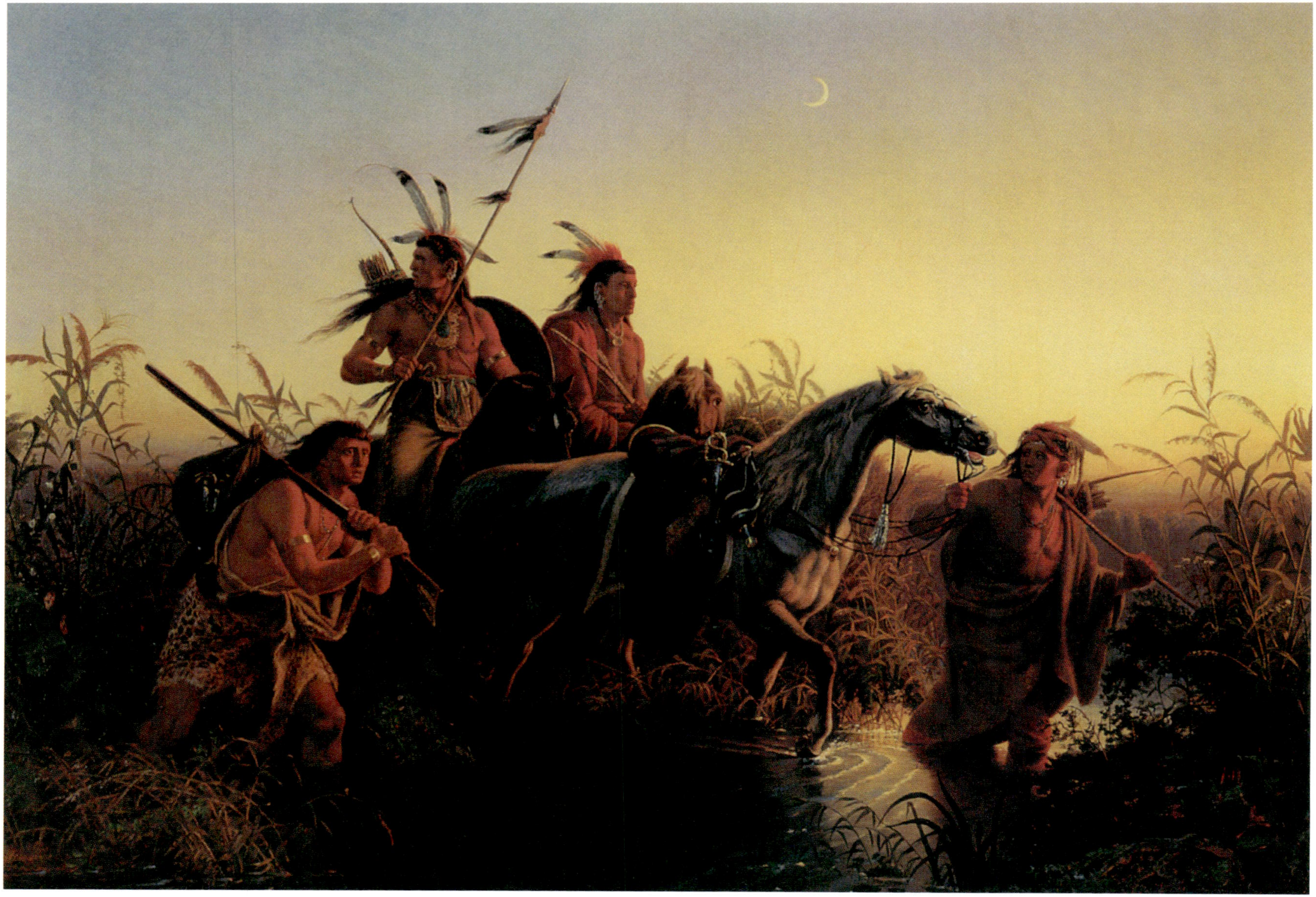

118. CHARLES WIMAR (1828–1862)
The Captive Charger, 1854
Oil on canvas. 30 x 40½ in. (76.2 x 102.9 cm)

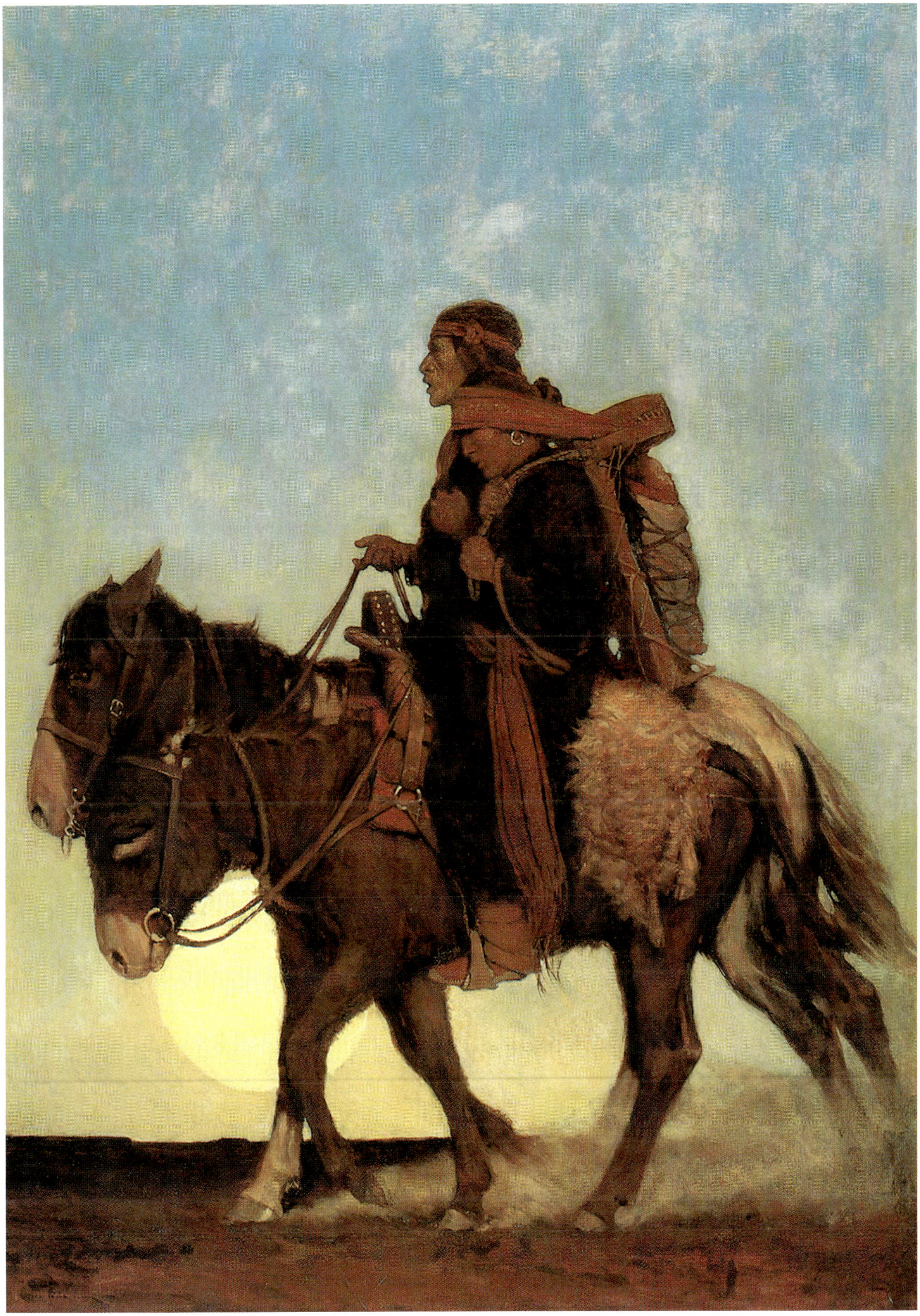

119. N. C. WYETH (1882–1944)
On the October Trail (A Navajo Family), 1908
Oil on canvas. 41¾ x 29¼ in. (106 x 74.3 cm)

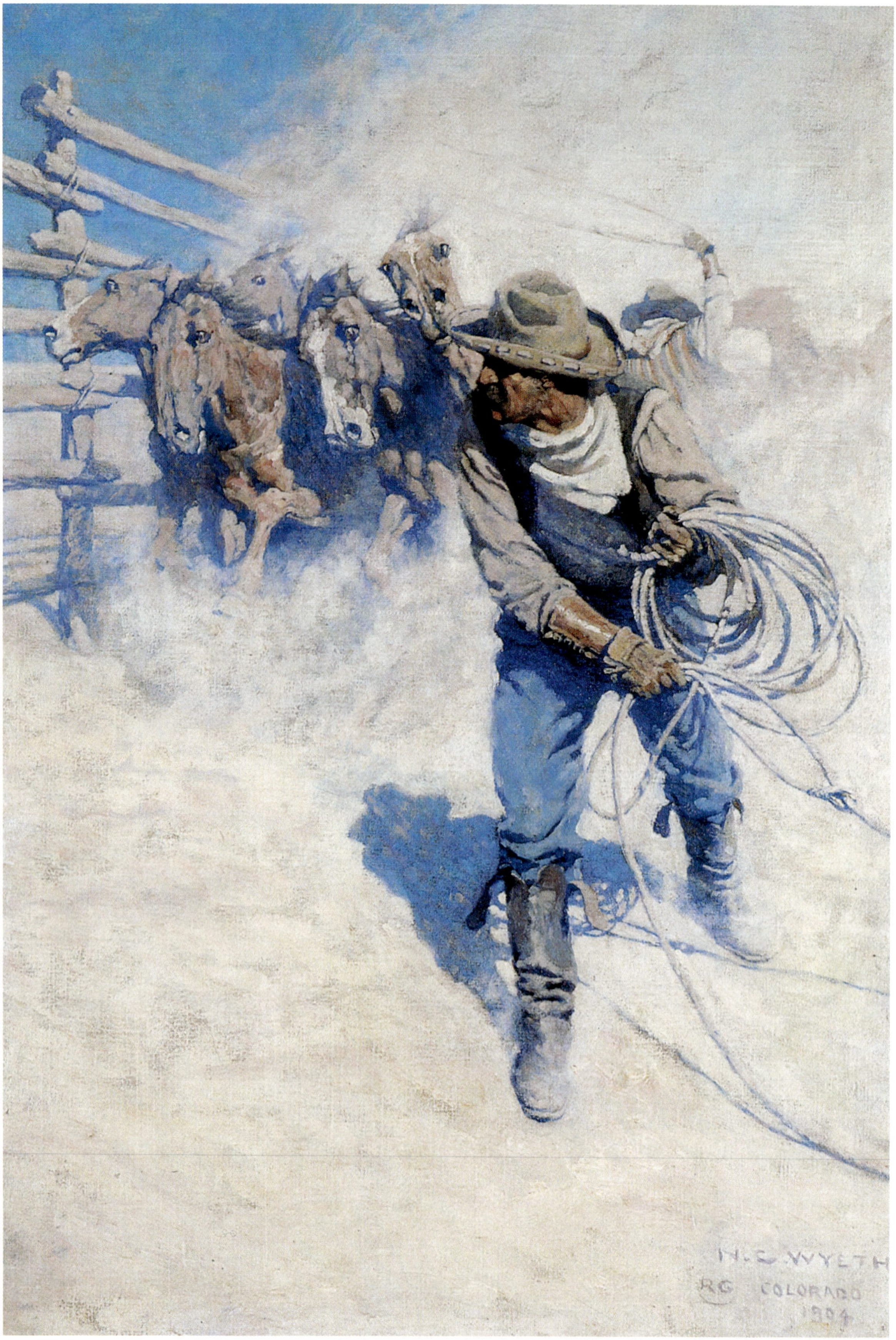

120. N. C. WYETH (1882–1944)
Above the Sea of Round, Shiny Backs the Thin Loops Swirled and Shot into Volumes of Dust, 1904
Oil on canvas. 38¼ x 26 in. (97.2 x 66 cm)

BIOGRAPHIES OF THE ARTISTS

Kenneth Miller Adams (1897–1966). PLATE 001. Born in Topeka, Kansas, Adams was the youngest member of the Taos Society of Artists, a group specifically organized to promote and exhibit the work of its members. Adams was strongly influenced by the Mexican muralists.

Irving R. Bacon (1875–1962). PLATE 002. Born in Fitchburg, Massachusetts, Bacon was a sponsored protégé of Henry Ford. Bacon studied art under William Merritt Chase, and is best known for his Ford family portraits, political portraits, and Wild West themes, including several images of Buffalo Bill.

George Bellows (1882–1925). PLATE 003. Born in Columbus, Ohio, Bellows was taught by Robert Henri, and painted in the Realist style of the Ashcan school. Bellows, noted for his dynamic paintings and lithographs, often portrayed vibrant scenes of everyday life, including his famous series of boxing matches.

Thomas Hart Benton (1889–1975). PLATE 004. Born in Neosho, Missouri, Benton, a painter of rural genre scenes, was the leader of a group of artists known as the Regionalists, who emphasized American themes in art to bolster the nation's flagging spirit during the Great Depression.

Oscar E. Berninghaus (1874–1952). PLATES 005, 006; BONUS IMAGE 1. One of the original six founders of the Taos Society of Artists, Berninghaus settled in Taos permanently in 1925. Among his favorite themes were his paintings of Indians and the southwestern landscape.

Albert Bierstadt (1830–1902). PLATES 007–010; BONUS IMAGE 2. German-born landscape artist Albert Bierstadt was a key figure of the Hudson River school of painters, who glorified the wonders of nature. Bierstadt's picturesque scenes of natural beauty captured the essence of the American wilderness.

George Caleb Bingham (1811–1879). PLATE 011. Bingham, reared in Missouri, studied law and theology before attending the Pennsylvania Academy of Fine Arts. He exhibited genre scenes in New York, painted portraits in Washington, and returned to Missouri, where he was elected to the legislature. Scenes of river life became his favorite subject matter.

Ernest L. Blumenschein (1874–1960). PLATES 012, 013, 014. Born in Pittsburgh and raised in Ohio, Blumenschein studied the violin for one year before pursuing his interest in art. For two decades, he studied and worked in London and Paris. A successful commercial illustrator, Blumenschein was instrumental in founding the Taos Society of Artists, and moved permanently to Taos in 1919.

Karl Bodmer (1809–1893). PLATE 015. A native of Zurich, Switzerland, Bodmer studied art in Paris, where he became adept as a draftsman and watercolorist. While on an expedition in the Upper Missouri area, Bodmer captured on paper spectacular landscapes, artifacts, and portraits of Native Americans.

Carl Oscar Borg (1879–1947). PLATES 016, 017. Born in Sweden, Borg was a self-taught artist who worked as a scene painter for the theater in both London and America. Borg was commissioned by William Randolph Hearst's mother to paint the ceremonies of the Southwest Indian tribes. In 1936 he published a book of etchings devoted to Navajo and Hopi Indians.

Gutzon Borglum (1867–1941). PLATE 018. Born in Idaho Territory, Borglum held a deep respect for frontier life. He studied art in San Francisco and Paris, and exhibited small sculpture and paintings of the American West. His most famous and monumental work, the four presidential portraits on Mount Rushmore, is typical of his patriotic ideals.

Maurice Braun (1877–1941). PLATE 019. Hungarian-born Braun moved to the U.S. when he was four years old. His early interest in art led to his copying works at the Metropolitan Museum of Art. Skilled at showing the varying effects of light in a landscape, his compositions reflected the Impressionist style. He founded the San Diego Academy of Art in 1912.

Valentine Bromley (1848–1877). PLATE 020. Born in London to a family of engravers, Bromley was a proficient draftsman who received commissions from such journals and publications as *Punch* and *Illustrated London News*. In 1874 a patron requested that Bromley accompany him to portray his hunting adventure to the American West.

Albertus del Orient Browere (1814–1887). PLATE 021. Born in Tarrytown, New York, Browere was the son of a sculptor. Largely self-taught, he established himself in New York City, and executed scenes from the work of Washington Irving.

George de Forest Brush (1855–1941). PLATE 022. Born in Tennessee and raised in Connecticut, Brush was formally trained in New York City and Paris. Beginning in 1881, Brush embarked on multiple trips West to Wyoming, and produced views of Arapaho and Crow tribes for *Harper's* and *Century* magazines.

William Cary (1840–1922). PLATE 023. One of the last artists to portray Native American themes before railroad developments opened up the West, Cary, born in Tappan, New York, had firsthand knowledge of Plains Indian life before the tribes were confined on reservations.

Gerald Cassidy (1879–1934). PLATES 024, 025. Kentucky-born Cassidy was raised in Cincinnati and attended the Art Students League and the National Academy of Design in New York. A successful commercial artist and lithographer, Cassidy moved to Albuquerque to improve his health, and his art soon focused on Native American themes.

George Catlin (1796–1872). PLATES 026–029; BONUS IMAGE 3. Pennsylvania-born Catlin was a self-taught portrait painter who was so inspired by his first glimpse of Native Americans that he sought to devote his life fully to painting their way of life. His "Indian Gallery," a fastidious collection of 500 paintings that included portraits, ceremonies, and other customs, is now part of the Smithsonian Institution.

Eanger Irving Couse (1866–1936). PLATES 030, 031. After formal art training in Chicago, New York, and Paris, Couse gained a solid reputation in both the United States and France. In 1915 he was the first president of the Taos Society of Artists. His fascination with the Taos Indians is reflected in his art.

Henry Cross (1837–1918). PLATE 032. Exhibiting an early talent for drawing, Cross left his upstate New York home to study with noted animal painter Rosa Bonheur in Paris. Upon his return to the U.S., he traveled West with the P. T. Barnum Circus, and painted many authentic portraits of Native Americans.

Charles Deas (1818–1867). PLATES 033, 034, 035; BONUS IMAGE 4. Strongly influenced by George Catlin's Indian Gallery exhibition, Deas left Philadelphia to travel West. By 1841, Deas had moved permanently to St. Louis, painting frontier life and depicting the everyday life of the Indian.

Maynard Dixon (1875–1946). PLATE 036. Born in Fresno, California, during the days of the gold rush, Dixon briefly attended the San Francisco School of Design before traveling to New Mexico, Arizona, and Utah, where he worked as a wrangler. Sympathetic to the plight of the Indians, Dixon was known for his portrayals of Native Americans and for his landscapes.

William de Leftwich Dodge (1867–1935). PLATE 037. Painter and muralist Dodge was born in Virginia, and studied art in Paris and Munich. He was commissioned to decorate the dome of the central building of the Columbian Exposition in Chicago, and his murals are also on display at the Library of Congress in Washington, D.C., as well as in various theaters and hotels.

William Herbert Dunton (1878–1936). PLATES 038, 039. Maine-born Dunton is best known for his lively illustrations, executed and painted with remarkable technical ability. He moved to Taos in 1912, at the urging of artist Ernest Blumenschein. During the Depression, Dunton rendered Western themes for lithographs and produced murals for the Missouri State Capitol.

Thomas Eakins (1844–1916). PLATE 040. Born in Philadelphia, Eakins attended anatomy classes in America and studied art in Paris and Spain, where he was inspired by Diego Velázquez's naturalism. Celebrated for his realistic depictions, Eakins exerted a considerable influence through his teaching.

Seth Eastman (1808–1875). PLATE 041. Eastman was a career officer who gained his formal artistic training at West Point. While stationed in Minnesota, Eastman would paint the various Native American tribes in the area.

Henry Farny (1847–1916). PLATES 042, 043. Farny studied art in Germany, Austria, and Italy before supporting himself by illustrating books and stories for U.S. magazines. Farny's chief subjects for his oil paintings in the 1890s comprised Indians, hunting parties, and pueblo scenes.

William Hahn (1829–1887). PLATES 044, 045. Born and trained in Germany, Hahn was greatly influenced by Emanuel Leutze and developed his genre painting style. When Hahn first arrived in the U.S. in 1871, his paintings had already been exhibited in New York and Boston. He lived in California during his later years, sketching Yosemite, the Sierras, and the Napa Valley.

Marsden Hartley (1877–1943). PLATE 046. Hartley, born in Lewiston, Maine, moved to Ohio with his family after winning a scholarship to the Cleveland School of Art. In 1899, he studied in New York under William Merritt Chase. Hartley visited Taos and Santa Fe in 1918 and 1919, and produced several New Mexican landscape paintings during this time.

Childe Hassam (1859–1935). PLATE 047. A notable figure in the American Impressionist movement, Hassam was called the "American Monet." He was born in Dorchester, Massachusetts, and began working as a freelance illustrator. In his mature paintings, his brushwork became looser and more delicate, utilizing brighter, richer colors.

William Jacob Hays (1830–1875). PLATE 048. Born in New York City, Hays journeyed up the Missouri River in 1860, painting animals and western themes. He later exhibited his game animal paintings in New York City and London; some works were reproduced as lithographs.

William Penhallow Henderson (1877–1943). PLATE 049. After an itinerant childhood, Henderson attended art classes in Massachusetts and traveled abroad before moving to Santa Fe. Residing in the Southwest region sparked his interest in representing Indian and Hispanic subjects. His work included pastels, oils, murals, stage designs, and architecture projects.

E. Martin Hennings (1886–1956). PLATE 050. A native of Pennsgrove, New Jersey, Hennings studied art in Chicago and Germany, where he met fellow art students Walter Ufer and Victor Higgins. He later moved to Taos, joining the Society of Artists, in 1924. Between 1916 and 1938, Hennings won twelve national art prizes.

Robert Henri (1865–1929). PLATE 051. A member of the Ashcan school of painters, Henri worked as an art teacher in New York City before visiting Santa Fe for the first time in 1916. He became an associate member of the Taos Society of Artists. Born in Ohio, Henri was a staunch advocate of Realism in art.

Herman Herzog (1831–1932). PLATE 052. Herzog was born in Bremen, Germany, and entered the Dusseldorf Academy at seventeen. He later went to Norway to paint, finding his inspiration in landscape painting. Herzog traveled extensively, and he emigrated to the U.S. in the early 1870s. He produced a large volume of drawings, sketches, watercolors, and oils.

Victor Higgins (1884–1949). PLATE 053. Higgins left his native Indiana to pursue art studies in Chicago. He spent time abroad, where he met artists Walter Ufer and E. Martin Hennings. He joined the Taos Society of Artists in 1917, and produced a varied body of work, including still lifes, landscapes, and figure painting.

Thomas Hill (1829–1908). PLATES 054, 055; BONUS IMAGE 5. English-born Hill emigrated to the U.S. in 1844 and worked as a carriage painter, furniture decorator, and interior designer. He made his first trip to Yosemite in 1862, returning there regularly to paint and sketch. He was acclaimed as an eminent artist, earning high praise for his work.

Edward Hopper (1882–1967). PLATE 056. Born in Nyack, New York, Realist painter Edward Hopper studied commercial art before switching his efforts to fine art. He studied with Robert Henri, a member of the Ashcan school of painters. Hopper visited New Mexico only once, at the prodding of John Sloan.

Henry Inman (1801–1846). PLATE 057. Born in Utica, New York, Inman was hired to copy Indian portraits, most of which were originally illustrated by Charles Bird King. Inman established his own art studio in New York City in 1827, and later moved to Philadelphia to be a partner in a lithography firm. An apprentice to John Wesley Jarvis, he was also a noted historian of the West.

George Inness (1825–1894). PLATE 058. Born in Newark, New Jersey, Inness was apprenticed to a map engraver in New York, but was disinterested in that career. He soon turned to painting landscapes in the Hudson River school tradition. A patron sent him to study in Europe, where he would return on a regular basis over his lifetime.

John Wesley Jarvis (1780–1840). PLATE 059. English portrait artist Jarvis was brought to America as a child. Around 1814, Jarvis taught artist Henry Inman, who worked in Baltimore for a time. His most important work was a series of portraits of military and naval heroes for the city of New York.

William Smith Jewett (1812–1873). PLATE 060. Born in South Dover, New York, Jewett was a prominent portrait painter during the mid-nineteenth century. He studied at the National Academy of Design, and moved to California in 1849 to paint portraits of the newly rich gold miners. In addition to portraiture, Jewett also painted landscapes.

Frank Tenney Johnson (1874–1939). PLATE 061. Using colorful landscapes, Johnson's themes centralized on the working life of the cowboy, portrayals of Western horses, and Indians of the early West. He spent time in both the Southwest and New York City, where he was a successful magazine illustrator.

Charles Bird King (1785–1862). PLATE 062. Primarily a portrait artist, Charles Bird King was working in Washington, D.C. when he was hired by the War Department to document visiting Native American dignitaries during the 1820s and 1830s. At twenty, he studied under painter Benjamin West at the Royal Academy in London.

Leon Kroll (1884–1974). PLATE 063. Encouraged by Winslow Homer to pursue a painting career, New Yorker Kroll attended art classes in both New York and Paris. After exhibiting works in the 1913 Armory Show, Kroll traveled to New Mexico with Robert Henri and George Bellows. While there, he painted some southwestern scenes, but he is best known for his New York figure paintings and portraits.

William Robinson Leigh (1866–1955). PLATES 064, 065; BONUS IMAGE 6. Leigh, born in West Virginia, was already a successful illustrator when *Scribner's* sent him to North Dakota on assignment in 1897. Over the next three decades, Leigh returned to the Southwest, concentrating on his favorite subjects, the Hopi and the Navajo.

Emanuel Gottlieb Leutze (1816–1868). PLATE 066. Among the most popular historical painters in America in the mid-nineteenth century, Leutze was born in Germany and reared in Philadelphia. His most famous work was *Washington Crossing the Delaware* (1851).

Louis Maurer (1832–1932). PLATES 067, 068. Inspired by the Western-themed work of George Catlin and Karl Bodmer, Maurer specialized in portraying horses in great detail. The German-born artist took a job in the U.S. as a lithographer for Currier & Ives. His first trip West was as a guest of Buffalo Bill.

Alfred Jacob Miller (1810–1874). PLATES 069–072. Inspired by Catlin's journey West, Miller embarked on a trip to the Rocky Mountains in 1837. While there, he attended a bash where traders and fur trappers exchanged goods; he remains the only artist to record the boisterous era of the American fur trade. In 1842 Miller returned to his home in Baltimore, Maryland, and worked as a portraitist.

Thomas Moran (1837–1926). PLATES 073, 074, 075. Born in England, Moran came to the United States at a young age, and was influenced by the work of J. M. W. Turner. Moran was commissioned in 1871 to document an expedition to Yellowstone; his paintings helped to designate it as a national park.

Charles Christian Nahl (1818–1878). PLATES 076, 077. Illustrator and engraver Nahl was born in Kassel, Germany, to a well-known family of artists. He painted portraits, scenes of the California Gold Rush, and other Western themes.

Bert Geer Phillips (1868–1956). PLATES 078, 079. While studying art in Paris, Phillips met fellow American artists Joseph Henry Sharp and Ernest L. Blumenschein, with whom he toured the West in 1898. A founding member of the Taos Society of Artists, Phillips was captivated by the lifestyle of the Taos Indians.

Henry Cheever Pratt (1803–1880). PLATE 080. Born in New Hampshire, Pratt was a portrait and landscape painter whose artistic talent was discovered by Samuel F. B. Morse, who brought him to Boston to work as his assistant. Greatly influenced by artist Thomas Cole, Pratt joined the Mexican Boundary Survey in 1851 as the official artist. In 1852 Pratt presented his work in the first art exhibition in California.

Howard Pyle (1853–1911). PLATE 081. Founder of the Brandywine school of illustration, Pyle was a gifted artist, writer, and teacher. He was born in Wilmington, Delaware, and established his own teaching studio in Chadds Ford, Pennsylvania. N. C. Wyeth, Frank Schoonover, and Maxfield Parrish are counted among his students.

William Tylee Ranney (1813–1857). PLATES 082, 083, 084. Born in Middletown, Connecticut, Ranney had an art studio in New York City during the 1840s. After serving in the Southwest during the Mexican War, Ranney devoted the remainder of his life to depicting frontier scenes at his home in New Jersey.

Frederic Remington (1861–1909). PLATES 085–090; BONUS IMAGE 7. Reared in upstate New York, Remington came from a wealthy family, and first traveled to the West in 1881. In great demand as an illustrator, he produced several thousand paintings and drawings, and his art helped promote a popular image of the West.

Charles M. Russell (1864–1926). PLATES 091–095. At the age of sixteen, Russell left his native St. Louis and settled in Montana to work as a night wrangler. Russell—known as "The Cowboy Artist"—had ample opportunity to sketch cowboys, horses, and camp activities. He became a full-time artist by 1893.

Charles Schreyvogel (1861–1912). PLATES 096, 097. Schreyvogel, who learned about the West through study and travel, was a diligent researcher and successful illustrator. He often painted the cavalry during the Indian wars. In *Breaking Through the Line*, the central figure fires his weapon directly at the viewer, a typical technique of this artist.

Olaf C. Seltzer (1877–1957). PLATE 098. As a teen, Seltzer emigrated from Denmark to Great Falls, Montana, where he worked as a cowboy. For thirty years, he worked as a railroad machinist, painting and sketching in his spare time. His chief artistic influence was his neighbor, Charles M. Russell.

Joseph Henry Sharp (1859–1953). PLATES 099–102; BONUS IMAGE 8. Sharp studied art for several years in Cincinnati, and spent another year at the Antwerp Academy in Belgium. Intrigued by Native American culture, Sharp was a founding member of the Taos Society of Artists, and inspired other artists to visit the Southwest.

John Sloan (1871–1951). PLATE 103. Sloan was a member of The Eight, a New York-based group of urban Realist painters. He began spending his summers in Santa Fe in 1919, and his Southwest subjects included landscapes as well as Native American images.

De Cost Smith (1864–1939). PLATE 104. Born in Skaneateles, New York, Smith was raised near the Onondaga Indian Reservation. He attended formal art classes in New York City at the McMullin School and the Art Students League. Inspired by the work of artist George de Forest Brush, Smith embarked on his first journey West in 1884.

John Mix Stanley (1814–1872). PLATES 105, 106. Greatly influenced by Catlin's work, Stanley abandoned portraiture in 1842 and headed West to aid the documentation of Native American life before its demise. Raised in upstate New York, Stanley traveled for ten years through the Southwest, and then journeyed to the Northwest to paint Indian portraits.

Arthur Fitzwilliam Tait (1819–1905). PLATES 107, 108. Born near Liverpool, England, Tait emigrated to the U.S. in 1850. Best known for his depictions of wildlife, Tait studied and sketched in his summer studio in the Adirondack Mountains, where he painted sporting scenes. Beginning in 1852, Currier & Ives published lithographs of his animal works.

John Henry Twachtman (1853–1902). PLATE 109. Originally from Cincinnati, Ohio, Twachtman began offering summer classes in Impressionist-style *plein-air* painting in Greenwich, Connecticut, in 1889. He taught at the Art Students League in New York City during the winter.

Walter Ufer (1876–1936). PLATES 110–113. Kentucky-born artist and lithographer Ufer studied and worked in both Chicago and Germany. Upon his first trip to New Mexico, Ufer fell in love with the Southwest countryside, and returned there for several months every year as a member of the Taos Society of Artists.

James Walker (1819–1889). PLATE 114; BONUS IMAGE 9. Walker was born in England, but grew up in New York City. After working as an interpreter during the Mexican War, he set up an art studio in New York in 1848, traveling extensively on commissions. He is well known for his battle scenes and his depictions of the Spanish-American *vaquero*.

Thomas Worthington Whittredge (1820–1910). PLATES 115, 116. Remembered chiefly as a painter of Eastern landscapes, Whittredge was born in Ohio and became part of the second generation of Hudson River school painters. After ten years studying abroad, Whittredge traveled West in the 1870s, instilling in him a deep love of nature and the countryside.

Charles Wimar (1828–1862). PLATES 117, 118. Born in Germany, Wimar came to America with his family in 1843, settling in St. Louis, where he became intrigued by Native American culture. He studied at the Dusseldorf Academy under Emanuel Leutze before scheduling several steamboat trips up the Missouri River to sketch the American Indian.

N. C. Wyeth (1882–1944). PLATES 119, 120; BONUS IMAGE 10. Best known as an illustrator of children's classics, Wyeth was born in Needham, Massachusetts, and studied art under Howard Pyle. His son, Andrew, and his grandson, James, are also well-known artists.

ALPHABETICAL LIST OF WORKS

BONUS IMAGES

See the link in the "Info" folder on the DVD to download your bonus images.

1. OSCAR E. BERNINGHAUS (1874–1952)
Indian Farmer, 1926
Oil on canvas. 35 x 40 in. (88.9 x 101.6 cm)

2. ALBERT BIERSTADT (1830–1902)
Sunrise, Yosemite Valley, c. 1870
Oil on canvas. 36½ x 52⅜ in. (92.8 x 133.1 cm)

3. GEORGE CATLIN (1796–1872)
Stu-Mick-o-súcks, Buffalo Bull's Back Fat, Head Chief, Blood Tribe, 1832
Oil on canvas. 29 x 24 in. (73.7 x 61 cm)

4. CHARLES DEAS (1818–1867)
Long Jakes, 1844
Oil on canvas. 30 x 24⅞ in. (76.2 x 62.9 cm)

5. THOMAS HILL (1829–1908)
Bridal Veil Falls, Yosemite, c. 1870–84
Oil on canvas. 72 x 95 in. (183 x 241.4 cm)

6. WILLIAM ROBINSON LEIGH (1866–1955)
The Scout, c. 1922
Oil on canvas. 48 x 36 in. (121.9 x 91.4 cm)

7. FREDERIC REMINGTON (1861–1909)
Dismounted: The Fourth Trooper Moving the Led Horses, 1890
Oil on canvas. 34 1/16 x 48 15/16 in. (86.5 x 124.3 cm)

8. JOSEPH HENRY SHARP (1859–1953)
Crow Encampment, Montana, c. 1902–10
Oil on canvas. 30 x 36 in. (76.2 x 91.4 cm)

9. JAMES WALKER (1819–1889)
Vaqueros Roping Horses in a Corral, 1877
Oil. 20 x 36 in. (50.8 x 91.4 cm)

10. N. C. WYETH (1882–1944)
The Pay Stage, 1909
Oil on canvas. 38 x 26½ in. (96.5 x 67.3 cm)

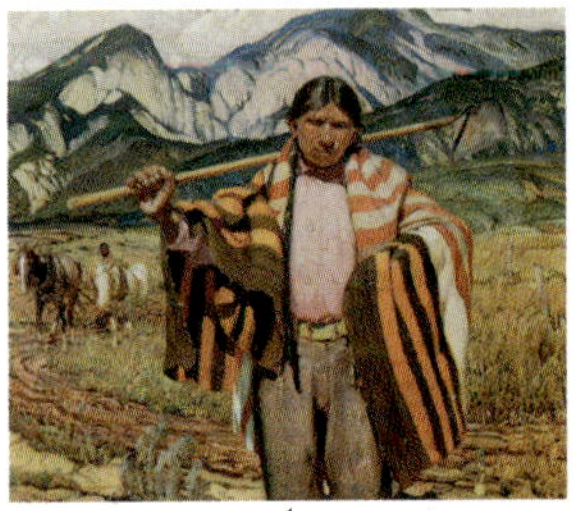
1

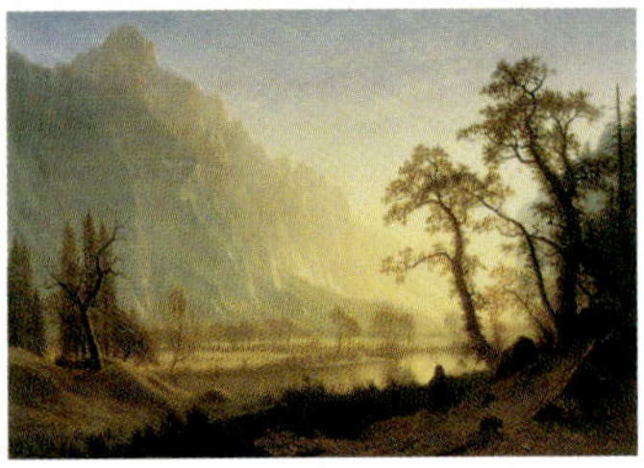
2

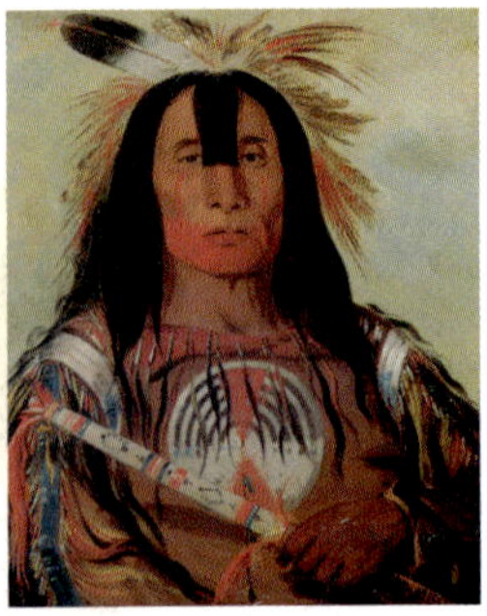
3

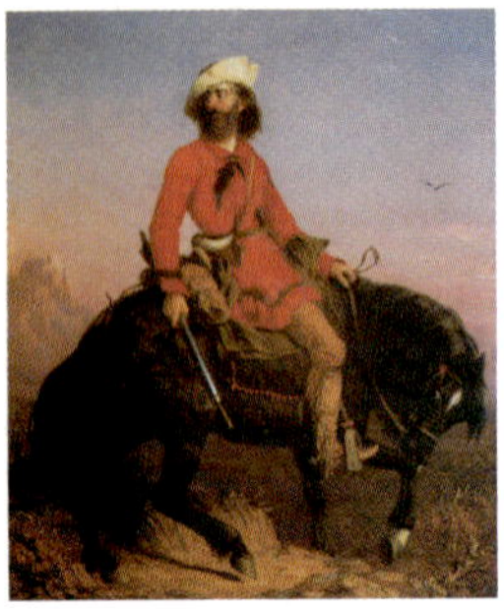
4

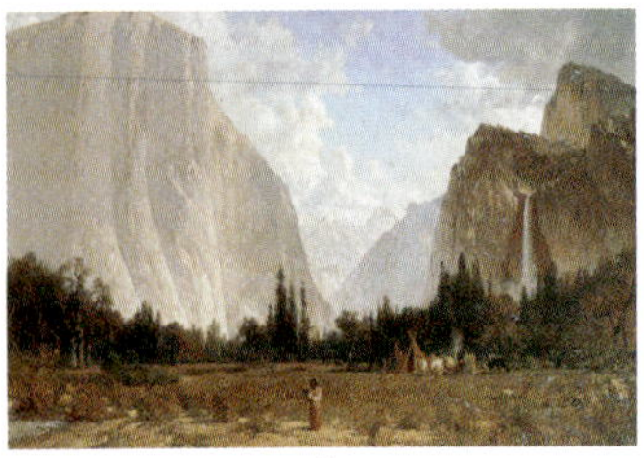
5

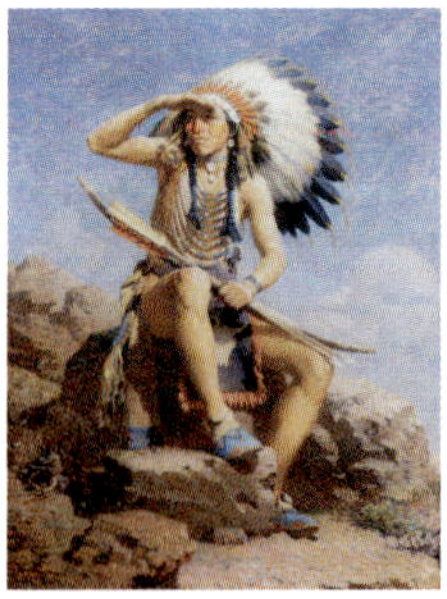
6

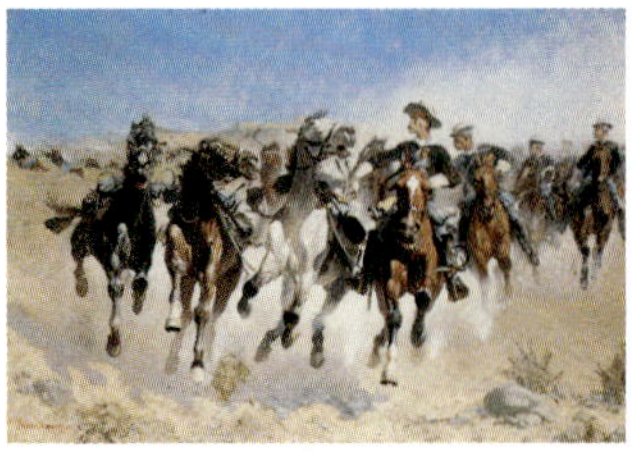
7

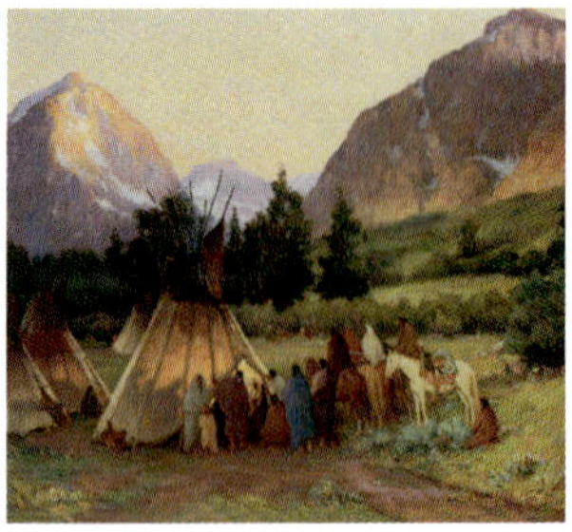
8

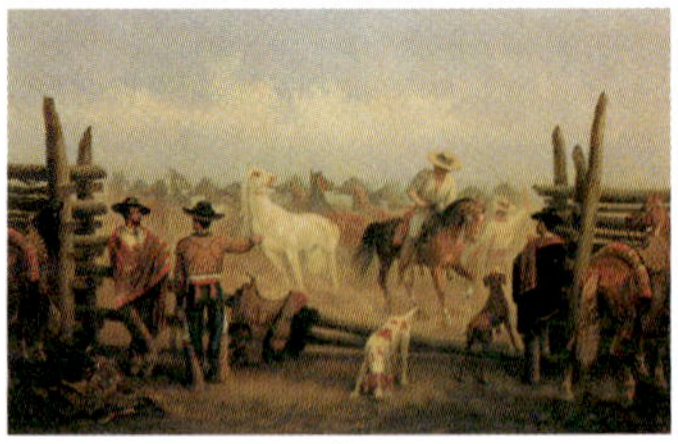
9

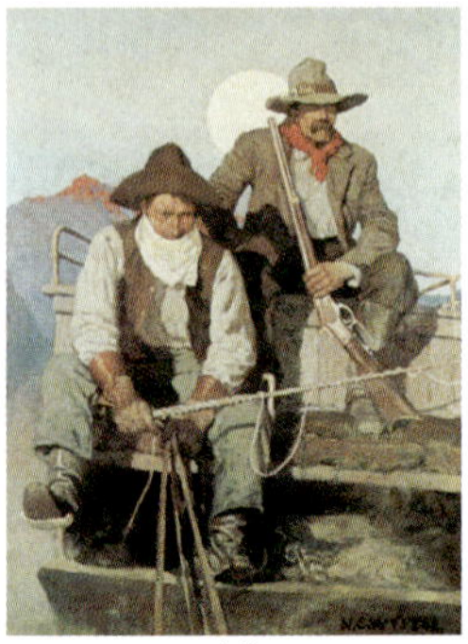
10